CRAFTING IDENTITY IN ZIMBABWE AND MOZAMBIQUE

T0374639

ROCHESTER STUDIES in
AFRICAN HISTORY and the DIASPORA

Toyin Falola, Senior Editor
The Frances Higginbotham Nalle Centennial Professor in History
University of Texas at Austin

(ISSN: 1092–5228)

A complete list of titles in the Rochester Studies in African History and the Diaspora, in order of publication, may be found at the end of this book.

CRAFTING IDENTITY IN ZIMBABWE AND MOZAMBIQUE

Elizabeth MacGonagle

UNIVERSITY OF ROCHESTER PRESS

First published 2007
Reprinted in paperback and transferred to digital printing 2013

University of Rochester Press
668 Mt. Hope Avenue, Rochester, NY 14620, USA
www.urpress.com
and Boydell & Brewer Limited
PO Box 9, Woodbridge, Suffolk IP12 3DF, UK
www.boydellandbrewer.com

ISSN: 1092-5228
hardcover ISBN: 978-1-58046-257-0
paperback ISBN: 978-1-58046-365-2

Library of Congress Cataloging-in-Publication Data

MacGonagle, Elizabeth.
    Crafting identity in Zimbabwe and Mozambique / Elizabeth MacGonagle.
        p. cm. — (Rochester studies in African history and the diaspora, ISSN 1092-5228
; v. 30)
Includes bibliographical references and index.
    ISBN-13: 978-1-58046-257-0 (hardcover : alk. paper)
    ISBN-10: 1-58046-257-X
    1. Ndau (African people)—Ethnic identity. 2. Ndau (African people)—Social life and
customs. 3. Ndau (African people)—History.
I. Title.
    DT3328.N38M33 2007
    305.896'3975—dc22

                                                                        2007012900

A catalogue record for this title is available from the British Library.

This publication is printed on acid-free paper.
Printed in the United States of America

CONTENTS

ILLUSTRATIONS

ACKNOWLEDGMENTS

Chafamba chapenga.

One who has set out on a journey cannot help being foolhardy.

—Shona proverb

Numerous people, both at home and abroad, helped me navigate to the end of this project. Scholars gave generously of their time and knowledge, while friends and family kept watch as a supportive crew. I heartily recognize my mother, Cinny MacGonagle, who has always provided the right charts and the best harbor. Over the past several years, colleagues at the University of Kansas were there to see that I stayed on course.

The elders of the Ndau region made this work possible, and I am grateful for their willingness to share a small part of their history with me. I am deeply indebted to my four assistants: Pinimidzai Sithole in Zimbabwe, and Jaime Maconha Augusto, Farai (António Francisco) Raposo, and Pedro Castigo in Mozambique. Their contributions helped ensure successful fieldwork. Looking back, it is difficult to imagine working with anyone else, for these scholars made the many journeys and interview experiences among the Ndau enjoyable and productive.

This book began as a dissertation on history and identity in the Ndau region. As a graduate student at Michigan State University, I received support, assistance, and funding from the African Studies Center, Department of History, College of Arts and Letters, and the Graduate School. Advice and encouragement came from many places and professors, including the Africanist contingent of Bill Derman, Elizabeth Eldredge, Harold Marcus, John Metzler, David Robinson, and David Wiley. Peter Beattie, Harry Reed, and Steve Averill helped me explore other regions beyond Africa. Harold Marcus, David Robinson, and Peter Beattie deserve special recognition for seeing the dissertation through to the end with grace and wit. Paul Wendland drafted the original maps, and Darin Grauberger transformed them into their final state at the University of Kansas.

Fieldwork in Mozambique, Zimbabwe, and Portugal in the 1990s was carried out with grants from Fulbright-Hays, the Social Science Research Council, the Luso-American Development Foundation, and the National Library of Lisbon. The University of Kansas provided further assistance for writing and fieldwork in 2003 and 2004 with grants from the General Research Fund. A Fulbright to Iceland in 2004 allowed for more time to write. A fellowship with the American Philosophical Society in 2005 enabled me to conduct further research in Mozambique. The Friends of the Hall Center for the Humanities at the University of Kansas supported publication with a subvention award. I gratefully acknowledge all of this financial support.

I walked down many paths during the course of fieldwork, and I appreciate the cordial receptions I received at the end of them. In Mozambique, Gerhard Liesegang not only shares his insight into Mozambican history each time I visit, but he also provided me with a place to stay during the elections in 1994. David Hedges, Solange Macamo, Amélia Neves de Souto, Luís Covane, and Benigna Zimba have been helpful fonts of knowledge at the Universidade Eduardo Mondlane, along with the libraries of the Centro de Estudos Africanos and the Archaeology and Anthropology Department. I would also like to thank Fernando Dava and ARPAC (in Maputo, Beira, and Chimoio) for their support. The staff at the Arquivo Histórico de Moçambique were most accommodating, and this work is enriched by the many sources that António Sopa brought to my attention in the archives. In Machaze, the staff of CARE graciously provided lodging in their compound. The acampamento in Moribane, a very special place, also hosted us. Rachel Chapman, James Pfeiffer, and Wendy Johnson provided good food and company in Chimoio. In Maputo, Carrie Manning, John Fleming, Heidi Gengenbach, Lloys Frates, Anne Pitcher, Martin Murray, Allen Isaacman, Sidney Bliss, Eric Allina-Pissano, Rob Marlin, Daphne Sorensen, Kathleen Sheldon, Sherilynn Young, and Jeanne Marie Penvenne provided support, encouragement, and companionship. Research in Maputo would have been an entirely different endeavor without their presence over the years.

In Zimbabwe, the Mpofus provided me with a home away from home in Chikore that was much appreciated. I would also like to thank Lorraine and Bill Giles and Mbuya G. for providing transport and conversation in and around Chikore and Chimanimani. David and Melanie McDermott Hughes hosted us in Chipinge and provided not only a ride to Vhimba, but also more importantly an entrée into the community. Ruben Zuze was a gracious host in Vhimba, where alas, my time was too short. Elias Nyamunda made fieldwork in Vhimba run smoothly. His keen sensibilities allowed us to meet and interview many elders in the area. Elias also conducted several interviews in Vhimba for this study. Gilbert Pwiti, Innocent Pikirayi, and the staff at the University of Zimbabwe's History Department made sure that my time at UZ was productive. Likewise, the staff at the National Archives of Zimbabwe facilitated my archival research in Harare. Colleagues in Zimbabwe including Diana Jeater, Tony King, Mark Guizlo, and Heather Holtzclaw provided company and support for this endeavor. Others, in ways both large and small, were there to assist and encourage—including many unnamed in the United States and Portugal.

This project builds on the careful and thoughtful work of other scholars steeped in the region. Allen Isaacman always offered warm guidance as this project progressed over the years from a dissertation to a book. James Bannerman (and his detailed maps) provided insight into early Shona history. Anne Pitcher has served as a wonderful guide both in Mozambique and the United States. Finally, I deeply regret the loss of David Beach of the University of Zimbabwe, who died in February 1999. His copious work in Shona history is unparalleled, and he displayed an unwavering enthusiasm and support for my investigations into precolonial history. From our very first correspondence and meetings in 1994, I appreciated his indefatigable encouragement and kind assistance. This manuscript, regrettably not enriched directly by his comments, builds upon his scholarship and enthusiasm. I worked on this book with fond memories and a shared passion for the study of the region's early history. *Nhasi haasiri mangwana*—Today is not tomorrow.[1]

1

A MIXED POT

THE CRAFTING OF IDENTITY

> We cannot say there is still Ndau. People are now modernized. Ndau is
> disappearing. I do not want to lie to you. . . . When you come here you call
> us VaNdau.
>
> —Sarai Nyabanga Sithole
>
> Ndau is difficult.
>
> —Jona Mwaoneni Makuyana

This study examines the complicated and ambiguous process of identity formation over several centuries in a corner of southeast Africa. In the region
of eastern Zimbabwe and central Mozambique, the Ndau of the highlands
and coastal plain drew on cultural, social, and political aspects of their identity to craft a sense of Ndauness between 1500 and 1900. The histories and
material culture that shaped this sense of identity form the subject of this
book. Ndau speakers came to be called Ndau long before the arrival of formal colonialism in the late nineteenth century, and I trace here the relationship between social identity and political power as far back as the
fifteenth century to reveal how intriguing historical factors led to shifts in
Ndauness before the arrival of missionaries and colonial officials on the continent. Drawing on rich historical data gathered from Ndau elders and
gleaned in written documents, I contend that the shared Ndau identity that
emerged in twentieth-century Zimbabwe and Mozambique stems from a long
period of transformation that included the development of common cultural
traits, mutually intelligible dialects, and a political history of both state formation and fragmentation.

Reconsidering Tribalism and Identity Formation

The findings presented in this book challenge popular notions about "tribalism" by pushing the study of identity formation back several hundred years. A tendency persists among many to perpetuate stereotypes and think of Africans as tribal in nature throughout time. Yet, scholars in African Studies have countered this commonly held perception over the past twenty years by showing how Europeans, with African assistance, forged identities during the colonial period that "created tribalism" and divided their African subjects. Rigid identities did indeed emerge out of earlier permeable ones when ethnic identities were manipulated and fixed under colonial rule. However, this popular "invention of tribalism" thesis does not adequately explain how identifications such as that of the Ndau took shape over a much longer span of time. What is new in this work is my contention that the long history behind ethnic identities reveals African agency in the precolonial period as central to the formation of "tribalism." Precolonial rulers, as I will demonstrate, also used ideology to promote group identification. I employ a groundbreaking methodological approach that considers the period between 1500 and 1900 to show how the development of political and cultural systems in southeast Africa prompted the Ndau to craft a collective identity long before formal European colonialism.

Neither primordial nor the product of colonialism, ethnic identities arise from collective historical experiences. Identities are fluid; they cross borders and they have a long and messy history in this region of southeast Africa. Writing about identity gives rise to questions about the concept itself. What are the meanings and ways of expressing identity? Like the term "tribe," identity can mean many things to different people—and, therefore, at times perhaps almost nothing at all. However, in the end, identity still means something to many, and I am not prepared to abandon the term as many have done with their use of "tribe."[1] Certainly, the concept of identity is imprecise and full of baggage that accompanies any use of such a problematic term. Other substitutes or alternatives, such as self-understanding, identification, or groupness have their weaknesses as well.[2] I use the term identity here without surrendering to it.[3] Identities can be strong or hard and weak or soft, as Frederick Cooper and Rodgers Brubaker note.[4] Calls by these authors either to abandon the use of the term identity or to move "beyond identity" point to the ambiguous and elusive nature of the concept.[5] Yet, recent scholarship recognizes how indispensable the concept is, not only as a category of practice, but also as a category of analysis. Identities have a story and a meaning behind them; thus, they have a contribution to make to history.

I define identity here as a broad sense of group belonging, or being something. This state is relational and opposed to the existence of an "other." Thus, the identities of a particular people exist "in a context of oppositions and relativities" as groups classify "others" during their own acts of self-identification.[6]

Although the feeling of sameness may be a strong pull or a weak push, the existence over time of a collective phenomenon begs historical investigation.[7] I examine the development of ethnic identities, since these are so closely tied to debates about "tribalism" in Africa's past, present, and future. The historical relevance of ethnicity, and its tenacious character that "refuses to vanish," deserves further exploration.[8] What, then, gives a group its identity? Is it perhaps history, behavior, appearance, customs, language, or culture? This is difficult to answer since identities are not static—they change in intriguing ways and often shift in a slow, imperceptible manner. Despite their fluid nature, cultural identities derive from somewhere in the past. As Kwame Anthony Appiah observes, "Cultures are made of continuities and changes, and the identity of a society can survive through these changes."[9] In this book the focus is on culture, broadly defined, and the continuities and changes of historical, social, political, and economic characteristics that distinguish the identity of a society. Ndauness, and my reconsideration of it, crosses temporal, geographic, and theoretical boundaries.

The story of how the Ndau came to be Ndau tells us something about the importance of examining long histories and cultural processes to understand more about both Africa's history and modern realities on the continent. A sense of being Ndau continues to exist into the present, albeit in a modified form, despite different colonial histories, postcolonial trajectories, and official languages in Zimbabwe and Mozambique. The investigation of ethnic identities among a marginalized group such as the Ndau has compelling importance for contemporary societies. History matters, and the past informs the present. An understanding of this region's history sheds light on conflicts and divisions that haunt southeast Africa today. In this book I describe the world the Ndau knew before 1900, when the study ends, and turn to introduce that world now.

The Ndau Setting

Most of the several million inhabitants living between the Pungwe and Save Rivers, two waterways that originate in Zimbabwe and flow eastward through Mozambique on their way to the Indian Ocean, speak a dialect of the Shona language called Ndau (see map 1.1). However, the Portuguese, who left an extensive written record about this region, did not use either Shona or Ndau in their early precolonial vocabularies. Both words came into use only in the nineteenth century, before formal colonialism took hold under the Portuguese in Mozambique and under the British in Southern Rhodesia, now Zimbabwe. Yet, a common identity was evident in the unified linguistic and cultural history of those in the east who spoke what came to be called the Ndau language. This work reconstructs how the Ndau formed and maintained a sense of being Ndau over the *longue durée*.

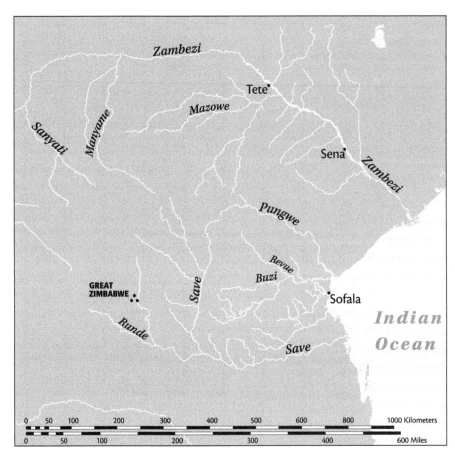

Map 1.1. Major rivers between the Zambezi and the Save.

When the Portuguese established a presence along the Mozambican coast at Sofala in the sixteenth century, the population living between the Save and Zambezi Rivers spoke several dialects of the Bantu language known today as Shona. Arab traders used the famous port of Sofala and the surrounding coastal region, probably since at least the ninth century, until the Portuguese established a fortress at Sofala in 1505 and began interfering with established trading relationships.[10] Even though the Portuguese soon realized that Sofala failed to offer the best access to the gold found to the northwest on the Zimbabwe Plateau, the settlement remained a strategic location that the Portuguese exploited long after their arrival in the region.[11] The port, located south of the mouth of the Buzi River on a low-lying sandy coast, remained an important local center for the export trade in ivory, gold, and other goods from interior markets such as the *feiras* of Manica and Teve.[12]

Early on, Portuguese documents refer to the peoples along the Sofala coast and in the hinterland as Karanga. The Portuguese applied the label indiscriminately throughout the region even though the word denotes an imprecise ethnic reality. Variations of the term Karanga appear in very early Portuguese documents, the first time probably in 1506, when a Portuguese chronicler referred to the gold at Sofala coming from a king called Ucalanga.[13] Local inhabitants had their own terms of self-identification that included not only Karanga for the northern plateau region, but also more specific names such as Teve, Danda, and Sanga for areas in the east and southeast (as shown in map 1.2). Yet, despite these local names of territories that in turn became separate polities, a sense of collective identity among eastern Shona speakers was acknowledged by early Portuguese observers when they used the term Karanga to refer to the peoples along the coast and in the Sofala hinterland. Ceremonies at the court of Teve in the east, for example, resembled royal customs at Mutapa, a large and famous state on the plateau known to the Portuguese for its gold supply.[14] Succession patterns in particular are similar throughout the region.[15] In this study I follow current practice and refer to the larger Shona-speaking group as the Shona people, but my focus is on those who live in the eastern region and speak a distinct version of Shona known as Ndau.

Bounded to the north by the Zambezi River, to the east by the Indian Ocean, and to the south by the Save River, the lands of the Karanga encompassed a wide area that included not only the immediate Sofala hinterland, but also other Shona-speaking regions to the north and west. The western boundary of this Shona area was unknown to the early Portuguese, for the Karanga inhabited much of the Zimbabwe Plateau that indigenous traders crossed on routes stretching from the Kalahari Desert to the Indian Ocean. Throughout the entire Shona area flourishing communities constructed elaborate stone settlements on the Zimbabwe Plateau, including Great Zimbabwe (1250–1450 CE), as well as at related sites on the Mozambican coastal plain. These centers contain archaeological evidence of a shared material culture in Mozambique and Zimbabwe before the arrival of the Portuguese in the sixteenth century.[16]

In the early history of southeast Africa, political divisions and alliances were formed within and across ethnic boundaries to mark cultural identities. Between the sixteenth and eighteenth century, boundaries were fluid when both the Mutapa state and smaller eastern territories in the Ndau region vied for political control and economic power to regulate trade in the Sofala hinterland. Economic pursuits, particularly trade, influenced Ndau politics and the formation of a cultural identity from the sixteenth century onward. Political power was inextricably linked to external trade, and these precolonial contacts highlighted and reinforced cultural identities for the people who came to be called Ndau.

The Karanga of the northern Zimbabwe Plateau were the dominant aristocracy in the Shona region in the sixteenth century when the Portuguese

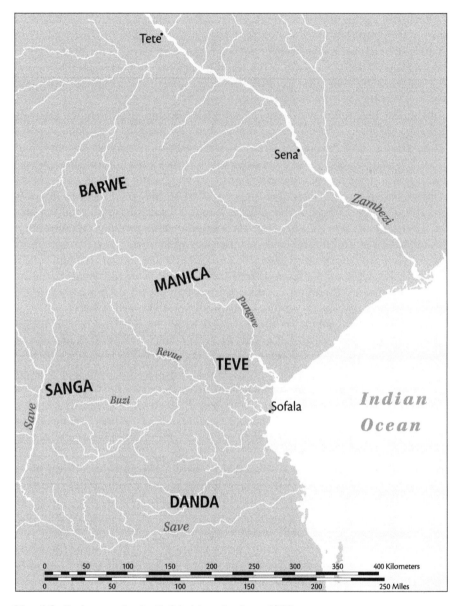

Map 1.2. Early states in the Sofala hinterland, ca. 1700.

arrived.[17] The first and most prestigious Karanga state, the Mutapa state, relied on its own military power for support. Damião de Goes wrote of the Mutapa leader: "Whether in time of peace or war he always maintains a large standing army, of which the commander-in-chief is called Zono, to keep the land in a state of quietness and to prevent the lords and kings who are subject to him from rising in rebellion."[18] The Karanga rulers symbolized their prestige by building small *madzimbabwe*, or houses of stone, in the areas where they settled, and they had better living standards than the groups they conquered.[19] Although few small stone ruins remain, ruins at Chibvumani are shown in figure 1.1. Despite the casting by the Mutapa rulers of a common political identity known as Karanga over much of the eastern region, there were some Ndau who refused to accept Mutapa overrule. Local chiefs, for instance, could decide to withhold tribute or carry out clandestine trade. Those within the sphere of the Mutapa's influence referred to others outside of his control, such as groups residing south of the Ndau region near the port of Inhambane, as *Tonga* to signify their status as outsiders.[20]

Eventually external pressure from the Portuguese presence, combined with a lack of unity among the Karanga aristocracy, led to rivalries that resulted in the formation of a series of separate secondary states in the hinterland of Sofala.[21] The formation of these smaller states over two centuries complicated the process of crafting the identity that was to become Ndau. States in the Ndau region such as Teve, Danda, and Sanga relied on the once large and powerful Mutapa state for symbolic legitimacy, and they all claimed, along with Manica, that sons of the Mutapa ruler founded these states.[22] The Portuguese persistently recognized the Mutapa ruler in the northern interior as the overlord of the entire region, for they thought that this leader controlled the gold mines in the area and thus held the key to untold wealth.[23] This led to some hostility between the Portuguese and smaller states such as Teve and Danda that continued to trade with their Swahili partners from city-states along the East African coast.[24] In the eyes of the Portuguese, the Afro-Arab Swahili were economic competitors. As the Portuguese challenged Swahili influence both in the hinterland and along the coast, a wider sense of being Karanga faded. In turn, states in the greater Ndau region came to develop their own political identities that lasted into the nineteenth century.[25] In the early twentieth century Europeans and local inhabitants nonetheless revitalized these identities as ethnic markers in their quest to classify and sort the "tribes" of southeast Africa.[26] Even though these secondary states were indeed distinct political entities over several centuries, a wider cultural identity based on a shared history and the Shona language permeated the region.

A majority of people in Zimbabwe and a considerable number of Mozambicans living between the Zambezi and Save Rivers speak the language of Shona. And on maps and in the literature on ethnicity today most of the people in Zimbabwe and central Mozambique are labeled as Shona. On twentieth-century ethnographic maps, such as maps 1.3 and 1.4, the classification Shona stretches across central Mozambique and into most of Zimbabwe. These maps are the products of scholarship that focuses on Zimbabwe and Mozambique, often separately. Although these two examples show the Shona as an ethnic group that stretches across the border, the Ndau are only vaguely mapped as a subgroup in map 1.4. Yet, the use of the term Shona to encompass the various

Figure 1.1. Building in stone, Chibvumani ruins in southeastern Zimbabwe. Photo by author.

identities—historical, cultural, ethnic, or linguistic—of the people living in central Mozambique and Zimbabwe is problematic.

Shona is neither an apt ethnic or "tribal" label, but its usage as a blanket term usually implies that being Shona means speaking the same language, having similar cultural traditions, and experiencing a shared history. Shona is

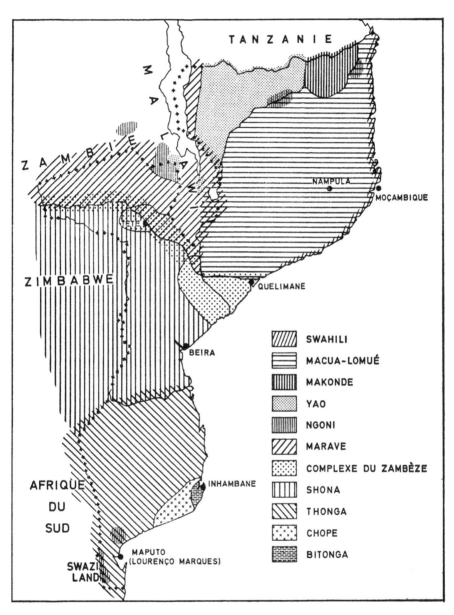

Map 1.3. Ethnographic map showing the eastern Shona region. Reprinted by permission of the publisher from Pélissier 1984.

an accepted linguistic term that identifies speakers of the Shona language, which falls within the south-central zone of the Bantu language group. Ndau is one of six main dialects of Shona, and in the wider region language is often equated with ethnicity. Even though a Shona identity in south-central Africa

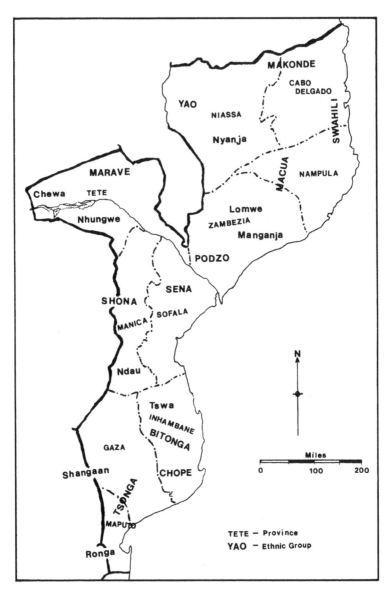

Map 1.4. Twentieth-century ethnographic map of Mozambique. Reprinted by permission of the publisher from Vines 1991.

is based heavily on language, Shona speakers have shared cultural practices and historical experiences over the *longue durée*.

The Nguni-speaking Ndebele, migrants from the south, first used the term Shona to refer to the Rozvi people they encountered after entering the

Changamire state in the southwestern area of the Zimbabwe Plateau in the 1830s.[27] At that time Shona speakers described themselves in terms of their region or clan, and they apparently only began to use the term Shona themselves sometime after 1890.[28] Terence Ranger describes his view of the sense of identity among Shona speakers who shared a common language and political culture in the nineteenth century:

> There certainly existed a very wide zone of common culture, which scholars have come to call "Shona", but in the nineteenth century the people who shared that common culture did *not* feel themselves to be part of a single "Shona" identity. People defined themselves *politically*—as subjects of a particular chief—rather than linguistically, culturally, or ethnically.[29]

In the nineteenth century other outsiders besides the Ndebele were describing some Shona speakers as Shona too. Maps from this period include the term, but it was not a comprehensive label for most Shona speakers on either the Zimbabwe Plateau or the Mozambican coastal plain. Indeed, one Portuguese map from 1867 (a portion of which is reproduced in map 1.5) has Machona in the southern area of the plateau near Muzururos and Quissanga.[30] A later map in 1889 (part of which appears in map 1.6) places Machona farther north and over a wider area, but Manica is another label that covers about the same amount of territory.[31] The southern portion of the plateau was called Matabeleland by the middle of the nineteenth century after the Ndebele settled there, and a large part of the north-central plateau came to be known as Mashonaland sometime after that. White settlers commonly referred to the east, including the Ndau-speaking area, as Manyikaland. Manyikaland (or Manicaland), Mashonaland, and Matabeleland are three provinces in Zimbabwe today, but "Ndauland" is not a province or a commonly used term.

After the Southern Rhodesian government commissioned a study on the unification of the dialects of Shona speakers in the 1920s, the term Shona was recommended by the linguist Clement Doke to be the official name of the language.[32] His report, published in 1931, described the quandary that the members of the Language Committee faced when they chose a unifying name for the language:

> It has been widely felt that the name "Shona" is inaccurate and unworthy, that it is not the true name of any of the peoples whom we propose to group under the term "Shona-speaking people", and further that it lies under a strong suspicion of being a name given in contempt by the enemies of the tribes. It is pretty certainly a foreign name and as such is very likely to be uncomplimentary.[33]

As missionaries turned the spoken Shona language into various written dialects in the early twentieth century, they meddled with "tribalism" and tradition by fixing ethnic boundaries.[34] Missionaries and colonial officials drew language borders and demarcated dialect territories in many parts of Africa.

Map 1.5. Portion of 1867 map showing the wider Shona region. *Source*: Randles 1975.

Map 1.6. Portion of 1889 map of Mozambique. *Source*: Randles 1975.

American missionaries in southeast Africa, for instance, championed Ndau so that they could work with just one language that would cover their entire sphere of influence from the Save River to the coast.[35] European explorers, colonists, and missionaries erected similarly suspect linguistic borders based on problematic spatial categories among neighboring Tsonga speakers living south of the Save River. Patrick Harries has shown how European discourse, rather than local Tsonga histories, shaped an emerging ethnicity in the region. "A bounded and written language altered peoples' perceptions of reality and influenced their course of action," according to Harries.[36] Just as delimitations of language had an effect on power structures among the Tsonga, the Ndau faced similar changes at the hands of the linguist Doke.

On examining the developing language situation in Southern Rhodesia, Doke arrived at six main "Dialect Groups": Ndau, Manyika, Korekore, Zezuru, Karanga, and Kalanga (as shown in map 1.7).[37] Three of these classifications—Ndau, Manyika, and Korekore—stretched into Mozambique, which by that time was the colony of Portuguese East Africa. Within each area there were also various dialects. For example, among the Ndau cluster, there are subdivisions that Doke labeled Ndau, Danda, and Shanga.[38] I question Doke's neat boundaries within the wider Shona region, for this South African linguist did not visit many of the areas shown on his map.[39] The imprecise template reflected in Doke's map (reproduced in map 1.7) became a reality and influenced the shaping of linguistic, and subsequently cultural, identities in the region. Throughout Africa language became central to European definitions of "tribe," people, and nation.[40] The push to standardize language played an important role in the development of expanded identities. Thus, in the twentieth century identities among speakers of the Shona language moved beyond historical political units within the region to broader realms of language and culture across the Shona-speaking zone.[41]

This relatively recent and broad characterization of people as Shona or Ndau does not correspond with identities grounded in a history that signified membership within one political unit.[42] Before 1890 Shona speakers were conscious of local chieftaincy groups rather than one overarching cultural or political identity that could be called Shona.[43] Historians such as Terence Ranger have therefore concluded that precolonial states in this region "had never pulled their subjects together into self-conscious identities, nor had they manipulated concepts of group identity in a manner which left a lasting legacy."[44] While this appears to be the situation in some cases, I contend that Ndau speakers drew on their history of a shared language and culture to develop a wider sense of identity. Ranger's argument does not work for the case of the Ndau, and this becomes especially apparent in the nineteenth century when the Ndau endured overrule at the hands of the Gaza Nguni, as will be discussed in chapter 7.

Some speakers of Ndau—particularly residents of Zimbabwe, where today about 80 percent of the population speaks Shona—would identify themselves as both Shona and Ndau, but their ancestors would not have considered themselves to be Shona or even Ndau before the late nineteenth century. Ndau speakers most likely identified with a region such as the lowland Danda area, or a political entity such as Sanga in the highlands or Shanga on the coast. As two elders interviewed in Machaze, Mozambique, explained, "All north of the Save [River] speak Ndau, but the Ndau spoken in various zones is different."[45] Ironically, Doke's 1931 report stressed the need for "a linguistic term to use in connection with the unified language, a term by which the people need never call themselves."[46] His recommendation of Shona did

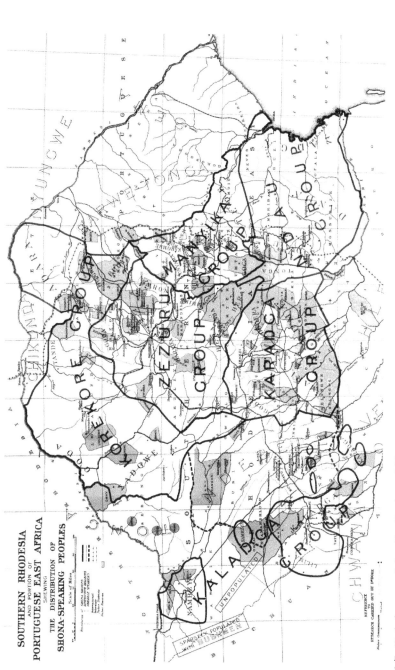

Map 1.7. Doke's map of the distribution of Shona-speaking peoples. Reprinted by permission of the University of the Witwatersrand Press from Doke 1931.

indeed come to be used as an identifier by many of the people themselves, despite the term's failure to develop *from within* the linguistic group.[47] Similarly, usage of the name Ndau has grown to denote about the same area of the Ndau Group marked on Doke's map. A second, significant irony is that the use of Ndau as an ethnic identity today covers a larger area than the local dialect of Ndau spoken only in the highlands.[48]

Just as the label Shona has ambiguous origins, the exact derivation of the term Ndau is also unclear. Today many Ndau speakers say that the term was first used as an exclamation of deference in their customary greetings. In the late nineteenth century the Ndau would say *Ndau-we, Ndau-we*, which translates as "We salute you! We salute you!"[49] These words served as a sign of humbleness and respect, and the use of *Ndau-we* as a greeting has become a point of pride that symbolizes the friendliness of Ndau speakers.[50] One elder related her thoughts on being called Ndau when she explained, "For me, we are called Ndau because we say 'Ndauwe', that is why we are called VaNdau."[51] In a similar vein, several elders explained that the term is derived from *ndau-ndau*, or *ndau* (with a low tone), a saying people used "long ago" when entering a homestead.[52] Another elder from Nyanyadzi, Zimbabwe, said, "I think the Ndaus are called Ndau because when they get to a home they say 'Ndau.' "[53] This expression "meant that if you were busy, that would be a signal to notify you so that you pay attention."[54] Those in the compound would respond by saying *Gumai*, meaning "Come in."[55] Thus, Ndau became a nickname used by others to describe the people who said *Ndau*.[56] Today visitors to a homestead respectfully announce their presence by calling out *Do-do-do*. This phrase serves the same introductory purpose as *ndau-ndau*.[57] In contemporary usage, the dweller calls for the visitors to enter the compound by responding with *Pindai*, meaning "Enter." Although many Ndau speakers no longer utilize *Ndau* or *Ndau-we* in their greetings, elders recognize the meaning behind the word today and describe this usage as common in the late nineteenth century.

In fact, the use of the word Ndau may even extend back to the eighteenth century. One historian argues that the earliest reference is apparently from a Portuguese document that mentions "Mujao" traders who crossed the Save River in 1739 to trade their gold for cloth at Inhambane to the south.[58] This reference to "Mujao" is similar to "Ndjao," the Inhambane version of Ndau.[59] About one hundred years later, a Portuguese writer referred to "Mataos" as well as "Madandas" and "Madandas Vatombozis" in the hinterland of Sofala in a report from 1844.[60] Soon afterward a British explorer reported "Mandanda" in the lowlands near the Save River, and he placed the term "Maandowa" on an 1875 map of his journeys.[61] These written references suggest an earlier existence of the term Ndau and an established distinction from Danda long before the recollections of twentieth-century elders in the Ndau region. Whenever the term originated, Ndau was not widely used to designate a specific people until the nineteenth century.

The two groups of Ndau and Danda were not always that different, and over time the Danda came to be Ndau as well. Several elders talked about aspects of this process during interviews. "In Nyabanga there are many Ndaus and Dumas," explained Sarai Nyabanga Sithole of Zamchiya.[62] "I want to tell you clearly," she said while giggling, "VaDuma and VaDanda were the enemies of the Ndau."[63] Jona Mwaoneni Makuyana recalled that the Danda were "outsiders" who came from Mozambique to marry local people in the highlands so that both groups could "become one flesh."[64] Makuyana, born in Mozambique and now a resident of Zamchiya, Zimbabwe, explained, "The VaDanda can speak Ndau; our languages are almost the same."[65] He further emphasized, "They are one and the same thing. The slight difference is [in] the tones. After the Danda region, we could not hear their language, deep within Mozambique."[66] Noting the limits to understanding what Ndau is exactly, he concluded, "Ndau is difficult. If you go to the south, they are now Hlengwes, and they do not speak Ndau."[67] When Ndau elders made distinctions between themselves and others, they often turned to language to define the wider Ndau identity. For instance, Mucherechete Dhlakama of Zamchiya explained, "I am Ndau because I was born by Ndaus. I do not have a Duma tone or language; neither do I have that of Hlengwe. That is why I say I am Ndau."[68] Unlike the Danda, the Duma to the west and Hlengwe to the south are the "other" and distinctly *not* Ndau.

Among Ndau speakers, being Shona is replaced for the most part by a sense of being Ndau, or being something else such as Danda or Tomboji, but nevertheless speaking the Ndau language. In the highland region, there are Ndau known as either Ndau, Garwe, Sanga, or Tomboji along the Zimbabwe-Mozambique border. Some in the highlands refer to those in the valley as *mugowa*.[69] Lowland Ndau near the Indian Ocean coast are called Danda or Shanga. Northern neighbors of the Ndau identify as Manica or Teve and speak Shona dialects of the same name. Even though Teve is distinct from Ndau today, the precolonial Teve state was in the greater Ndau area under study here. In addition, many Mozambicans of the late twentieth century who live in the wider Ndau region do not see themselves as being Shona, even though linguists designate Ndau as a dialect of Shona.

The amalgamation of dialects in Doke's Ndau Group, combined with the differences in accent and vocabulary between Ndau and other Shona dialects, have all contributed to confusion over Ndau as a language and relegated it to the fringe of the Shona-speaking world. The remoteness of Ndau to most Zimbabweans is apparent in its oversight in two prominent Shona-language dictionaries published in Zimbabwe. The authors of these dictionaries avoid mentioning the Ndau dialect. For example, the Shona-English dictionary by D. Dale specifies words common to the dialects of Karanga, Korekore, Manyika, and Zezuru, but not Ndau.[70] M. Hannan's comprehensive *Standard Shona Dictionary* also leaves out Ndau but includes dialect variations from Karanga, Korekore, Budya, and Zezuru.[71] As the ethnographer H. P. Junod argued in

1934, the Ndau are "certainly the most loosely connected group," although their affiliation with other Shona speakers is undeniable.[72] The history of the Ndau region in Zimbabwe and Mozambique casts the most doubt on the straightforward nature of ethnic and linguistic classifications in this area.

Uncovering History in Southeast Africa

Although the creation and shaping of ethnic identities is ongoing for any particular group, ethnicity remains tied to a sense of group belonging. Shared characteristics may include a language or dialect, geographic region, common origin or ancestry (historical or mythical), religious bond, or political entity. The shifting identities and changing polities among groups such as the Ndau pose a challenge for scholars, since both Africans and Europeans transformed ethnic identifications through social and ideological means at various historical moments. Even though select histories are constantly used to produce identities, ethnic identities tend to take on a powerful salience and appear to be natural, essential, and even primordial.[73] It is possible to discern how group identities respond to political and cultural changes over time, but continuities and differences in the creation of ethnicity during the precolonial, colonial, and postcolonial eras have yet to be explored in much of Africa. Throughout history, social stratification and struggles for power have intensified ethnic awareness among people who view themselves as sharing a common culture and historical origin.[74] Although ethnic identities may arise at any given time, they are most prominent when violence is used to satisfy group aspirations at the expense of others.

Ethnic identities among the Ndau were created through social and political institutions, cultural practices and expressions, economic activities, and relations between humans and the environment. For example, social structures such as families, extended kinship ties, and patron arrangements shaped ethnic identification. Language, religious beliefs and rituals, oral traditions, and aspects of material culture served to foster ethnicity in both subtle and obvious ways. In many instances, diverse socioeconomic activities and unequal access to environmental resources intensified ethnic awareness. Gender relations, shifting class structures, and leadership patterns all influenced ethnic identification, and the unequal allocation of power and wealth heightened perceptions of group distinctiveness and exclusion. In this study I document how people speaking the same language maintain ethnic distinctions, at times more subtle than obvious, despite a history of overlapping political structures. I trace the forging of common identities as well as the processes of exclusion to offer a more meaningful analysis of long-term shifts in identities.

In order to identify the many patterns and processes of change, I map the existing evidence of material culture over several centuries in the Ndau-speaking region. I examine markers of identity such as language, body art, religious

beliefs, rituals, and gender roles in the context of changing social and political structures. I discuss cultural affinities in ceremonies and social gatherings
while also analyzing the abundant information on Ndau dress, jewelry, and
markings on the face and body. The technologies of material culture as well
as specific objects such as tools, clothing, pots, crafts, and houses reflect
changes in self-identity.[75] Since ethnic awareness shifts over time, it is necessary to analyze the combined evidence of written documents, oral interviews,
and material culture to trace continuities and changes in the cultural identity
of the Ndau.

In the written record, I have found evidence of a Ndau cultural identity in
early travelers' accounts, reports by European officials, writings of missionaries, and other miscellaneous documents. Portuguese records are rich in
descriptions of material culture, and many important primary materials exist
now in published form. Obscure ethnographic studies, despite their ahistor-
ical framework, are also very informative. A critical reading of these sources
has yielded ample evidence of material culture and expressions of identity at
different historical moments. I offer a historical analysis of the evidence of
material culture and strive to make a contribution that bridges the divide
between the social sciences and the humanities. A deeper historical study of
the manner in which people constructed new ways of seeing themselves and
others has relevance beyond Africa, for the phenomenon of ethnicity is world-
wide. People call on various identities in the midst of ethno-political conflicts,
and my study addresses how the ambiguities and complexities inherent in the
fluctuations of ethnic boundaries speak to larger historical processes.

Oral interviews with Ndau elders and European documentation are the two
main types of source material used in this study. At the start of one interview,
Riyarwi Mushoma joked about my cassette recorder saying, "That is the thing
that will record me. We will go to America together."[76] Indeed, the more than
two hundred interviews I conducted during fieldwork in the Ndau region
from 1998 to 1999 did "go to America" as recorded interviews painstakingly
transcribed into written form. The comments of Mushoma and others now
join the written record of southeast Africa's history alongside archival documents housed in Mozambique, Zimbabwe, and Portugal as well as published
versions of select archival evidence. Although there are some obvious differences between oral and written sources, I draw from each as an interpreter
with a critical awareness of their biases and errors. Yet, the data is rich, with
the documentary evidence often complementing the information gleaned
from interviews with elders. Portuguese documents, beginning in the early
1500s, describe local societies on the coast as well as the activities of inhabitants farther inland. Even though European writers were often firsthand
observers of the period under study here, I learned just as much about Ndau
history from the true historians of the Ndau—elders who have an incredible
memory of events and traditions passed down from earlier generations. With
a wealth of documentary evidence, combined with information gathered from

Ndau elders, it is possible to reconstruct early Ndau history since the sixteenth century and gain a sense of Ndauness over time.

The act of interpreting the meaning of errors can be a difficult business. Alessandro Portelli writes about how the telling of "wrong" tales enhances our knowledge, since "errors, inventions and myths lead us through and beyond facts to their meanings."[77] In this book I have attempted to glean some truths and understand errors as more than casual mistakes. The large number of interviews I conducted during fieldwork allows me to assess both the similarities and the wide range of responses to many of the same questions asked of elders. Yet, I also have stories from elders that inadvertently answered my questions and raised new lines of inquiry. Elders recalled events from over sixty, seventy, or eighty years ago, for most of those interviewed were in their eighties and nineties. They were very friendly and willing to speak at length about their knowledge of history and customs long ago. When someone claimed to know little about history, I explained that the subject at hand was also *magariro netsika akare*, the way of life and customs long ago. Thus, they had knowledge passed down from earlier generations that was not necessarily history, but nonetheless essential information for my inquiry.

The area of this study is relatively large, since I wanted to speak with elders from one end of the Ndau region to the other. Traveling across an area of about 17,000 square miles (as shown in map 1.8), I spoke with elders from Chisumbanje to Hot Springs in the west and from Machanga to Buzi in the east. To this day the lower Pungwe River marks, roughly, the northern frontier of the Ndau-speaking area and the Save River forms a southern boundary.[78] I interviewed elders in both the capitals and the outlying areas of all districts inhabited by a majority of Ndau speakers. Throughout my fieldwork I worked with an assistant when conducting interviews.[79] Three Mozambicans— António Francisco (Farai) Raposo, Jaime Maconha Augusto, and Pedro Castigo—as well as one Zimbabwean, Pinimidzai Sithole, facilitated my introduction into communities, asked questions during interviews, and transcribed the taped interviews. Their assistance was invaluable for this study.[80] At each field site I conducted interviews on a daily basis when logistics permitted, and I recorded each interview on an audiocassette only if informants were willing and comfortable.[81] Questions during interviews were open ended, but we guided the conversation when necessary. Sociopolitical structures, gender roles, language, religious beliefs, and rituals were the main themes raised in each interview. Many questions focused on the technologies of material culture and household production. Other studies of material culture have shown that muted voices, particularly those of women, can be expressed in the decoration of rooms and pots.[82] I spoke mainly with elders over eighty years of age—both men and women—to record their recollections of earlier times.[83] The information gathered from these interviews, although clearly subject to interpretation by both the sources and the researcher, helps to counter the class and gender biases often present in the written record.[84]

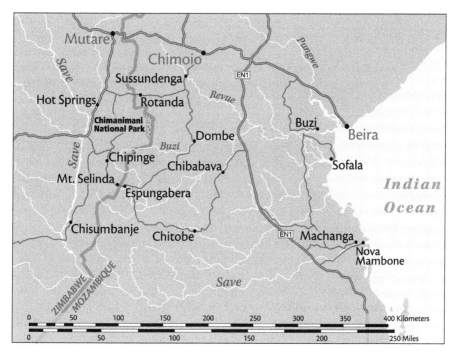

Map 1.8. Fieldwork area in Zimbabwe and Mozambique, 1998–99.

During fieldwork near the border, it was clear that the international boundary separating Zimbabwe and Mozambique is an artificial border that runs through the Ndau-speaking area dividing kin, culture, and speakers of the same language. Most people on or near the border in the 1990s were oriented toward Zimbabwe, partly due to the infrastructure on that side. With better roads and more frequent transport, well-stocked shops, and greater educational opportunities, Zimbabwe lured Ndau speakers residing on the Mozambican side of the border. Children crossed the border to attend school in Zimbabwean communities such as Zamchiya and Zona, and some Mozambican residents used only Zimbabwean currency.[85] Since my extensive fieldwork experiences in the 1990s, the situation has changed dramatically and taken a reverse turn. A visit to the Mozambican city of Chimoio in the province of Manica in 2005 revealed well-stocked stores in Mozambique frequented by former residents of Zimbabwe, including relocated white farmers. Living across an international boundary with fluctuating political conditions on either side, Ndau speakers find themselves once again between borders.

Both different colonial experiences and postindependence fighting in Mozambique during the war with Renamo created distinct histories on each side of the border. Those on the Mozambican side who fled to Zimbabwe over time "simply traded one set of obligations to their chief for a less severe one" on the other side, as David Hughes has convincingly shown in his research.[86] Yet, bonds of marriage, language, and culture tie Ndau speakers to one another across the border. They share common interests and a common identity, but they do make distinctions among themselves.[87] The border is a marker and a tangible facet of the Ndau region. People refer to it in conversation and acknowledge its existence, making this a hard border in some respects.[88] Yet, it is also a border with soft edges as well. Elders such as Jona Mwaoneni Makuyana noted few differences in the customs and way of life on either side of the border earlier this century.[89] Comparing his birthplace in Mozambique to his current home across the border in Zamchiya, Zimbabwe, he noted, "The only difference was that a school was built earlier in Zamchiya than in Chikwekwete. That is the only difference."[90] My focus here is on this region's past long before the existence of any border.

This book is an attempt to cut across a former colonial boundary and transcend the intellectual frontier defining ethnicity in terms of the colonial and postcolonial age. To conduct this study of the shared cultural, political, and linguistic heritage that has provided the basis for a larger Ndau identity, it was necessary for me to conduct research in both Mozambique and Zimbabwe since the territory of the Ndau stretches across central Mozambique into southeastern Zimbabwe. Unfortunately, the imposed boundary running through this region has divided much of the existing scholarship. I have discovered the importance of talking to Ndau speakers on both sides of the border and envisioning the wider history of the Ndau region.

The idea of crafting Ndauness emerged from many interviews with Ndau speakers in the region. When Idah Manyuni of Chikore, Zimbabwe, was asked if there were outsiders living in her area near the border between Mozambique and Zimbabwe, she replied, "Oo-oh yes! They are so many now. . . . We are now a mixed pot, it is no longer Ndaus only."[91] Her comment about the Ndau region as a "mixed pot" reflects the internal contributions and outside influences that shape a sense of place for the Ndau today. In this study I focus on the somewhat messy process of crafting identity in the Ndau region in order to discern the ambiguities, distinctions, and layered complexities inherent in an earlier sense of Ndauness. The metaphor of a "mixed pot" or several different pots also reflects the many facets of Ndauness in the twentieth century, since the Ndau have distinct uses for various pots. For instance, there is a specific pot for water, another for beer, one for cooking greens, and a special pot for maize meal, or *sadza*.[92] When women bring these different pots together, they create a delicious meal—or in a larger sense, a Ndau cultural identity.

In this book I seek to clarify our understanding of the creation of ethnicity and the shaping of African identities before the onset of the colonial period through an examination of the case of the Ndau. Many historical studies over the last two decades, while groundbreaking for their time, have only highlighted

African and European manipulations of ethnic awareness since the end of the nineteenth century. To move beyond the contemporary scholarship that focuses on recent identities, I look back in time. A wealth of documents from the Portuguese presence in Mozambique and Zimbabwe since the sixteenth century combined with rich historical information preserved by elders of the twentieth century offer us a tremendous opportunity to gain insight into the crafting of identity in southeast Africa over the *longue durée*.

Outline of the Study

The chapters that follow note how history and identity are both salient and inconspicuous features of the cultural landscape. I begin in chapter 2 by theorizing identities and revisiting both the rewards and the pitfalls of examining ethnic identifications over time. Despite the heated discourse often associated with the terms ethnicity and identity, I argue that an examination of the fluidity of ethnic identification and its historical baggage is needed to understand and combat the threat posed by those who use race and ethnicity to create sociopolitical divisions.

Trade and political relations form the subject of chapter 3. Both local and regional economies are examined, for the Ndau produced and exchanged diverse commodities such as hoes, pots, cattle, gold, ivory, copper, and salt. I discuss how important chiefdoms and powerful rulers sought to shape the contours of Ndau identity and benefit from economic production through tribute and trade. I also analyze the disintegration of several dynamic and extensive political systems and assess the smaller polities that remained. Although Ndau history is marked by multiple levels of political identification that are often unclear and contradictory, I show how economic and political ties in the wider region were central to the formation of linkages that cultivated a sense of being Ndau in spite of changing political units.

Chapters 4, 5, and 6 consider how Ndauness is shaped within Ndau communities. I examine cultural practices and social structures—the ties that bind—in chapter 4. Through marriage alliances, women reproduced a local political order and played an integral part in maintaining a common language and culture over a wide geographic region. In chapter 5 I consider cultural affinities in adornment and beauty and analyze the abundant information on Ndau dress, hairstyles, jewelry, and markings on the face and body such as tattoos (*pika*) and scarification (*nyora*). The technologies of material culture as well as specific objects such as houses and pots reflect changes in identity. Three important activities for the Ndau are the focus of chapter 6: brewing beer, making rain, and holding court. I analyze both the practical and the symbolic aspects of these rituals and emphasize the steadfast importance of shared beliefs among the Ndau.

Chapter 7 examines more recent manipulations of ethnic awareness. The Gaza Nguni created tremendous upheaval when they left southern Mozambique with their army to rule over the Ndau area in the nineteenth century. I explore the legends surrounding the leader Ngungunyana's rule, generally considered harsh, and examine the effects of his decision to force large numbers of Ndau to follow him back to the original Gaza Nguni capital in southern Mozambique at Bilene. Around this time Ndau men began to pierce their ears as the Gaza Nguni did, and this practice later served as a symbol of being Ndau among migrant laborers in South Africa. I examine the forging of common identities and the processes of exclusion that took place in the region under the shadow of Ngungunyana. Ultimately, inhabitants of southeast Africa were influenced profoundly by the presence of these outsiders.

The final chapter addresses negotiations between past and present to consider continuities and changes in a Ndau identity. The local population draws on historical memories and oral traditions to foster and alter ethnic identifications. I address the prickly problems of "tribalism" and recent reconsiderations of ethnic identities to illustrate how this work provides a foundation for examining conflicts and divisions in the area today. I conclude by showing how the Ndau have responded over time to alterations in the political and cultural terrain by actively crafting their own identity and giving it meaning.

2

THE HISTORICAL LANDSCAPE OF SOUTHEAST AFRICA

Kare haagari ari kare.

The past will never remain the past.

—Shona proverb

A survey of the historical landscape suggests how to give meaning to identity formation and interactions between insiders and outsiders that occurred before formal colonialism took hold in southeast Africa. Although internal and external dynamics were both at play (and often intertwined), local populations shaped their own histories as agents of their own collective experiences. By looking at early written sources from Europeans who lived and traveled in the region, it is possible to trace the precolonial history of the Ndau since about 1500. Evidence of the development of identities from as early as the sixteenth century allows me to overturn the prevailing habit of dating African identities from the period of the Scramble for Africa in the late nineteenth century. In this chapter I turn to theoretical concerns that influence the study of ethnicity, identity, and history and then discuss the written record that informs a history of the Ndau from 1500 to 1900.

Ethnicity, Identity, and History

Previously, scholars and postcolonial leaders avoided questions surrounding ethnic identities on the continent. They tended to view ethnicity as a "retrogressive and shameful" topic, as Crawford Young notes, that could "summon forth from the societal depths demons who might subvert nationalism."[1] A popular phrase in Mozambique after independence, for instance, was "Down with tribalism!" Similarly, in neighboring South Africa ethnicity was viewed as the false creation of an apartheid state and feared as a divisive force.[2] More recently, scholars and some political leaders have acknowledged

25

that ethnicity is a motivating force in the world today, for indeed past cultural practices, social structures, and political orders help explain relationships and conflicts in the present. For Edwin Wilmsen and Patrick McAllister, ethnicity is "politically constructed and may arise anywhere at anytime,"[3] just as events in Rwanda so disturbingly revealed. But members must view their group identity as natural or real for the identity to work, or "to work best," as Kwame Anthony Appiah argues.[4] Current notions of primordial ethnicity that justify either "new or continued suppression of dispossessed groups"[5] are problematic, for when ethnicity gains "the 'natural' appearance of an autonomous force"[6] the phenomenon *appears* to be primordial. Although ethnic identities are an integral aspect of the historical landscape, they are not primordial. Rather, they are constructed over time through a process that I unravel in this book.

An insidious neoprimordialism, a combination of primordialism and instrumentalism, is currently receiving attention in the discourse about ethnicity. With this "theoretical bricolage," as noted by John Comaroff, ethnic identities call on some sort of primordial infrastructure in times of crisis or opportunity.[7] This view legitimizes a racist politics of difference. In South Africa, for example, both Inkatha and conservative Afrikaners express their ethnonationalist claims in primordialist terms. Ethnicity is attractive, for it simplifies the social world in a diffuse and unspecified manner and couches complexities "in the emotive language of identity, being and belonging."[8] An assessment of the fluidity of ethnic identification and its historical baggage is needed to combat destructive consequences of ethnicity, such as those arising from subnationalism among Zulu and Afrikaner groups.

In the social sciences, Fredrik Barth's work on the persistence and permeability of ethnic boundaries has shaped theoretical concerns about ethnicity over the past thirty-five years.[9] He argues that ethnic groups maintain discrete categories such as observable cultural features of dress, language, or architecture as well as basic value orientations. He also shows that movement across ethnic boundaries and relationships with outsiders, often adversaries, can strengthen ethnic recognition. These distinctions, which often add to an ethnic group's vitality, demonstrate that ethnic groups are energetic structures with outside contacts, rather than isolated, primordial "tribes." Expanding on Barth, social scientists studying the Maasai in East Africa conclude that ethnic ideologies shape identity formation and social action.[10] For these scholars "ethnicity need not be strictly defined," as I argue for the Ndau, since individuals in East Africa become Maasai as both active and latent identities are transformed during a continual process.[11] The interplay of various ethnic dimensions across the social field underscores the importance of understanding the idea of culture for the study of ethnicity. John Comaroff and Jean Comaroff provide a useful working definition of culture as "a historically situated, historically unfolding ensemble of signifiers-in-action, signifiers at once material and symbolic, social and aesthetic."[12] In this work I examine shifts in cultural and political indicators that affect Ndau identity by focusing on the historical landscape.

To explain the fashioning of ethnic identity during the colonial period, historians developed their own theories of ethnicity. Studies that examine the "creation of tribalism" in colonial Africa suggest that cultural, social, and political boundaries were fixed during the colonial period. For southern Africa, Leroy Vail's model of the process of ethnic construction stresses the importance of culture brokers and African intermediaries in shaping popular ethnic ideologies.[13] Language, a central element of the "cultural package," serves to either foster unity or create divisions.[14] Vail's arguments, while helpful in understanding the issues of "tribalism" during colonial rule, can also be applied to the precolonial period. Precolonial rulers used inventions of ideology to heighten ethnic awareness and reinforce the loyalties of their subjects.[15] My study expands on Vail's model to address gaps in our understanding of the precolonial era and to look further into the past for the motivating forces of ethnicity.

Through an examination of the shaping of ethnic identity over several centuries, I have determined shifts that are apparent only over long time periods. The pioneering work of the historian Fernand Braudel has led me to consider the value of analyzing continuities and changes in social, political, economic, and cultural systems and traditions over centuries. Braudel's method spurs scholars to look at different conceptions of time. He measures time on three scales by examining the very slow history of people's relationship to the environment (*la longue durée*), the social history of groups over several generations, and the exciting yet dangerous history of events. Although the traditional history of events is, in Braudel's words, the "richest in human interest of histories, it is also the most perilous. We must beware of that history which still simmers with the passions of the contemporaries who felt it, described it, lived it, to the rhythm of their brief lives, lives as brief as our own. It has the dimensions of their anger, their dreams, and their illusions."[16] For Braudel, events act as a smoke screen to obscure the economic and social realities of the past. By adopting all three types of approaches, historians are able to reflect on both rapid events and slower periods to move beyond traditional narrative histories.[17] Only by looking at the *longue durée* do scholars offer deeper understandings of history with nuances of change and continuity.

For this study I also draw on the methodological and analytical approaches used by historians who have extended the discourse on the phenomenon of ethnicity by tracing its evolving course over several centuries. Ronald Atkinson, for instance, relies primarily on oral traditions to make conclusions about early Acholi ethnicity in Uganda.[18] He argues that the period from the mid to late seventeenth century was the crucial moment when a distinctive collective identity emerged among the people who came to be called Acholi. David Newbury's work contests the traditional understanding of clans as static structures.[19] Using oral traditions and comparative evidence of ritual practices and political forms,

Newbury shows that clan identities, rather than being descent-based, were continually transformed over time in the Kivu Rift Valley. And Jan Vansina reconstructs political tradition in the rain forests of Equatorial Africa by using "words as history" to examine cultural interpretations and collective representations.[20] He argues that a single tradition, evident in a sense of cultural unity and common institutions, flourished for centuries among small political units previously thought to be unconnected. Vansina redefines tradition as a process with "concepts, values, institutions and tools" and declares that it "must continually change to remain alive."[21] A careful examination of change over time in the Ndau region reveals a long history of dynamic traditions.

In the Zambezi region that includes parts of Mozambique, Zimbabwe, Zambia, and Malawi, Allen Isaacman and Barbara Isaacman draw on the lived experiences of slave soldiers and their descendants to highlight the shaping of a collective identity among the Chikunda.[22] In this unstable part of south-central Africa the Chikunda emerged from the slave armies of Portuguese *prazos*, or crown estates, first established in the late sixteenth century. Going beyond the master-slave relationship, the authors explore the inner realm of Chikunda men where "real men" were "made" in the interior far from the gaze of the Portuguese. Describing the culturally exalted activities of a male-centered world, the Isaacmans provide a rich explanation of the gendering of ethnicity. Although the Portuguese may have created the phenomenon of the Chikunda through enslavement, the Chikunda made themselves over time by giving social meaning to a sense of being Chikunda. Thus, the nuances of a longer encounter with Portuguese colonialism are revealed in this work, along with the relatively weak nature of the Portuguese presence.

Another framework for tracing the course of ethnicity comes from Elizabeth Eldredge's study of nineteenth-century Lesotho.[23] She describes processes of amalgamation among southern African chiefdoms that led to the political consolidation of a kingdom and subsequent cultural assimilation. She uses oral traditions, evidence of material culture, and archaeological data to demonstrate the feasibility of tracing regional cultural linkages in spite of changing social and political units. Eldredge argues that the involvement of women in politics contributed to political reproduction. Through marriage alliances "women produced and reproduced the regional political order" and played an integral part in maintaining a common language and culture over a wide geographic area.[24]

Although women play important roles in reinforcing and transforming ethnic identification, politics and ethnicity are often mistakenly viewed as solely the affairs of men. In her history of the Anlo-Ewe of southeastern Ghana, Sandra Greene challenges the way in which most historians of Africa have studied gender and ethnic relations as two separate fields of social history.[25] She argues that both fields should be studied together since they are inextricably connected to each other over the *longue durée*. Greene's study of Anlo social groups known as *hlowo*, or clans, offers an exciting approach to the analysis of the intersection of gender and ethnicity over several centuries. Dismissing the idea that "women have no tribe," she argues that Anlo women, since the late seventeenth century, consciously and explicitly supported and shifted ethnic boundaries within the lineages and clans of Anlo society.[26] Although many other studies of ethnicity have focused mainly on elite Africans, Greene notes that marginalized men and women were actively involved in transforming ethnic identities as they defined and redefined their own identities. Disadvantaged people challenged their social definitions as the "other," and some outsiders were able to alter their identities. Greene's emphasis on the connections between gender and ethnicity over the *longue durée* is a very different, and welcome, conception of ethnicity.

In addition to these theoretical influences, my research builds on the work of others studying ethnic identity in the wider Shona region. In a well-known argument, Terence Ranger claims that missionaries and colonial administrators played a central role in the "invention of tribalism" among the Manyika in northeast Zimbabwe.[27] Although Ranger creatively shows how ethnicity was tampered with in the colonial period, he gives colonialists too much credit for inventing "tribalism." My work joins a growing body of scholarship contesting Ranger's conclusion that the origins of ethnicity do not lie in the precolonial past.[28] Others following Ranger have informed the debate by demonstrating how missionary linguistic politics "fixed" the ethnolinguistic map. Herbert Chimhundu, for instance, views the creation of "new and wider ethnic identities" in the Shona-speaking region to be a result of missionary influence in Zimbabwe, but it is still not clear how these linguistic identities spread beyond the missions' sphere of power.[29] A study of Christianity and nationalism among the Ndau in Zimbabwe by J. Keith Rennie shows how Ndau speakers could adopt new identities in the nineteenth and early twentieth centuries.[30] I expand on Rennie's work here and extend the scope to consider the precolonial situation on both sides of the arbitrary colonial border.[31] While these studies have highlighted the manipulation of ethnic awareness during the colonial era, I shift the focus to encompass a much longer period of time.

Portuguese Writings as Historical Sources

After consulting early sources on the history of southeast Africa, it is clear that the pen of the Portuguese was mightier than their sword. Although most of the first Portuguese arrivals carried either the sword or the cross, they put these down to wield the pen and leave a written record of their triumphs and travails. Portuguese soldiers, religious men, and others in the service of the crown left documents that provide details about Portuguese experiences and the lives of those they encountered. Rich portraits of local customs and appetizing snippets of daily life are embedded in various writings. The abundant written records left by the Portuguese shed light on changes and continuities in Ndau history and provide evidence of identity formation from as early as the sixteenth century.

The Portuguese pen detailed favored hairstyles and common spices much to the delight of not only contemporary readers in Portugal, but also today's scholars interested in the past. Fragments of evidence about a type of brewed beer or a manner of dress were heretofore overlooked and most likely over-shadowed by other official documentation such as the voluminous cor-respondence between the king of Portugal and his viceroy overseeing Mozambique. All of these materials are mere pieces of a larger historical puz-zle about the early history of southeastern Africa. An analysis of the reports, letters, and other data that have survived demonstrates the feasibility of recov-ering African perspectives from colonial sources, albeit tainted and pre-judiced ones. Rather than dismissing this colonial record in its entirety, I acknowledge the inherent biases in these documents and subject them to a healthy interrogation, for they yield amazingly detailed and valuable evidence of local realities in what is today central Mozambique and eastern Zimbabwe.

Sofala and the Hinterland

Before the arrival of the Portuguese in the early sixteenth century, the Sofala region of Mozambique thrived as an important trading center. About ten thousand residents lived around the Bay of Sofala in 1505 when the Portuguese first established a fortress and began competing with local traders, some of whom were Muslim.[32] Known for its gold exports, Sofala was an important East African commercial center similar to Kilwa and Zanzibar far-ther north. Sofala was linked to wider trade networks that connected the Arabian Peninsula, India, Indonesia, and Madagascar. However, its distant southern location meant that it was difficult to access because of the mon-soon, and this lower frequency of contact placed it on the fringe of the sophis-ticated Indian Ocean exchange system.[33] The most powerful man at Sofala was a sheik related to the Swahili living farther north along the East African coast.[34] This ruler directed exports of gold and ivory from the interior and enjoyed considerable prosperity until the Portuguese gained control of Sofala in the sixteenth century.[35]

In the half century before Portuguese ships first entered the bay of Sofala, trade, particularly in gold, shifted toward the north and away from Sofala.[36] This reorientation soon eclipsed Sofala so that the coastal region of Angoche, along with the Zambezi River settlements of Sena and Tete to the north, grew into thriving urban centers. These trade centers relied on the increased min-ing activity and new gold trade fairs, known as *feiras*, on the northern part of the Zimbabwe Plateau.[37] Swahili traders and their local partners probably accelerated the shift in trade routes to the north as they moved to escape the new presence of the Portuguese at Sofala. The Portuguese did not cooperate well with Muslim traders and tended to assert their power through violence.

Although Sofala did not offer the best access to these sources of gold to the northwest of the region, the settlement continued to be a strategic location that the Portuguese managed to exploit after their arrival. At spring tide Sofala offered good entry to the innovative, deep-keeled Portuguese ships known as *naus*.[38] A small number of Portuguese maintained a fortress at the port and capitalized on the trade in ivory with the population around Sofala.[39] A combination of larger kingdoms, confederations, and smaller polities existed at various times in the Sofala hinterland. The Portuguese tapped into the established trading networks and lines of communication that stretched into the interior to facilitate their commercial interests. Many rivers crossed this well-watered region known for its abundance in meat, fish, and grains. Details from early Portuguese documents help historians form a picture of the early period, although the regional economic and political situation was not always clear to the Portuguese themselves at the time.

As Portuguese writers described events in the Sofala hinterland, they focused their attention on the Mutapa state, located on the Zimbabwe Plateau northwest of the Ndau region. In the interior, extensive Shona political systems such as the Mutapa, Torwa, and Changamire expanded rapidly but eventually disintegrated while decentralized, segmented political structures survived.[40] The Ndau and the Manica, both Shona-speaking peoples in the east, declared their independence from Mutapa overrule shortly before the beginning of the sixteenth century. From these new political subdivisions the larger states of Teve, Manica, and Barwe were formed, along with smaller territories such as Sanga and Danda, located southwest of Sofala. The Portuguese left extensive evidence about their trading activities with the Mutapa state, but documentary evidence about smaller polities within the realm of the Ndau is scattered. However, various sources describe commercial activities, political maneuvering, and details of Ndau daily life that reveal aspects of identity formation.

Chroniclers and Missionaries

Portuguese chroniclers and missionaries wrote about this part of the world for the pleasure of their readers, while other officials corresponded with the Portuguese king and those in the government out of duty and necessity. The Portuguese monarchy initially solicited information about kings, wars, and riches after their first contacts with the population at Sofala and the surrounding region in the early sixteenth century. Often "the noise of gold drowned the thoughts of danger" for the Portuguese who sought their fortunes in this part of the world.[41] Some of the Portuguese who ventured into the interior were illiterate, so they described their observations to others who then created a written record secondhand. Missionaries proved to be the best observers and recorders of events. Many learned local languages such as Ndau and came to understand facets of Ndau culture. A long line of writers whose works have survived as written documents, with many now available in published texts, provide a wonderful sample of data.

The Jesuit father Francisco Monclaro was one of the first Portuguese observers to describe local customs in detail in his report of Francisco Barreto's 1569 expedition to "conquer" the ruler of the Mutapa state.[42] Despite the aggressive nature of this famous mission and Monclaro's perception of the population as "barbarous," his account offers precious evidence of customs and politics that can be compared with other great works of the period.[43] Monclaro stated that he either observed various "customs and principal affairs" of inhabitants firsthand or "learned upon trustworthy information."[44] For most of the Ndau area, Monclaro had only secondhand knowledge. As Portugal learned more about the region in the sixteenth century and locals continued to interact with Europeans in their midst, any initial considerations of each other as equals seemed to fade. Early on, the Portuguese displayed violent tendencies when they attempted to gain control (unsuccessfully) over access to mineral wealth and exact revenge for the death of a Portuguese priest in 1561 at the Mutapa court.[45] They also tried to expel Swahili traders and subjugate local rulers, often to no avail, to achieve their commercial goals.[46]

One of the main sources of information about southeast Africa at the end of the sixteenth century comes from Father João dos Santos, a Dominican friar who lived in Sofala for a total of five years and also spent time in the Zambezi Valley before writing his narrative.[47] His monumental encyclopedic work, *Ethiopia Oriental*, discusses the geography and culture of the Sofala region and the Zambezi Valley.[48] He also provides details about missionary activities and the military and commercial penetration of the Portuguese. His writings are valuable, for dos Santos had contact with Ndau speakers around Sofala who lived either in the land of Teve or just outside its borders. He also resided at the Mutapa court.[49] In *Ethiopia Oriental* dos Santos argued that the region "is the most barbarous and brutal that there is in the world."[50] Dos Santos and others such as Monclaro made these statements in a religious context, referring to the dearth of Christians in the region.

Father Manuel Barreto, a chaplain who spent several years with missionaries and Portuguese officials in the region, wrote another account in 1667 based on firsthand knowledge of the Zambezi and Mutapa region.[51] He urged the Portuguese king to support the conquest of Mokaranga, Manica, Maungo, Barwe, and Butua to secure "endless rich lands, like large counties, with revenues of from five to ten thousand, with which it would be possible to build up many houses and reward many services."[52] He points out that the conquest of Maravi and Teve could be left for a later enterprise since these kingdoms would be more difficult to subjugate and yield less lucrative spoils.[53] In one glaring exaggeration, Manuel Barreto overstated the southern boundary of the kingdom of Teve in his report, claiming that the territory ends at the Cape of Good Hope on the southern tip of the continent.[54]

The large amount of documentary evidence generated by an assortment of prolific Portuguese writers in Mozambique during the sixteenth and seventeenth centuries whets the appetite of the researcher.[55] Unfortunately, events of the next two centuries are not as well known since the Portuguese were expelled from most of the Zimbabwe Plateau in the 1690s.[56] Just as the early Portuguese were obsessed with the Mutapa state in their quest for gold, later historians were drawn toward the Mutapa state because of the extensive documents generated by four centuries of Portuguese contact. Thus, scholars have written about the history of the Mutapa state, but the Ndau region to the southeast has not received the same attention. In this study I draw on many of the early narratives by the Portuguese and rely heavily on these documents because they provide some of the best evidence of the precolonial period. The richness of these sources led archivists and scholars to select these documents for publication in multivolume collections with English translations.[57]

This account relies heavily on two well-known collections of primary materials, totaling eighteen volumes, which both provide a wealth of information about the early history of south-central and southeast Africa. George McCall Theal's *Records of South-Eastern Africa*, first published at the end of the nineteenth century, was followed over 60 years later by *Documents on the Portuguese in Mozambique and Central Africa* (*Documentos Sobre os Portugueses em Moçambique e na África Central, 1497–1840*). This recent collection was an attempt to update Theal's *Records*, and it includes nine published volumes of documents on the Mozambican coast and the interior from 1497 to 1615. Theal's volumes are valuable for the reports and chronicles from mainly the sixteenth and seventeenth centuries. They include informative selections from *Ethiopia Oriental*, the sixteenth-century account written by the Dominican friar João dos Santos mentioned above. There are also important excerpts from chronicles known as the *Decades* (*Décadas*), a history of the Portuguese in India and Asia, written by João de Barros, Diogo de Couto, and Antonio Bocarro between 1552 and 1649. It is possible to discern the early history of southeast Africa by relying on documents such as these, for they provide the richest data about the period.

Eighteenth-Century Writers

Although the Portuguese crown was mainly interested in gold and ivory, the early accounts that Portuguese writers dutifully returned to the king in Portugal also included details about the uses and customs (*usos e costumes*) of local peoples. Trustworthy information from the interior was scarce in both the early and middle part of the eighteenth century due to distant relations with the powerful Rozvi of the Changamire state, but Portuguese documents from the end of the eighteenth century are especially profuse. There was an impressive increase in the number of requests from the crown for information on Mozambique between 1781 and 1805.[58] The significant volume of responses sent from Mozambique during this time period provides scholars with an informative glimpse of social and cultural history. Many writers were interested in local traditions, daily customs, and the causes of conflict, and their manuscripts display a sincere, if at times misguided, attempt to describe the way of life of those they encountered. The accounts, like their predecessors, reflect an obvious Eurocentric view of the world held by the Portuguese at the time. This assortment of writings was followed by other important studies published later in the nineteenth century when the Portuguese and the British initiated powerful steps toward a firm control over the Ndau residing in their respective spheres of influence.[59] These records document how the European "civilizing mission" coalesced into the systematic exploitation of the Ndau and their neighbors.

Ethnographic reports are the most valuable sources about local daily life. The authors included their own observations as well as secondhand reports of others. João Julião de Silva (1769–1852), for example, consulted written primary sources housed in Sofala for his nineteenth-century *Memórias* about Sofala, and others may have done so as well.[60] Some accounts contain misleading tall tales, while others offer more accurate information. Ignácio Caetano Xavier appeals for sympathy from his European audience when he writes about the children of Portuguese settlers who are enslaved by the ruler Changamira in the interior.[61] Xavier is also critical of the activities of certain priests, and he accuses them of devising schemes to enrich themselves at the expense of the crown.[62] Yet, the author himself was looking for a royal favor in return for his work, and he managed to secure an appointment after his report was submitted in 1758.[63] Regardless of his motives, Xavier clearly stated Portuguese priorities when he declared that missionary operations should be followed by an influx of skilled mine workers.[64] Indeed, historians are pleased that Xavier was most efficient and detail-oriented in his undertaking, since scholars are able to benefit from the fruits of his labor. These Portuguese writers leave a meandering paper trail that combines informative musings with contradictory, erroneous, and humorous details. Here I attempt to make sense of these sources and carefully glean accurate information about the Ndau. Wherever possible, I have authenticated information through juxtaposition with other sources.

One of the most valuable documents is *Reposta das Questoens sobre os Cafres*, written in 1781.[65] This reply to questions about the indigenous population of central Mozambique is probably the first ethnographic survey of Mozambique.[66] Before this report appeared in 1796, earlier works included fragments of data on indigenous beliefs, customs, rituals, and other cultural aspects amid personal memoirs and reports of the Portuguese about plans to exploit the wealth of the region and develop favorable trading relationships.[67] This *Reposta*, conceived as part of a failed attempt to form a national museum, assembles ethnographic pieces about the Ndau into a substantial package of information.[68] The document describes traditions, religious rituals, aspects of social life, weddings and burials, death, divinations, prophecies about causes of death, various aspects of political life, agriculture and food, treatment of sickness, climate, topography, the manufacture of goods, and the use of plants found in nature. This report is attributed to Carlos José dos Reis e Gama, the governor of Sofala, but another writer was most likely the true author.[69] The *Reposta* deserves considerable attention as the most detailed example of evidence about the Ndau region from an eighteenth-century Portuguese source.

Although no detailed discussion of identities should overlook the value of the *Reposta*, the observations in this work are presented as biased comparisons with a Portuguese way of life rather than neutral observations about local customs. Many paragraphs begin with statements about what inhabitants do *not* do rather than what they do practice. For example, Gama (or the actual author) claims that the Ndau have no ideas about the origin of their polity.[70] He even contends that they do not think about this question.[71] He alleges that the Ndau are ignorant about the history of the region since they do not know of an apparent "revolution" that once occurred among them.[72] Bearing in mind this caveat about Gama's mistakes and incorrect information, scholars can turn to supporting evidence from other sources to confirm or reject some of the questionable observations in the *Reposta*.

Bridging a Cultural Divide

The methodology of both the early Portuguese authors of these documents and later colonial officials who compiled reports is somewhat similar. In the twentieth century colonial officials relied on interpreters or acquired a proficiency in a local language, depending on their length of time at a post and their personal views about African languages.[73] Missionaries in the region often learned local languages, including Ndau, and spoke them in their efforts to spread Christianity. Many Portuguese traders certainly developed some knowledge of languages spoken by the people, and those who married local inhabitants were intimately exposed to their cultural milieu. These men—and all surviving records of the early period come from men only—studied the "customs and practices" of the people.[74] Scholars are fortunate that some who were well informed recorded their observations. The friar dos Santos even conducted oral interviews, presumably in a manner similar to that of historians today. Dos Santos spoke with elderly women at Sofala who "perfectly remembered events that had taken place eighty years before."[75] Most of his writings were the result of direct observations and experience, such as his comparison of women's agricultural practices in Mozambique and northern Portugal.[76] At times the valuable observations of dos Santos and others describe realities that still exist in Ndau culture.[77] The documents also reveal a dynamic history, full of good stories with twists and turns along the way to keep the reader, and the historian, entertained.

The information garnered from the early Portuguese pen, combined with evidence from oral histories, aids the historian in mapping the contours of Ndauness over time. For instance, the documents tell us that hand clapping enjoyed widespread use as an important custom. This practice has endured in the Ndau region to this day. Chiefs have their own distinct order and rhythm for the clapping at their courts, and men clap differently from women in daily greetings and expressions of pleasure. It is unfortunate that the Portuguese chroniclers, missionaries, and officials—all men—focused mainly on the deeds of men. Women are often noticeably absent from many of the Portuguese descriptions, and thus information about their contributions must be sought elsewhere to obtain a fuller picture. Despite shortcomings such as this, historians who consult the eclectic evidence left by the Portuguese can gain an understanding of Ndau history across a cultural divide.

The Portuguese sources reveal historical data about local perspectives and material culture from earlier centuries that can be compared with evidence from interviews with Ndau elders in the twentieth century. Interestingly, Gama insisted that the Ndau did not have "any memories or traditions of times past."[78] He was either misinformed about the importance of memory and oral traditions among the Ndau or perhaps felt that unwritten remembrances did not constitute an accurate recording of the past. It is clear today, however, that oral histories and traditions have proved to be an essential component for an in-depth study of the region's early history. Scholars can no longer rely solely on European documents, for their inherent biases, exaggerations, misinformation, and repetitions of false rumors often render them severely flawed. Although the documents do not tell the *whole* story of things past, they do contain a wealth of evidence that merits a thorough consideration and investigation. By comparing this written evidence with other sources such as the archaeological record and local oral traditions, scholars can ask and answer questions about southeast Africa over the *longue durée*.

In the Ndau region, a Portuguese presence that spanned several centuries did not lead to a significant European influence over local inhabitants. Only a relatively small number of Portuguese officials, *prazeros* (holders of leased crown estates), and traders lived in the area, and a viable Afro-Portuguese community did not develop (except along the coast), as was the case farther north near the Zambezi River.[79] For the most part, Portuguese institutions were not transplanted among the Ndau, and European technology and material culture did not take root. Elements of European culture were present in the form of firearms, some luxury items, and several churches with their accompanying ritual objects.[80] More often the exchange flowed the other way, with the small number of Portuguese in the area adopting the material culture and way of life of the population. Missionaries made few converts, but fortunately they left many documents. The Portuguese who resided in the area worked to exclude new settlers and officials so that the wealth remained among only a select few. Traders extracted the region's resources, in the form of gold, ivory, some slaves, skins, and base metals, and they exported these items through long-established trading routes from the interior to the coast.

Archaeological Contributions

Archaeology fills in some of the gaps in our knowledge of local history before the arrival of the Portuguese, but the evidence is scattered and scarce in the Ndau region. For eastern sites on Mozambique's coastal plain, the best evidence comes from studies of Manyikweni, a site 133 km south of the Save River that was first built in the twelfth century.[81] Manyikweni has an architectural style, *zimbabwe* stone building technique, contents, and dates that are contemporary with Great Zimbabwe on the plateau.[82] Building in stone, *zimbabwe*, occurred throughout the wider Shona-speaking region from the late thirteenth century to the first half of the sixteenth century.[83] At Manyikweni, agriculture, livestock, and hunting were the basis of the *zimbabwe* economy, but Chinese porcelain and glass beads present at the site are evidence of external trade.[84] Archaeologists have determined that stone structures in the wider Shona-speaking area indicate the existence of an elite living inside the enclosures separate from the rest of the population.[85] Evidence from *zimbabwe* structures such as Manyikweni and Great Zimbabwe suggests that a large degree of social and political change was occurring within these societies before the arrival of the Portuguese.[86] Archaeologists have excavated only a handful of *zimbabwe* sites in the greater Ndau region, but future archaeological work would likely yield valuable evidence to aid historians studying the Ndau and their neighbors.[87] These smaller *zimbabwe* sites to the east are similar to those on the plateau where archaeologists have focused their work.[88]

With more archaeological evidence historians could rethink how "to blend an archaeological reconstruction of an earlier period with a substantial historical one."[89] Few historians have shown much interest in material culture, yet both archaeologists and historians would benefit from systematic studies of these topics. Thus, historians need to turn to their sister discipline, or as Jan Vansina says, to their lost "siblings"—archaeologists—to enhance studies of precolonial history.[90] Archaeology provides "resonance to documentary evidence by placing it against its background, by eliciting the longue durée in which documented events and trends unfold," according to Vansina.[91]

Until recently, the historical scholarship was based mainly on Portuguese writ-ten records, but an incorporation of archaeological evidence and a careful use of oral traditions will enhance our interpretation of the documents, which have their own biases.

In the future, more work on the archaeological history of southeast Africa will help to resolve some of the gaps in the historical record. Further research on neighbors of the Ndau will provide a better understanding of the wider picture. We know much about the Mutapa state, for instance, yet the research program for other areas, including the Ndau heartland, remains unfulfilled. Differences in style variation—any change in material culture that is not related to the function of the object—offer clues about early ethnic identities. The elaborate stone ruins at sites such as Zembe, Messambuzi, Uzuma (Ussoma), Nhamara, and Magure are a fertile and scarcely explored ground for archaeological research and historical interpretation in the southeastern region.[92] Further investigations will enhance our understanding of the histor-ical landscape of southeast Africa. In the meantime, written documents tell us much about early exchanges, the subject of the next chapter.

3

EARLY EXCHANGES

POLITICAL AND ECONOMIC CONTEXTS

> There is plenty of ivory in Sofalla and some amber and also gold with
> which people come from Quiteve and Manica to buy merchandise.
>
> —Fr. Felippe da Assumpção, ca. 1698

> Therefore Kaffirs who are careful to choose laborious wives are the rich-
> est, and have the most provisions.
>
> —Fr. João dos Santos ca. 1580

As the Ndau exchanged gold, ivory, and other commodities in the Indian
Ocean trade, they developed relationships with neighbors in southeast Africa,
Muslims from the Swahili coast, and Portuguese in the region. This ebb and
flow of contacts over several centuries in turn strengthened group identities
and ideas about being interconnected for those living in the Ndau region. This
chapter discusses the economic and political contexts that shaped ethnic
boundaries in the wider world of the Ndau by examining trade (both local and
long-distance) and political relations between 1500 and 1900. The focus is on
activities between the Zambezi and Save Rivers, for similar patterns of trade
and related political systems influenced ethnic identities as well as notions of
the "other" across this space. Large states, confederations, and smaller polities
tied to commercial exchanges and flourishing economies existed at various
times in the region, and trading networks and lines of communication helped
maintain cultural similarities. Political identifications occurred at multiple levels as villagers and chiefs alike recognized overrule by larger states and paid
tribute to Shona-speaking dynasties in the north and west such as the Mutapa,
Torwa, and Changamire. Dynamic and extensive political systems expanded,
competed, and splintered long before the onset of formal colonialism by
European powers at the end of the nineteenth century.

The economic activities and political institutions of the Ndau were two
important aspects of a heritage that formed the basis of a shared identity.

Historically, ethnicity was used for political purposes and ethnic boundaries were drawn within overlapping political structures. Trade and politics influenced ethnic identification, along with other cultural practices and expressions such as language, religion, art, and architecture. As the term Karanga fell into disuse in Portuguese documents, existing political designations became ethnic terms, or "political ethnicities."[1] By examining the political and economic map of this part of southeast Africa, this chapter begins to unravel how the Ndau crafted history and identity before 1900. Although the Portuguese left a written record of early exchanges and political connections, they failed to settle in the Ndau heartland in large numbers or assert much control over the population. The activities of the Ndau and their neighbors, rather than Portuguese policies or maneuvers, shaped much of the region's history.

Early Trading Economies

For the Ndau, the long-distance trade in gold and ivory between the interior and the coast of southeast Africa brought wealth to the region and routine contacts with outsiders. Residents of Sofala and the surrounding area interacted with Swahili traders from East African ports farther north in a sophisticated Indian Ocean exchange system long before the arrival of the Portuguese at the end of the fifteenth century.[2] After the Portuguese arrived at Sofala and joined the trade with the Ndau and their neighbors in the sixteenth century, they plotted to expel the Swahili merchants who often acted as middlemen in the profitable Indian Ocean network. But the two groups of traders coexisted for some time, and both penetrated the hinterland to trade at inland towns.[3] By taking over strategic bases in key East African ports, the Portuguese became a formidable competitor in the Indian Ocean system. As a result, trade and commerce, rather than political domination or territorial possession, characterized early relationships between the Ndau and their trading partners—the Swahili and the Portuguese.[4]

The Ndau and their neighbors fueled a demand for the main imports of cloth and beads, but it simply was not feasible for most local inhabitants to gather gold and ivory directly for trading purposes in the region.[5] Either skilled hunters or the construction of large pits for trapping were needed to kill elephants for meat and ivory. Even though an attack on an elephant was a very dangerous undertaking for a hunter, an estimated four thousand to five thousand elephants were killed each year in the sixteenth century.[6] Yet, perhaps fewer than two thousand people hunted elephants in the wider region.[7] Gold was easier to secure than ivory, since about one in every five people lived near alluvial deposits or gold reefs.[8] Gold washing was much safer than mining, for many people were killed in accidents when they worked inside gold mines. Other items such as copper, iron, leopard skins, beeswax, rubber,

grain, and cattle were traded for the main imports of cloth, beads, iron implements, and porcelain.[9] An early Portuguese document from 1512, for
instance, notes that cloth, either imported or made locally, was "traded
throughout the land."[10] The Portuguese took note along the East African
coast in 1783 that cloth was "the currency that is accepted in ports."[11]
Inhabitants used gold, beads, cloth, guns, cattle, hoes, and ivory as currencies
in their trading activities.[12]

After the decline of Great Zimbabwe in the fifteenth century, the major
trade routes from the interior to the coast shifted farther north to run
through either settlements on the Zambezi River or into Teve and Manica
south of the river. Reports from the fortress at Sofala in 1580–84 note the
reduced trade in ivory, compared to the "extensive trade in gold and ivory"
earlier in the century.[13] Trade routes within the Ndau region along the Buzi
and Save Rivers were used less frequently for long-distance exchanges.[14] Boats
did navigate up the Buzi, Pungwe, and Save Rivers for at least fifty miles from
the coast, but the economic activities taking place to the north in the Mutapa
state overshadowed those involving the Ndau.[15] Communication links were
good among the Ndau, yet the long-distance trade declined as the Mutapa
state gained more power farther north.[16]

Long-distance trade routes that once passed through the Ndau heartland
from Great Zimbabwe were far from the Mutapa capital. Commenting on the
shift in trading to the north, one seventeenth-century observer noted, "Today
some gold from Manica is exported from Sofala, which I think does not
exceed five hundred pastas, whereas that annually exported from Quelimane
is nearly three thousand."[17] The Ndau also lost the interest of the Portuguese
when it became clear that gold deposits were scarce in the region.[18] However,
mining activities in neighboring territories to the north such as Manica (long
a focus of the Portuguese) supported a substantial trade in commodities
within Ndau communities. The Ndau also interacted with their southern
neighbors who used trade routes that ran through the Tsonga region to
Venda in the interior.[19] But as Sofala turned into a backwater under
Portuguese control in the 1530s, the bulk of long-distance trading activities
shifted away from the Ndau to flourish along the Zambezi River and into the
northern reaches of the Sofala hinterland.[20] The economic decline of Sofala
left parts of the Ndau region free from the gaze of the Portuguese for some
time.

Sofala did remain linked to lands inhabited by the Ndau and their neighbors in the *sertão*, or interior. The system of rivers south of the Zambezi River
allowed residents of Sofala to communicate with those in Manica via the
waterways, but contact with the trading center of Sena on the Zambezi was
hindered since there were no rivers connecting the two towns.[21] Trading
opportunities at Sofala continued to attract inhabitants of the region, as one
Portuguese observer noted at the end of the seventeenth century, "[T]here is
plenty of ivory in Sofalla and some amber and also gold with which people

come from Quiteve [Teve] and Manica to buy merchandise."[22] In fact, the abundance of ivory in Teve led to an expansion of the ivory trade among the Ndau up to the end of the seventeenth century.[23] The region of Teve was "very rich, fertile, and healthy" with an abundant supply of ivory and ambergris from the coast.[24] However, "not a grain" of gold was to be found, according to a report from 1667.[25] For locals, gold could be less important than cattle, and this frustrated the Portuguese to no end.[26] South of Sofala, pearls and seed pearls were harvested in the Bazaruto archipelago and around the port of Inhambane, where ivory was also traded.[27] Portuguese records about local economies and polities in the wider region provide a view of how early exchanges and encounters shaped the people who came to be Ndau.

Political Contexts

Important chiefdoms and powerful rulers influenced the contours of Ndau identity as they benefited from economic production through tribute and trade. But as the Ndau produced and exchanged diverse commodities such as hoes, pots, cattle, gold, ivory, copper, and salt, they experienced the disintegration of several dynamic and extensive political systems. Smaller polities formed in their wake to mark Ndau history with multiple levels of political identification that are often ambiguous and contradictory. Economic and political ties in the wider region, however, were central to the formation of linkages in spite of changing political units and a declining volume of trade. Through political and economic contexts over time, the Ndau came to see themselves as culturally similar to neighboring Shona speakers, with related little traditions, but distinct from outsiders such as the Swahili and the Portuguese.

After 1700, large state-building in the Shona-speaking region ceased as gold and ivory resources dwindled.[28] Despite exhausted goldfields in the southwest and a reduced elephant population, trade continued between the interior and the coast into the nineteenth century.[29] There was a shift to mining copper and other less precious metals in the eighteenth century to substitute for the shrinking gold resources.[30] The Mutapa, Torwa, and Changamire states—all on the periphery of the Ndau region—lasted into the eighteenth century, but no new large states emerged. Politically, Shona speakers were more divided after 1700, whereas during the previous two centuries there were several strong states and numerous united territories throughout the region.[31]

As an era of intense trade and state formation ended, Ndau rulers and other leaders in the east managed to hold on to their political power. Although this political strength was often on a much smaller scale, many ruling dynasties endured for centuries. The eastern territories of Barwe, Manica, Teve, and Danda controlled trade through their lands and collected a tax on trade goods and a *curva*, or annual gift, from outside merchants.[32] At times, coastal rulers demanded too much in taxes or gifts, and this led to a stifling of the established trading system and a decline in activity at ports such as Sofala.[33] Local leaders also disrupted commerce when they were at war. For example, when Teve and Manica engaged in hostilities in the 1570s, the ruler of Teve did not allow the Portuguese to pass through Teve territory to reach the gold mines of Manica.[34] Even though the Portuguese claimed to have "conquered" Teve in 1575, they agreed to provide an annual gift to the ruler of Teve to maintain an open trade route.[35] When the Portuguese reported problems, they acknowledged that these issues stemmed from an inability to control the politics and economies of the Ndau and their Shona neighbors.

External forces interrupted trade, and outside merchants often turned to alternate routes when the Mutapa state intervened or negotiated new commercial agreements.[36] The Mutapa leaders probably sent armies to newly formed territories in the region to collect tribute in the sixteenth century, but the evidence suggests that this larger state did not exert any regular rule over the east, home to the Ndau.[37] Rather, Mutapa rulers exercised a monopoly over the inland ivory trade that frustrated Portuguese traders who returned "with their hair standing on their heads after having been one, two or sometimes three years in the bush, away from their homes."[38] The Portuguese alleged that Mutapa leaders failed to cover transport costs and pay "a fair price" for ivory, thus reducing the quantity of exports overall.[39] From its location to the northwest, the Mutapa state always faced the logistical problem of distance and failed to monopolize trade or politics in the eastern region.

Although rulers in the wider Ndau world relied on trade to enhance their political power, their dependence on this commerce proved to be precarious. It was difficult for leaders to control the various aspects of exchanges. The Ndau and other Shona speakers had to secure relationships with outsiders and provide a constant supply of commodities for export. Little is known about the mediating relations that were formed out of trading activities among the Ndau, neighboring groups, and the Portuguese in this early period. How exactly were identity boundaries formed, maintained, and crossed during an intense period of trading and state building? What follows here is a discussion of the connections between political power and commerce and an investigation of how everyday encounters affected the emergence of an identity that came to be Ndau.

Political Structures in the East

In their struggle to control commerce in the Sofala hinterland, both large states and smaller territories depended on the extensive trading networks developed over centuries of contact with outsiders. Political solidarity in the east was fragile as rulers formed alliances to suit their own economic and political needs. These smaller states used diplomatic maneuvering and military force to guarantee a continued hold over trade. Both the Mutapa state and the eastern territories vied for control over trade in this manner during the sixteenth and seventeenth centuries. Despite the political fragmentation that occurred after the decline of the Mutapa state, ethnic identities in southeast Africa drew on a shared culture that came to be called Ndau. Economic ties and political alliances helped the Ndau to maintain links to a wider Karanga or Shona identity while also strengthening their own ethnic boundaries. As polities changed and those in the east were no longer united under the reaches of Great Zimbabwe or Mutapa, cultural identities shifted from Karanga to less inclusive labels such as Ndau, Danda, and Teve.[40] Today these local identities tied to the political realm still exist alongside a resilient sense of Ndauness retained over centuries.

Political leaders maintained their power by fostering a sound economic base and asserting an ideological legitimacy over others. A second tier of territorial chiefs ruled under the aristocracy with elders, headmen, and household heads governing below these chiefs. Although rulers increased their economic power base by taxing traders, they also relied on their role as administrators of justice to strengthen their economic position.[41] For example, in Teve, according to dos Santos, "nobody could see the king of Teve without bringing clothes or a cow, and if he could not afford that the supplicant brought a sack of earth to signify his obedience to a territorial ruler, or a bundle of grass for thatching."[42] A ruler could also order a seizure of goods "to avenge some injury he has received, or pretended to have received, from the Portuguese . . . this is what they call an *empata*, and in this way he liberally pays himself what is due and takes satisfaction for the affront he has received."[43] Dos Santos also reported that merchants "with their bags of gold" could travel "much more securely than if they were in Portugal" save for the occasional *empata*.[44] Thus, local rulers used the proceeds of trade to sustain their power, while also relying on internal production to increase their economic base.

Below kings and their courts, chiefs of the intermediary aristocracy were called *nyamasangos*, or rulers of the woodland.[45] These chiefs came from various origins. They were members of royal lineages, older leaders recently incorporated into the state, or recent immigrants invited into the community.[46] *Nyamasangos*, rather than kings, took the obligatory ground tusks of elephants killed on their land.[47] *Nyamasangos* also received cloth for burials, and some collected tribute, announced court decisions, and conveyed messages for their rulers.[48] Ideology was "a critical factor" in perpetuating an economic arrangement in which "the aristocracy as a whole enjoyed considerable control over the accumulation and redistribution of wealth."[49]

Leaders in the political hierarchy did not use ideology alone to win followers. They used elaborate methods that incorporated symbolism, apparent in descriptions from many Portuguese documents, to create consensus and support the cohesive nature of states.[50] Political authority and social inequality were legitimated both symbolically and historically in a number of ways. For example, local leaders could claim to control aspects of the environment, such as rain, or maintain a royal grave cult with annual offerings.[51] Symbolic ties to an external political authority, such as the Mutapa state, were maintained through the annual relighting of local fires from a main fire at the ruler's court. Rennie's research reveals that when the Rozvi state farther south eclipsed the power of the Mutapa, the "fire ritual was re-enacted from that quarter, and the legitimating charter was adjusted."[52] Smaller states also maintained traditional connections to the Mutapa state with the claim that sons of the Mutapa ruler founded the eastern territories of Teve, Danda, and Sanga.[53] Legitimating factors among local rulers shifted to retain validity when powerful institutions such as the Mutapa state declined at the end of the seventeenth century.

Much of southeast Africa in the eighteenth and nineteenth centuries came to be characterized by the unstable great society of paramount chiefs as well as the more durable little society of smaller villages.[54] Although state formation on a grand scale among the Shona ceased, what followed had a profound effect on the Ndau to the east. Changamire ruled the last renowned Shona state, Rozvi, as a large military power on the southern part of the Zimbabwe Plateau, until this state (like the Mutapa) declined in the eighteenth century after succumbing to internal problems and outside pressures. The gold and ivory resources that helped support great political systems in the region dwindled during this time.[55] At the close of the seventeenth century, *mwoyo* totem clans from the Rozvi state migrated eastward and occupied the Ndau area in the western reaches of the Sofala hinterland.[56] In 1698 Portuguese residents described this movement as an invasion by the "rebel" Changamira who attacked in 1684 and again in 1694.[57] These clashes reflect both the continued state-building efforts of the Rozvi and the determination of their rulers to keep the Portuguese out of the interior.[58] But for the Ndau, the Rozvi presence was another encounter that served to shape a sense of Ndauness.

By the early eighteenth century, this Rozvi confederation asserted some control over both the Ndau in the Save Valley as well as parts of a weakened Mutapa state.[59] In 1758 the Portuguese official Ignácio Caetano Xavier summarized the political situation while describing the Rozvi invasion and the Changamira's rise to power:

At the time when Francisco Barreto and other captains tried to conquer the great Empire of the Senna Rivers, the Manamotapa [Mutapa] was obeyed by all the tenants and the land of Butua that now belongs to the Changamira was his, but one of his shepherds ripped it away from his empire and proclaimed himself its owner, taking the name of Changamira and gradually increased his power in the native style to the point it has reached now; all the Régulos [rulers] used to unite forces to fight as if for a common cause.[60]

The bold actions of the rebellious Changamira were similar to earlier attempts, some less successful, by the Ndau and their neighbors to declare independence from the Mutapa. The Ndau were on the fringes of this empire building and less likely to unite "for a common cause" under the leadership of a powerful ruler like the Mutapa as Xavier noted above. Rather, the power and influence of both the Mutapa and later the Rozvi were weak in the eastern region inhabited by the Ndau. Yet, the presence of these larger and stronger states in southeast Africa forced the Ndau to face the reality of living under the shadow of powerful neighbors.

Amid the great society of Shona speakers, the Portuguese maintained a foothold in the east and remained on fairly good terms with the leaders, known as *régulos*, of the smaller polities of Teve, Manica, and Barwe.[61] The early Portuguese documents focus much more on trade than on the inner workings of local political institutions. However, since trade went hand in hand with politics, trading practices influenced the design of political systems. For example, those who paid tribute to the Mutapa ruler identified on one level with the state and the wider society. But at the local level, people were loyal to their village chief and paid tribute to this leader too. The individual economies of some families were even independent of a chief, as was the case among the Duma to the west of the Ndau region.[62] When leaders such as the Rozvi rulers demanded regular payments from subjects, there is evidence from the case of the Duma that chiefdoms located on the southern plateau traded independently with the coastal Ndau region.[63] North of the Duma, villagers and chiefs who recognized overrule by the Mutapa dynasty also resisted this domination at times. For instance, people found ways to circumvent tax and tribute and benefit more from their own labor. They hid gold, failed to report new discoveries of mines, offered less grain to chiefs, or never surrendered elephant tusks to their rulers.[64]

The Eastern Territories

Several states in the Ndau region, either offshoots of the Mutapa state or just territories providing tribute, trace their origins to the Mutapa state. A traditional tale, most likely part myth and part reality, states that three princes, all sons of the Mutapa king, were given distant lands that became the states of Teve, Sanga, and Danda in the east.[65] Another version of the story claims that one brother was the founder of Manica, thus providing Manica's rulers with political legitimacy and a direct link to Mutapa. A fourth son remained in the Mutapa's central lands on the northern Zimbabwe Plateau as the designated heir. According to tradition, after the death of the Mutapa king the three princes forged their own political identities in their new territories. Other leaders apparently followed suit so that, according to one account, there were one hundred chiefs wielding substantial power in the hinterland of Sofala by the end of the eighteenth century.[66] These rulers did not see themselves as beholden to the Mutapa king or any other leader, and a version of this diffuse political situation remains in place today among the Ndau, as many local chiefs claim autonomous rule over their own small territories.[67]

Despite the political independence of states in the east such as Manica, Barwe, Teve, Danda, and Sanga, these territories cultivated political and economic relationships with formidable local neighbors as well as the Portuguese. As independent polities, the eastern territories also benefited from long-distance trade between the coast and the goldfields in the south-western interior. In the sixteenth century, the powerful state of Torwa con-trolled these sources of gold as a close successor to Great Zimbabwe before Changamire's Rozvi conquered the Torwa rulers in the 1680s. And a group of Soko chieftaincies along the Buzi River examined by Rennie "suggests a pos-sible early creation of interlinked political authorities controlling the eastern half of the trade route between Sofala and the Great Zimbabwe area."[68] Danda, for example, probably acted as a mediator in the trade between Torwa (and later Rozvi) on the southern plateau and Muslim communities remain-ing in coastal areas such as Buweni and Chiluane.[69] Farther north, the Mutapa state continued its attempts to monopolize trade routes, but at times some of the smaller territories may have charged a tax of up to 15 percent on trade goods.[70] The Portuguese also attempted to exert continuous control over the trading fairs of the Mutapa state and its tributaries, but the eastern territories supported themselves by relying on a tax on the trade originating in the Torwa state.[71] Powerful states in the interior either escaped the grasp of the Portuguese or negotiated collaborative agreements that helped support the economies of the Ndau and their neighbors in the east.

Much of the information about the eastern region centers on Teve, which was the focus of the writings of João dos Santos. Teve was quite powerful even before dos Santos wrote his lengthy account, *Ethiopia Oriental*, at the end of the sixteenth century.[72] Dos Santos recorded that Teve and other lands in the east were "all free and independent, and some of them make war with Monomotapa [Mutapa]."[73] An earlier account from 1512 described the king of "Ynhacouce" as the *capitão-mor* of the Mutapa.[74] Noting the precariousness of the documents, scholars suggest that Ynhacouce was a part of Teve known as High Teve.[75] Given these major commercial connections, Teve developed close relations with its neighbors in the Ndau region during its early history.[76]

By about 1550 Teve ceased to have political relations with the Mutapa state, and Teve, despite Portuguese influence, maintained a separate identity until the nineteenth century.[77] After the Portuguese attacked Teve in 1575, Teve leaders appear to have maintained a fairly good relationship with them. The treaty after the 1575 Portuguese military expedition required the Portuguese captain of Sofala to make an annual gift of two hundred pieces of cloth to the ruler of Teve.[78] This gift ensured the safe passage of Portuguese merchants traveling through Teve. The rulers of Teve demanded both taxes and gifts from all foreign traders, and Teve had fairs on Mondays where traders sold their merchandise. Many locals brought goods to trade, and the only currency in the early sixteenth century was said to be "gold by weight."[79] Gold came from the area of Teve between the Buzi and Pungwe Rivers that contained small goldfields.[80] The Portuguese traders relied on the ruler of Teve, known as Sachiteve, to ensure peace in the region and protect markets and trade routes from outside attacks.[81] The ruler had a regular force of about two hundred to three hundred armed men, but at the end of the seventeenth century, when Teve came under the control of a crown estate, the Portuguese traders were forced to abandon their lucrative business at the trading fair.[82] As Teve's sense of identity waned, a wider Ndau identity came to encompass much of the territory over time.[83]

Despite the cultural similarities that territories in the east inherited from the Great Zimbabwe tradition of building in stone, states such as Teve displayed regional variation as they dealt with the Portuguese, the Mutapa state, and other neighbors. For instance, in the early sixteenth century, when the Portuguese arrived in the region, the ruler Nyamunda controlled the southern portion of greater Teve's territory between the Buzi and Save Rivers.[84] After Nyamunda succeeded his father to become the king of Teve, he installed his son (the first Sedanda) to rule over the southern area. This region became known as Danda (or Madanda) and formed a core part of the Ndau lowlands. In the early sixteenth century, Nyamunda capitalized on his gold supply and trading relations with some of the Portuguese to break away from the influence of the Mutapa state, according to Portuguese records and local traditions.[85] Nyamunda began to frustrate the Portuguese early on at the Sofala factory in 1516 by blocking trade routes to the coast.[86] In 1518 D. António da Silveira described the drastic change in the relationship with Nyamunda:

> Whilst he could and it seemed to him that we might be of some use, he was a good neighbour and allowed a lot of gold to come to the factory; now that he has no need and knows what, in truth, the captain of Sofala can do, he bursts with laughter at the thought of him and blocks all the routes and then writes to the captain to send ambassadors to him, accepts the gift they take him, detains them with words every three years and finally kills him [*sic*].[87]

Clearly, Nyamunda held the upper hand at this point in trading relations with the Portuguese. His actions forced the Portuguese at Sofala to seek out an alternate route to the north through Teve to reach the gold supplies of the Mutapa state.[88] The little society ruled by Nyamunda manipulated the balance of power in the region successfully to thwart control by either the Portuguese or the Mutapa state.

Unfortunately for eastern territories such as Teve and Danda, these relations proved to be tenuous. Wars with the Mutapa must have exhausted their resources and reduced their revenue from trade.[89] Salt from Danda was traded in the mountains to the north with Manica, but changing political relationships among rulers in southeast Africa and the growth of the Portuguese *prazos* in the seventeenth century overshadowed the economic power of these smaller states.[90] As Danda declined in the eighteenth century, chiefs were reported to be in open warfare by 1822.[91] Despite this political fragmentation, the ruling dynasties of the eastern territories proved to be quite enduring. This is evident with Danda's dynasty, an offshoot from Teve that can be traced back to at least the beginning of the sixteenth century.[92] Even if Danda's founding by the son of a Mutapa ruler is a mythical one, there are demonstrated, real connections among the inhabitants of the eastern region. Even the term Danda has survived as an ethnic classification in the Ndau world, albeit with changing meanings. Danda was used to distinguish inhabitants of the coastal plain from those of the highlands, who were called Ndau.[93] Thus, despite political disintegration, people continued to maintain ethnic boundaries by using political ethnicities or labels such as Danda in contradistinction to the term Ndau. Today, however, it is the term Ndau broadly conceived that encompasses the Danda region of the lowlands.

Other political units in the southeastern region, although much smaller than Teve or Danda, played an important role in the crafting of a Ndau identity. The Portuguese were not interested in this area since it lacked extensive wealth in gold, and unfortunately, the documentary evidence is scarce for these smaller dynasties. Often, it is difficult to match a name mentioned in a Portuguese document with any particular area on a map. References cite rulers of small political units, but we only know some scattered details about territories inhabited by the Ndau today such as Sanga and its Mutema dynasty or the Musikavanhu territory of Dondo.[94] One of the best accounts is attributed to Senhor Ferão, the captain of Sena who was based at a distance on the Zambezi River in the early nineteenth century.[95] Rennie's work on the Nyakuimba-Musikavanhu dynasty shows that traditions link this dynasty with the area of Great Zimbabwe far in the interior, just as others claim a similar connection to the *zimbabwe* culture as well.[96]

Sanga's Mutema chieftaincy was probably founded in the mid to late seventeenth century after the ruler Mutema clashed with Changamire and consolidated his power to create the independent state of Sanga.[97] Previously, Sanga was a client state of Changamire, but under the leadership of Mutema, the state gained its independence by the early eighteenth century.[98] The power of naming was evident in areas under Mutema's control where the terms Sanga and Rove (Rozvi) were no longer used.[99] Mutema's state developed a close alliance with the chieftaincy of Musikavanhu.[100] The court was at Ngaone (Gaonhé), in the highlands east of the Save and a journey of fifteen days from Sofala.[101] Copper mines were located in the southern portion of Sanga near the border with Musikavanhu's Dondo, but the details of trading relations are quite sketchy.[102] These copper mines provided wealth that likely made Sanga the richest of the lands ruled by the *moyo* chiefly lineage in the southeast.[103] More importantly, Sanga may have been the basis for a Ndau ethnic identity.[104]

The Ndau of Sanga were connected to their neighbors through extensive trade links in the eighteenth century. Traders from Sanga ventured south to the port of Inhambane to bring gold that originated from deposits farther afield.[105] In a pattern often repeated throughout the region, gold was moved from one region in the interior to another at the coast through the hands of the Ndau. As these wider economic links in the eighteenth century influenced the development of a political ethnicity arising out of Sanga, missionaries in the nineteenth century were involved in the artificial shifting of ethnic classifications. In the case of Sanga, missionaries eager to place their audience into one linguistic and cultural group applied the term Ndau to a larger group—all southern speakers of what came to be called the Shona language who lived east of the Save River.[106] This assigned identity remains as an ethnic legacy today for those who came to be Ndau.

At the mouth of the Save River, Machanga was the last polity formed in the Ndau region during this period of intense political activity.[107] Machanga, like Danda, may have been part of Teve, but by the end of the eighteenth century, it was already independent.[108] With its low-lying location, Machanga had a coastal identity shaped by geography that set it apart from highland neighbors like Sanga. Portuguese and Swahili traders occupied Mambone on the opposite bank at the mouth of the Save River and also established trading settlements at Chibuene and Chiluane not far to the north. In addition to the emergence of Machanga, there are "shadowy beginnings" of other smaller polities known as Budya, Maungwe, Buhera, and Dondo, but unfortunately, there is scant historical information about these inland polities.[109]

Solid evidence about Sanga suggests that changes in ideology are linked to the economic and political structures of precolonial societies in the Ndau region. Rennie has explored how ideology is shaped not only by changing economies and polities but also "from an internal dynamic at the level of ideology itself."[110] He argues that ideology has three dimensions of identity, cosmology, and values. Although ruling groups are obvious agents of ideological construction and reconstruction, oppressed groups also form their own ideologies to assert a group identity.[111] Ultimately, ideology helps legitimize the position of those in power and foster ethnic premises, as Wilmsen and McAllister have argued. The mere presence of "outsiders"—be they Portuguese, Swahili, or neighboring Shona speakers—reinforced a shared identity that came to be defined as Ndau for those living in the east.

Not far from Sofala, to the south near the mouth of the Save River at Mambone, the Portuguese established *prazos*, grants of land made by the Portuguese crown, in the early seventeenth century.[112] Many other *prazos* also existed to the north of the Ndau region along the Zambezi River. These *prazos*, became Africanized institutions as territory was acquired from local chiefs and the Portuguese interacted and intermarried with the local population.

Prazeros, or estate holders, and other Afro-Portuguese backwoodsmen, known as *sertanejos*, along with their private armies, tended to act independently of the crown and refuse to recognize royal authority.[113] *Prazeros* and *sertanejos* negotiated a coexistence with the Ndau and other groups while also taking advantage of any local conflicts to strengthen their positions. Thus, Portugal's overall "colonial" presence during this "precolonial" period was limited in practice to a slim degree of control over most of the trade routes leading to the interior.[114]

The power and reach of the *prazos* disrupted trade in the region even though the Portuguese presence in the area was relatively small. For example, after *prazero* Sisnando Dias Bayão won a large portion of Teve territory on the Buzi River, the king of Teve was forced to keep "a good understanding" with the Portuguese, apparently out of fear.[115] The *prazos* exerted political power in the area through marriage alliances, mercenary activities, and concessions from local chiefs.[116] With demands for tribute, gold mining, and ivory trading, some *prazos* were "essentially chieftaincies" within the regional economic network.[117] For the Ndau and their neighbors, the "parasitic nature of the *prazo* system" led to periods of violence and disruption in the region.[118]

Assessing Early Encounters

Political and economic situations day in and day out influenced identities for the Ndau, and over several centuries these everyday encounters led inhabitants of the region to develop a sense of being Ndau. As the Great Zimbabwe state on the southern edge of the plateau declined in the early fifteenth century, major trade routes shifted farther north to run through settlements on the Zambezi River. In tandem with this reorientation, the Mutapa state, located northwest of the Ndau region, grew to dominate the northern part of the Zimbabwe Plateau as well as portions of the central Mozambican coastal plain. The Mutapa state's influence extended to the coastal areas south of the Zambezi River by the middle of the sixteenth century, yet rulers never controlled all of the Sofala hinterland. Dynasties of the Ndau and others in the east declared themselves independent from larger states such as the Mutapa, and they began to develop their own smaller political units in the sixteenth century that benefited from trade to the coast.

The Portuguese intervened in the politics of the Mutapa state to regulate the export of trade goods, but they never completely conquered the Mutapa state or managed to maintain long-term control over the eastern territories in the Ndau region or neighboring Manica. The Mutapa rulers, meanwhile, demanded taxes and tribute from subjects in their sphere of influence and attempted to exert some form of rule over outlying areas. Yet, territories in the east, inhabited in large part by those who came to be called Ndau, successfully maintained their independence from the larger and more powerful Mutapa state. Other Shona-speaking groups closer to the plateau remained subordinate to the Mutapa state. These subjects supplied an annual tribute (*curva*) to avoid the threat of military intervention. Thus, many villagers preserved a sense of relative independence, and perhaps protection, by honoring this system of tribute. For the Ndau living in the Sofala region, the Portuguese fortress was a mere symbolic foothold rather than a major center of trading operations in the Indian Ocean. By the eighteenth century, the fort was in decline and the waves of the encroaching sea pounded against the structure.[119] There were only four Portuguese settlers, described as "rich," living at Sofala in the mid-1700s.[120] But in the interior local leaders, and at times some Portuguese as well, actively sought power over people and natural resources.

With a shared history of large states, confederations, and smaller chiefdoms, the Ndau faced pressure from several political entities in southeast Africa. Even though the Ndau were politically subordinate to larger states, they actively shaped an identity of their own amid contacts with others over time. Political power was intricately linked to external trade. Leaders relied on imported goods for income and to secure the political loyalty of their subjects.[121] Steady trading patterns strengthened the position of rulers, but the actual relationship between external trade and political power remains a point of debate among scholars.[122] Evidence from Portuguese documents suggests that when trade was erratic or trade routes were threatened in this part of Africa, political power became precarious.[123] Rulers of the Mutapa state asserted their dominance over a large area, and they demanded tax and tribute from subject peoples within this sphere. Their power, however, was often threatened by outsiders, such as the Maravi north of the Zambezi River and shrewd Portuguese who interfered with earlier trade patterns established between local inhabitants and the Swahili of the East African coast.[124] Although smaller chiefdoms in the interior were incorporated into the Mutapa state, the larger eastern territories maintained their independence, in part by exerting control over the trade routes passing through their lands.

In the end, neither the Mutapa state nor the Portuguese were able to dominate the coastal rulers who traded out of Sofala and the Ndau chiefs of territories in the surrounding region.[125] Rather, these early encounters with outsiders heightened group awareness among the Ndau. The chapters ahead discuss the formation of identities within the world of the Ndau in the context of changing sociopolitical structures. A sense of belonging tied the Ndau to each other over time as they went about their daily lives.

4

TIES THAT BIND

SOCIAL STRUCTURES AND CULTURAL PRACTICES

> Bridewealth into the family!
> —Midwife's announcement after the birth of a girl

> *Kuwanikwa igwara, vasikana vose vanofamba naro.*
>
> Marriage is like a path which all girls have to use.
> —Shona proverb

This is the first of three chapters that look at how Ndauness was shaped within societies in this corner of southeast Africa. Several long-standing, interdependent social structures and cultural practices bound Ndau communities together over successive generations and across a vast region. Modes of social and political organization such as households, lineages, totems, clans, villages, and chieftaincies were crucial elements of a Ndau sociocultural milieu. The Ndau regulated life-cycle events such as birth, marriage, and death through practices that reinforced the social order. A hierarchical system ensured, in most cases, that power flowed from paramount chiefs to lesser chiefs and their village headmen. A council of male elders assisted leaders in making decisions at the village level, and patriarchy was reinforced in daily household life where male authority was evident.[1] The Ndau responded to stresses in their social world by relying on the judgment of their leaders and established "safety nets" designed to deal with problems such as troubled marriages and food shortages. People turned to their own granaries or the more abundant food reserves of chiefs, for instance, in times of drought or locust plagues.[2] The Ndau consciously initiated changes in their social structures and cultural practices in response to shifts in the political and economic landscape. Although threats to a secure livelihood could have divided Ndau communities, the continuities and adaptations that emerged among sociocultural patterns and practices over the *longue durée* served instead to reinforce a sense of shared Ndauness across the region.

Even though all of their cultural practices and social structures are not unique to the Ndau, these customs held a particular meaning for them. Written evidence, some of it from as early as the sixteenth century, reveals certain myths and rituals that helped to sustain identities. Some of the continuity that persisted over time appears later in interviews and colonial documents from the twentieth century.[3] In this chapter, I use ethnographic data drawn from within the world of the Ndau to argue that the Ndau shared markers of identity over several centuries. Certainly, aspects of Ndauness changed in the ongoing, shifting process of identity formation, but the focus here is on the ties that bound the Ndau through time and space. The Ndau experienced movement within and across ethnic boundaries that strengthened their own ethnic recognition, just as Barth has detailed in his work on the nature of boundaries between ethnic groups.[4] The vitality and identity of Ndau society was reinforced amid "a context of oppositions and relativities," when internal dynamics and outside influences led the Ndau to see differences as they classified themselves and others.[5] Social structures and cultural practices are important characteristics for the construction of an ethnic identity, or the imagination of a community, as the case of the Ndau makes clear.

Totems and Clans

Clans and totems were two underlying principles of Ndau social structures, and membership in a Ndau totemic group was one enduring identity marker. Each person belonged to a clan that claimed descent from a common ancestor and had its own distinctive totem, *mutupo* (pl. *mitupo*). Although totems themselves varied throughout the region, the act of belonging to a totem—a Ndau totem—was a collective sign of identity that has a lingering relevance today. Totems have maintained their significance much more than clan groups, given the growth of clan populations and subsequent subdivisions and dispersals. Totems such as Sithole, Dhiliwayo, and Dhlakama serve as family names for the Ndau, and since overrule by the Gaza Nguni in the nineteenth century, the Ndau now use the Nguni versions of the older local equivalent.[6] These Nguni translations adopted by the Ndau have now become very much Ndau and serve once again to set the Ndau apart from other Shona speakers. This distinction, created through difference that resulted from outside contacts, is now a significant internal tie that binds the Ndau together.

In Ndau society, intermarriage was strongly discouraged among people of the same totem, thus promoting the maintenance of exogamy. However, large clans were divided into subclans with their own totems and lineages so that endogamous marriages could take place between members of different subclans with their own totems.[7] This occurred in Zamchiya, for instance, among the large Sithole totemic group. One elder explained that the Ndau created Makuyana, Gwenzi, and Komo from Sitholes as "distinctions so that they can marry one another."[8] In the Mutema chieftaincy farther north, a fine of a white cow was imposed in the past for any marriages within the same clan.[9] Given the scarcity of white cows, this penalty served to discourage intraclan marriages.[10] Today people of the same totem who wish to marry in the Mutema area must pay a cash fine.[11] Another elder from Chikore commented that Sitholes often marry each other, and "they are like a chieftaincy lineage" that "reigns supreme because wherever you go you will come across a Sithole."[12] John Woka of the Dhiliwayo totem withheld information about his true totem so that he could marry a woman of the same totem. His wife, Grace Chirawo, is also a Dhliwayo, but she is not closely related to Woka.[13] As these examples illustrate, there are some elements of flexibility within the totem system.[14] Although classifications shifted over time and restrictions could be ambiguous, the idea and practice of totems remained symbolically important for the Ndau.

Most totems are associated with an animal that is sacred, and members of a totem are not allowed to eat that animal or a particular part of it. Some totems revere an insect or a physical feature such as a river or the pool of a hippopotamus. It is said that people who eat the meat or restricted animal part associated with their totem will lose their teeth.[15] However, it is also possible to treat the meat with traditional medicine to prevent any loss of teeth, and some elders joked that they still had teeth after eating their totem.[16] People of the Sithole (*mwoyo*) totem, prohibited from eating beef several generations ago, now consume beef except for the heart.[17] And although Sarai Nyabanga Sithole of Zamchiya said that her sacred animal is cattle, or *mombe*, she eats beef.[18] Usually, however, the totem offers some protection from danger and is not to be sacrificed. In the past people shared a sense of spirit, or *mweya*, with their totem.[19] A member of the zebra (*mbizi*) totem remarked in 1933, "The zebra has got our manners; we have the same way of living."[20] A person always inherited the totem of the father and not the mother.[21] The food avoidance custom extended to a fetus, for a pregnant woman had to abstain from consuming both her own totem and that of her husband.[22] After she gave birth, she could eat the totem of her husband once again, but not her own. These examples illustrate an awareness of a common set of norms centered on totems.

Totems served to protect clan groups and make a spiritual connection with clan members.[23] Each totem has a special way of giving thanks that involves praising the totem in the form of a short praise poem. For example, a Sithole who was called Mazoje was thanked in this manner:

> *Mwaita Mazoje-ee*　　　You did it, Mazoje-ee
> *Mutupo uri mudanga-a*　The totem is in the kraal, i.e., cattle[24]
> *Sithole-ee Ganyamaope*

These praises reinforced the distinct identity of the members in a particular totem. People had strong feelings of affection for their totem and did not like to see any harm come to it. When an American missionary killed a snake at a chief's homestead in 1884, the chief accused the missionary of "killing his father."[25] A sense of protection was evident in 1933 when the anthropologist H. P. Junod allowed his European friend to kill a zebra in the presence of Office Muhlanga, who belonged to the zebra (*mbizi*) totem. According to Junod, Muhlanga was visibly upset over the death and "began a whole funeral oration" for the animal.[26] From this encounter, Junod concluded that a person's relationship with his or her totem "implies very deep feelings of affection, something like a sense of community of substance."[27] Presumably, Muhlanga followed a common code of conduct of the totem group after he witnessed the death of the zebra.

Each clan had its own particular greeting that involved a customary clapping of hands, and these salutations have changed little over time.[28] When men clap, they place their palms together so that their fingers are in front. Women cross their palms as they clap. This manner of greeting is not specific to the Ndau, for it is practiced among neighbors living in the wider Shona area.[29] In the early seventeenth century, this custom was part of the elaborate ritual surrounding all communication with the king. Subjects were required to crawl on the floor from the entrance to approach the king and then lie on their sides without looking at the king as they addressed him. While speaking to the king, they clapped their hands, in the customary manner of greeting, and when they finished their business, they exited by crawling on the floor just as they had entered.[30] Although crawling on the floor to indicate deference is no longer practiced, there is a continuation of displays of respect. Rather than clapping, in some areas today women perform a courteous lowering of their body when they encounter men. This practice is common in some rural areas, particularly in the Mozambican districts of Machaze and Chibabava. Junod noted the custom earlier in the twentieth century north of the Pungwe River as well.[31] Totemic praise greetings bound ordinary people together across the Ndau region just as marriages brought members from two families, and two different totems, together. These practices, though not unique to the Ndau, served as identity markers and continue to have relevance in the present.

Many totems found in the Ndau area were also common to other Shona speakers such as the Manica. This shared identity acted as a tie that not only brought the Ndau together, but also linked them to the wider cultural sphere of all Shona speakers. Despite the remarkable homogeneity of the Shona-speaking region, the Shona do not have a myth surrounding the creation of humanity.[32] Of course, they "have managed perfectly well without one," as David Beach has noted.[33] The clan identities of the Ndau, however, imply a common origin from one ancestor. According to highland "tradition" cited by Rennie, there were twelve original clans among the Ndau created by Chiphaphami Shiriyedenga.[34] The totems are listed here.[35]

moyo	heart
dziva	pool
mbizi	zebra
bumphi	wild dog
shoko	monkey
gwerekwete	ant-bear
nzou	elephant
gwai	sheep
shiri	bird
ishwa	termite
nungu	porcupine
nhuka	eland

Over time, branches emerged with their respective totems and lineages to accommodate population growth.[36]

Both the subdivisions of clans and the assumption of a common origin from Shiriyedenga blurred clan identities.[37] One history of Musikavanhu alleges that the founders of the Mutema, Musikavanhu, and Mapungwana chieftaincies were all brothers who were later given different clans to allow intermarriage among their descendants.[38] Yet, this story is similar to the myth surrounding the founding of Danda, Sanga, Manica, and Teve by sons of the Mutapa discussed in chapter 3. Both myths serve to unite groups by claiming a common ancestry. At the end of the seventeenth century, clans of the *moyo* (heart) totem migrated eastward from the Rozvi state in Mbire to the Save Valley. They conquered *dziva* (pool) clans located in both the Save Valley and settlements farther east. From the end of the eighteenth century, Chief Mutema dominated over the *moyo* dynasties in the southeastern highlands, but Beach points out that "important elements" remained from earlier polities reconfigured after the *moyo* migration from Mbire to the west.[39] Many Ndau chiefs in the highlands in 1900 claimed descent from Shiriyedenga and a common migration with the Rozvi from Mbire.[40] Chiefly lineages drew on this connection with the Rozvi to legitimate their political identity.[41] Rennie notes, "[W]e do not know to what extent the Rozvi identity was shared by non-chiefly lineages."[42] Chieftaincies in the twentieth century have more than one totem due to expanding households, an influx of migrants, and other developments.[43] Migration, incorporation, succession, and additional factors such as marriage all affected Ndau clans. The development of relationships within the Ndau sociocultural milieu was part of the complicated process of identity formation.

Marriage Ties

Role of Bridewealth

There are continuities in the practice of marriage among the Ndau that stretch back to the sixteenth century. Marriages created family alliances, and

Ndau chieftaincies relied on marriage arrangements to create ties among them.[44] Bridewealth, in the form of goods or services (and later currency), sealed a relationship between two families and acted as evidence of an established bond "for both family and ancestors."[45] At times the gift of a goat, from the husband's family, functioned as a symbol that tied the two families together.[46] Bridewealth also ensured reciprocity in the marriage arrangement by compensating the woman's family for the loss of their daughter and her labor.[47] The groom's family benefited from the incorporation of the new wife, and they held the rights to all offspring. In this way marriage helped provide increased security for the groom's family. Bridewealth ensured that the woman would be treated properly among her husband's family.[48] In a customary act, some men would bring cattle or even two mice to their potential father-in-law as a symbolic token of assurance that the bride would be cared for by the suitor.[49] Although the payments and negotiations of bridewealth have shifted during the colonial and postcolonial periods, the practice continues to be a central aspect of Ndau culture today.[50]

An account from 1569 describes what was perhaps the most common type of marriage involving bridewealth. A Portuguese priest wrote, "The method of marriage is to agree with the wife's father and give him a certain quantity of goods, for the wives bring nothing to their husband, but the latter buys them from their fathers in the manner aforesaid."[51] If marriages did not work out, women sometimes returned to their families and the goods were given back. In the instance above, the husband's family supplied cloth as bridewealth.[52] But hoes, chains of beads, and livestock were also used as bridewealth before the introduction of British pounds as currency at the end of the nineteenth century.

Portuguese observers occasionally misinterpreted local marriages as solely sales transactions. One writer at the end of the eighteenth century claims that marriage is the act of "purchasing a woman" from her father with a payment of cattle.[53] Describing the new wife as a "captive," the author makes it clear that bridewealth seals the marriage contract.[54] However, if the woman wishes to leave her husband and return to the homestead of her parents, she may do so only so long as her father either offers one of his other daughters as a substitute or returns the bridewealth to his son-in-law.[55] In either case, the son-in-law is assured of securing a wife. Although Ndau marriages bore a resemblance to the arranged marriages of the time in Europe, Portuguese observers viewed Ndau unions in a derogatory light.

In Ndau society, a father hoped that a wealthy man would be the husband of his daughter so that he could recoup a sizable bridewealth for himself and guarantee a secure future for the young woman.[56] A father knew that he could demand cattle as payment and then go on to buy sheep, goats, and poultry.[57] One elder described how a father might "look at a home and say, 'I want my daughter to be married at that home,' where there was enough food."[58] This often led to arrangements where older, more established men married younger women. Women also sought men who would be good husbands and providers of much bridewealth that would benefit their families.[59] Skilled hunters or dancers were popular men who received the attention of women.[60] Men who were not as talented or wealthy relied on the bridewealth of female siblings to assist them in securing a wife. Problems arose when one family had many more sons than daughters, for the bridewealth received after the daughters married would not be sufficient for all of the sons.[61] However, in a *ugariri* arrangement of clientage, a potential son-in-law could work for a prospective father-in-law for some time until he received a wife in exchange for his service.[62] Under this agreement, a young man without sufficient bridewealth had the opportunity to marry.

Just as other relationships required work, marriages often involved lengthy periods of courtship and intensive negotiations over bridewealth. If a man wanted to marry a particular young woman, he was expected to contact the woman's paternal aunt or grandmother to initiate a relationship. The paternal aunt, known as *vatete*, was a powerful figure in marriage negotiations and relations. Courtship between two adolescents, called *uchinde*, was an accepted practice among the Ndau.[63] Premarital sexual activity was also allowed so long as the hymen remained intact.[64] In some cases, courtship led to marriage after a process called *kufava* took place. This was when the young woman's parents accepted work from the groom in lieu of bridewealth.[65] The *kufava* arrangement allowed parents to fulfill a daughter's wish to marry her sweetheart.[66] The Ndau continued to engage in these agreements and courtship rituals into the twentieth century.[67] If a couple in recent times wished to elope or a man fell in love with a married woman, the man's father might attempt to provide money or the means for the couple to marry. The father may "borrow money from any person, even the chief," according to one elder living near the Zimbabwe-Mozambique border.[68] The son would then pay back the loan, most likely by working in Johannesburg, South Africa, as a migrant laborer. Or, the father may use bridewealth from the marriage of one of his daughters to assist his son.[69] Overall, the Ndau used various methods to facilitate courtship and promote marriage arrangements.

Strength in Numbers

One Portuguese observer noted in the middle of the eighteenth century that all of the efforts of the Ndau "aim at finding ways of acquiring more women and they do have as many as possible; Kings generally manage to have 1500 and more."[70] Men with many wives were considered wealthy. A large number of cattle also represented wealth, particularly in the southeastern Ndau area around the mouth of the Save River where large herds grazed at the end of the eighteenth century.[71] In Machanga and Mambone, for instance, rich men had three hundred or more cattle at this time.[72] Many children also signified a wealthy and prosperous head of household. Not surprisingly, the number of children of one man was generally proportionate to the number of his wives.[73] In the twentieth century, Freddy Sithole—with four wives and twenty-five children—boasts "no one can fight me here" at his homestead in Chikore, Zimbabwe.[74] He expresses a sense of security that comes from his wealth in people, knowing that his large labor force will bring plentiful harvests that will fill the granaries and carry him through times of famine. Reflecting on his situation, he commented that others would single him out to say, "[T]hat one is really wealthy."[75]

Relationships of Exchange—Mutengatore

The pursuit of food security among the Ndau was clearly played out in their marriage arrangements.[76] The custom of *mutengatore*, or the exchange of daughters or sisters, reflects the desire to strengthen social bonds and promote prosperous relationships. If two families did not have enough money or means to offer bridewealth, they would practice *mutengatore*. Each man would respect the other as a father-in-law, even though in reality each was a son-in-law as well.[77] If one wife initiated a divorce, her husband would go to her father and demand that the other exchanged wife be returned to his family as well.[78] Marriages were also arranged to benefit the brothers of young women. One elder recalled that if the brother of a young girl wanted to marry, "the family would sell the girl child to anyone willing so that the brother will get the proceeds from that trade in order to go and pay bridewealth for his would-be wife."[79] Some girls, often those reaching puberty, were betrothed to compensate for a debt. Marriages also involved loans, with a father borrowing what he needed and promising to give his daughter in return. In this instance, a young woman was betrothed to a family before members of the family decided on her intended husband.[80] These networks and agreements indicate the desire of Ndau communities to strengthen relationships and secure alliances.

After missionaries and British colonial officials settled in the highlands of Southern Rhodesia in the late nineteenth century, they prohibited African marriages based on clientage arrangements.[81] With the Native Marriages Ordinance of 1901, only cattle and cash could be used as bridewealth in Southern Rhodesia. This placed a burden on young men to work for cash wages in the colonial economy. Most of the elders interviewed spoke of 25 pounds as the average brideprice. "That money was not found here, but in Joni [Johannesburg]," remarked one elder who echoed a common sentiment.[82] As the use of cash for bridewealth increased, chiefs had more difficulty securing clients and accumulating wealth in people.[83] However, exchange marriages, *mutengatore*, continued despite the new law.[84]

Those who did not exchange daughters or sisters in a *mutengatore* arrangement could supply goods or livestock as bridewealth for a marriage. Before the introduction of money at the end of the nineteenth century, people married at times by using a thick chain of beads called *gapa reusanga* or *magoroza eusanga.*[85] This chain of beads was supposed to be as long as the future bride's height.[86] Some left the Ndau area and went south to the region of Bilene and Delagoa Bay to acquire beads known as *chuma.*[87] In the area of Zamchiya, chains of beads were often used in marriage exchanges until goats and an increased practice of *mutengatore* replaced them.[88] About six goats were given for a marriage, and people would weave baskets in exchange for goats.[89] "Only those with goats and sisters were able to marry," observed one elder.[90] But hoes were another common form of bridewealth, according to many elders. A man who wanted to marry would secure a hoe from a blacksmith and give it to his future father-in-law.[91] Some hoes were merely blunt stones.[92] Hoes without holes were used according to one elder from Mutema.[93] A less fortunate man would offer a wooden hoe, called *mutika,* to his potential father-in-law.[94] People in the Chikore region would exchange hoes from Bwanyi for a wife.[95] "You give out a hoe, you get a wife," explained Idah Manyuni.[96]

Incorporation of Women

At the time of marriage, a woman joined not only her husband, but also her husband's family, to strengthen the family group.[97] In a recent negotiation over bridewealth in the 1990s, a new wife was told, "Love the family of your husband, like the way you love your own family."[98] The bride kept her totem and could be referred to as a *mutorwa,* or outsider.[99] But if a man died, his wife usually remained with his family and received care from them in an arrangement where the widow was inherited and married to a close family member such as the deceased's brother or son.[100] This leviratic inheritance practice was a point of contention at times for widows. Women were expected to produce as many children as they could, with ten or twelve considered satisfactory.[101] If a woman was infertile, either a replacement—often one of her sisters—was given to her husband, or her family returned the bridewealth. After a woman passed her childbearing years, her husband might marry a younger woman to produce even more progeny. This new wife was often the daughter of the first wife's brother (a niece).[102] The relationship between the two wives could be characterized by either jealousy or a working partnership. Regardless, an additional wife increased the size of the husband's extended family and promised more security for the group.

Marriage Ceremonies

Much of a marriage ceremony revolved around the negotiation and payment of bridewealth, but elders recall ceremonies where the bride was ceremoniously escorted to the family of the bridegroom by a group of girls and women who prepared *sadza* (maize meal) and beer to take with them.[103] As they approached the bridegroom's home, they began singing, *"Tauya nayee. Makoti. Tauya nayee,"* to announce their arrival with the bride.[104] These women would then be invited to the homestead and given some token gifts. They would perform any chores that needed to be done and leave on the second day.[105] The Ndau expected all young women to marry and follow "a path" of marriage so that two families could forge a bond.[106] Marriage placed obligations on not only husband and wife, but also the family of the husband.

Through marriage alliances women "reproduced" the regional political order, just as Eldredge has demonstrated among BaSotho women, and they played an integral part in maintaining and transforming a common language and culture over a wide geographic region.[107] Through time, bridewealth, in its many forms, has remained a constant factor in Ndau marriages, except in cases of destitution, pawning, or warfare. In these times of extreme social stress, the Ndau did not always follow the standard custom of negotiating a marriage contract based on bridewealth. They sought other ways to acquire a wife, for "there is nothing that cannot bring about a marriage," according to local wisdom.[108] Themes surrounding marriage practices have remained constant in Ndau societies over several centuries, and the reliance on marriage customs, like totems and clans, provides the Ndau with a way to organize their society, marshal labor, and provide for the community.

Life-Cycle Events

Birth and Coming of Age

The Ndau reaffirmed family and clan alliances with rituals beyond marriage that marked the life cycle. Certain practices governed ceremonies that celebrated events from the beginning of life to its end. After the birth of a new child, people would assemble to offer congratulatory messages, clap their hands, and say, "*Wahuruka*. She has been honored."[109] A newborn remained inside the house until the umbilical cord fell off, and when this happened the family of the baby held a small party.[110] They would slaughter a chicken or a goat and invite close neighbors to celebrate.[111] During this party, known as a *musere*, the family thanked God and the ancestors for the child.[112] The baby was shown to the father, and if a boy, the father would declare a resemblance in appearance, perhaps as a means of declaring paternity beyond a doubt.[113] One elder claims that people ululated only for the birth of a girl, and this may be due to the prosperity a future young woman would bring her father in the form of bridewealth.[114] During a ceremony called *chinyuchila*, the paternal grandparents introduced the baby to the maternal grandparents, once again solidifying family alliances.[115]

Phrases accompanying the birth announcement demonstrate how the infant's sex could affect a family's future. Midwives, usually elderly women known as *mbuya*, delivered babies, and if the child was a boy the midwife would announce,

"Your bow has been snatched."[116] If a girl was born, the midwife would say, "Bridewealth into the family."[117] The midwife's role was an important one, and most of the gifts at the time of birth such as cloth, blankets, and grain went to the midwife.[118] The mother of the child also inscribed a starlike mark on the face of the midwife and the baby, expressing their connection at birth.[119]

As is the case in some societies, it appears that many Ndau considered the birth of twins to be a bad sign.[120] This attitude stems from the belief that it is not possible or "natural" to create two people together. One Portuguese writer at the end of the eighteenth century argued that the Ndau put one newborn twin into a pot that was cast off into a torrential river.[121] If both twins and their mother were to die during childbirth, they would all be cast off into a large river, according to this same source.[122] American missionaries, who first arrived in the Ndau region in the 1880s, also alluded to "many old customs" such as "the superstition about twins."[123] If infanticide did occur after twin births, it was most likely a recourse to deal with the unexplained phenomenon of twins. Above all, however, the Ndau coveted wealth in people, cattle, and abundant crops.

Elders report that when a young woman began to menstruate, she told her parents that she was mature and a celebration followed.[124] Similarly, at the end of the eighteenth century, the Ndau acknowledged the first menstruation of a young woman with food, drinking, and dancing.[125] The young woman dressed in the finest cloth and adornments of the household.[126] The Ndau also mark the coming of age of men with a celebration of food, drink, dancing, and the playing of drums.[127] In these celebrations of fertility and maturity from the eighteenth century, as well as during ancestral offerings, the Ndau played in a similar manner with the same drums.[128] Many of these same practices sustained by the Ndau lasted into the twentieth century.

Death

Funeral practices described in the late eighteenth century also remained in place during the nineteenth and early twentieth centuries. Soon after the death of an important leader such as a major chief, the Ndau would beat drums to assemble relatives and others, who would shave their heads and beards.[129] Those in mourning grieved on straw called *mulala*.[130] In recent times an announcement of the death of a chief was delayed and issued to the community after several days with a statement such as "the mountain has collapsed."[131] After a death some abstained from working as part of their mourning, and the number of days depended on the status of the deceased. A minor ruler such as a *nyamasango* merited six days, while princes required six months and a king was honored with one year, according to an eighteenth-century account.[132] To mourn the deceased chief, women would sing while pounding grain, *yowe, yowe, yowe-e! Chakadya mambo chinyiko?*, meaning, "Oh, Oh, Oh! What took our chief?"[133]

A writer from the end of the eighteenth century noted that in Teve, the body of a deceased king or queen was shrouded in a white cloth, called *samater*, that was imported to Sofala from Asia.[134] Elders and colonial documents describe a similar method followed by the Ndau in the twentieth century.[135] It was customary to slaughter a bull before the burial of a chief. After preparing the grave, in recent times the Ndau put a black and white cloth on the body. The cloth was covered with the fresh skin of the slaughtered bull. At the end of the burial, the pit was covered.[136] However, the late eighteenth-century account noted that before burial the corpse was placed on a bed and left to decompose, and several receptacles were placed underneath the bed to collect decaying matter from the body.[137] Various important men and highly esteemed women encircled the cadaver until it was severely decomposed. The material that fell into the vessels was saved, and eventually the bones were wrapped in the white *samater* cloth. Later the bundle of bones was put in the bloodstained skin of a black cow before the remains were deposited, amid a gathering of all relatives, in the cemetery of kings on a hill called Maôe.[138] This process often lasted for two or three years, and one Portuguese writer claimed that when the remains were buried, some influential men or women were sacrificed for the deceased king so that he had others to care for him and keep him company in the afterlife.[139] These assertions are not supported with evidence, and they may reflect European prejudice of the era. Ceremonies and burial practices seem to have remained consistent since at least this time, notwithstanding the unsupported allegations of human sacrifice.

There were similar rumors from 1609, almost two centuries earlier, of using human bodies at the Mutapa court. Dos Santos related the alleged practice of benefiting from cadavers there:

> It is related of this Monomotapa that he has a house where he commands bodies of men who have died at the hands of the law to be hung up, and where thus hanging all the humidity of their bodies falls into vases placed underneath, and when all has dropped from them and they shrink and dry up he commands them to be taken down and buried, and with the fat and moisture in the vases they say he makes ointments with which he anoints himself in order to enjoy long life—which is his belief—and also to be proof against receiving harm from sorcerers. Others say that with this moisture he makes charms.[140]

The Mutapa symbolically gained life from the death of others and maintained power over his subjects through this alleged ritual. Elders today note that although chiefs were mummified earlier in the twentieth century, ordinary people were not. The chief's *muzukuru*, an elder charged with naming the successor, would set a fire in the grave to mummify the body.[141] Once the body was mummified, the ash was removed from the pit and the chief was buried there.[142] A special object was removed from the chief's mouth after the mummification process and kept safely by his first wife.[143] It was later given to the chief's successor to swallow to repeat the practice and maintain a cycle of leadership.[144] The *muzukuru* spent about five months looking after the grave. People were not informed of the chief's death until a month, or longer, after he had died.[145] Sarai Nyabanga Sithole explained, "If anyone spoke about the chief's death, they were asked if they were the ones who killed him. So people kept quiet. They would only ask about his condition. They were told that the chief was very sick."[146] The wives of the chief and women who had not yet reached menopause were not permitted to visit the grave.[147] In recent times the site of a chief's burial remained sacred, and visitors were not permitted. Even when human remains were washed from graves after the massive floods of 2000, the sites of initial burials have maintained their sacred nature and remained off-limits to visitors.

Household heads "were regarded as guardians of the homestead," and the symbolic placement of their graves echoed this sentiment.[148] The male head of the household was buried in the center of the homestead, where children play.[149] The female head of the household was buried under the veranda of her house.[150] But when a person died, children were sent away, and the body of the deceased was removed from an opening in the wall of the house rather than the door so that children would not observe the removal.[151] When children later asked where the deceased was, they were told that the person was lost.[152] Mubayi Mhlanga explains, "Some children would go on and ask the elders to go and look for that person since when cattle are lost, people would go and look for them."[153] Although children may have been unaware of the custom, the burial of family leaders within the homestead connected family members to their ancestors.

Political Succession

Problems of succession could be a major crippling factor for polities in the wider region of southeast Africa.[154] With the system of *yafa yabara*, the first-born of the deceased chief became the new chief, regardless of the number of siblings.[155] The eldest son was given his father's ruling devices, including items such as walking sticks or knobkerries.[156] Unlike this recent practice of succession from father to son, Mubayi Mhlanga noted that "long back" succession followed "brotherhood seniority, from the eldest to the youngest."[157] An account from 1609 noted that chiefs nominated their successors, and the custom of ritual suicide by an ill or incapacitated chief may have been an attempt to maintain an orderly transfer of power.[158] Yet, even declarations of a successor by the ruler did not stop other descendants from attempting to take power, for not only sons of a chief, but also his brothers and the male descendants of past rulers, could make a claim for the throne. Before his death, a chief chose several young girls to take as his wives, giving some power to those with links to these women. The appointed successor sat with the new wives on an animal skin while people ululated and cheered in appreciation.[159]

People brewed beer and slaughtered a beast to celebrate the installation of a new chief.[160] Other chiefs from the surrounding area were invited to the celebration.[161] Women would sing, *Mambo wedu wauya tofara. Mambo wedu wauya tofara* (Our chief has come. We are happy).[162] The chief was installed while people danced, and "people would be overjoyed to have a new chief," according to one elder.[163] A new installation would not occur for another two years, creating an orderly if delayed transfer of power. Relatives and other chiefs were invited to witness the chief taking office. The new chief was hidden from the public and made to wait naked with a sister. Beer was poured over the new leader, and a small piece of black cloth was wrapped around him. Later both brother and sister were covered with a piece of cloth, and people began to cheer, ululate, clap their hands, dance, and celebrate. This sister of the chief was forbidden from marrying for the rest of her life. One elder from Zamchiya noted that the installation of a new chief differed across chiefdoms.[164] Only some poured beer on the head of a naked chief as part of the ceremony. The chief was usually installed with a woman, possibly one inherited from his deceased father. This was especially the case "long back," although the Ndau have not sustained this practice, most likely due to European influence during the colonial period.[165]

In Danda's history, the king's wives exerted power over the appointment of a new ruler, according to the 1609 account of dos Santos.[166] One king of Danda, suffering from severe leprosy, named a prince to succeed him before taking poison to kill himself.[167] However, the king's wives successfully maneuvered to seat another prince, described as diligent and well liked, on the throne.[168] This new king most certainly accommodated the interests of his new inherited wives. A similar system of succession took place during the same time in Teve, but in this instance the king reached the throne without any disturbances from the royal wives.[169] One Portuguese report from the seventeenth century describes an earlier Mutapa ruler from the previous century as having more than a thousand wives—perhaps a *slight* exaggeration.[170] The king's son displayed respect for these women by stopping to give way to all until they passed.[171] Another writer claimed that a sixteenth-century Mutapa had more than three thousand wives who cultivated in their gardens.[172] And a contemporary wrote that the king was a sovereign over many princes who tend to rebel; thus he "always keeps their heirs about him."[173] Although information about these royal women remains vague, it seems that they influenced certain political decisions with their proximity to the center of power. Both rituals of succession and stories of royal intrigue reflect the sociopolitical framework that sustained Ndau identities.

Local leaders also negotiated relationships with the Portuguese and attempted to deal with tension stemming from their presence. One incident in Teve from the end of the seventeenth century illustrates the tendency of the Portuguese to meddle in political matters. In this case the brother of the Teve king used Portuguese support to oust the king and assume the throne. The original king managed, however, to regain power after his expulsion and kill the brother who colluded with the Portuguese.[174] This episode was an attempt by the Portuguese to remove a leader who had entered into an alliance with "the enemy Changamira" and interfered with Portuguese trading interests through Teve's kingdom.[175] Although the Portuguese official involved in the overthrow claimed that the "grateful" brother of the king was the "legitimate heir" to Teve's throne, this new ruler turned out to be full of false promises and a propensity to start new wars.[176] After news of the incident and its repercussions reached the king of Portugal, the official was fired from his post.[177] Despite this fiasco, the following instructions from one document a century later clearly echo the Portuguese desire to gain control over Ndau leaders and trade routes:

> You must always be careful to put in charge a *régulo* [chief] that will respect the old conditions and to stop anyone from taking it without your consent as used to be the custom, and to open trade routes between Sofalla, and Manica; if that asks for any expense from the Royal Treasury, you will make it with the sense and economy required and will give the traders all the help they may need and be of use to them and the State.[178]

At times the Portuguese were intricately involved in local royal procedures in southern Africa, just as they were too across the continent in the Kongo kingdom. For instance, João Julião da Silva brought a *cabaia* (a red tunic with wide sleeves), a cap, and red cloth to the king at Bandire.[179] He also presented twelve rosaries of fake coral, twelve packets of beads, twenty-four bottles of *aguardente*, or firewater, and one kerchief to the king.[180] Although most chiefs in the Ndau region managed to maintain control over their own polities, they had to deal with the Portuguese as another factor in their external political and economic relations.

Social Stresses

The Ndau relied on sociopolitical structures such as the family and the chiefdom to deal with disasters and stress, but at times natural forces including drought and locust plagues led to famine. These events spurred migration and the development of new relationships among Ndau speakers. One great famine in 1912 came to be known as the year of *mutendeni.* Numerous elders referred to the hardship caused by this famine, which was named after a tuber that is peeled and pounded before being dried and mixed with chaff from pounded maize to neutralize the poison in the *mutendeni* grain.[181] Ndau suffering from famine would prepare a dark-brown meal out of the ground *mutendeni,* which is poisonous if eaten on its own or not prepared properly.[182] Famine victims would ask their chiefs for permission to dig out *mutendeni* or *diya,* a tuber that looks like cassava, to eat.[183] Some from Zimbabwe would go into Mozambique to find *diya,* probably creating new ties with other communities there.

Master farmers, known as *mukurudza,* had a better chance of surviving a famine with their abundant stores of grain.[184] During the famine of *mudiwa,* Sarai Nyabanga Sithole recalls "people from deep into Mozambique" coming to the border region because of the famine.[185] The Chikajara family perished except for "five men, two wives and one child" who managed to survive.[186] Sithole and her mother were refused assistance by her father's sister in Nyabanga, but the chief provided them with food and grain to take home with them.[187] After receiving this assistance from the chief, whose granaries were full, they did not have to dig for *diya* and *mutendeni.*[188] Meanwhile, her father survived by eating pumpkins with his other wives.[189] Women and girls were especially vulnerable during famine, with American missionaries reporting, "People are selling their girls for food."[190] In an earlier food shortage the missionaries lamented the death of a woman from starvation in the Save River Valley in 1909 after her husband deserted her.[191]

During other famines the Ndau also relied on *mutendeni* or wild fruits such as *masosote, maembe,* and *madzudzuonde* to survive.[192] Locusts would eat all of the maize plants in the fields,[193] but farmers also ate locusts and their eggs to survive.[194] After a locust plague, Chinungu Mtetwa remembers her mother grinding grain from grass into maize meal.[195] Mubayi Mhlanga recalls a famine known as *ndambi* and another one called *tsunu* that were caused by insects.[196] During the *mutendeni* famine, he survived by eating food called *gusha* prepared by his mother.[197] Those suffering from famine would also travel long distances to trade goods such as spears and arrows for grain.[198] In times of drought and other hardships, the Ndau traded grain, salt, and other goods with each other and with their neighbors such as the Duma to the southwest.[199]

The Ndau experienced their share of warfare over several centuries, but fighting was not an everyday occurrence. A late eighteenth-century comment by a Portuguese writer about the frequent warfare in the region dryly notes that the Ndau usually have weapons in their hands.[200] This account also describes the indigenous population of Sofala as "barbarously warlike," and claims that Ndau speakers are equaled in ferocity by the home guards of the Mutapa.[201] Most other observers do not repeat this characterization, and the people around Sofala do not have a fearsome, bellicose reputation. But occasional fighting did break out between the Ndau and either their rival neighbors or the Portuguese. Ndau speakers fought among themselves mostly over territory, according to the memories of elders such as Mateus Simango.[202]

Warfare occurred within Danda, the Ndau area located southwest of Sofala where the Ndau also faced hostile neighbors to the south, Nguni speakers who wished to assume control of the area.[203] The "production" of war was reserved solely for the Nguni, according to a late eighteenth-century Portuguese account.[204] Typically, winning parties would rob all whom they encountered after a victory.[205] This same source claims that the Ndau considered killing and stealing between leaders to be valiant acts.[206] Women, children, and male clients were all exchanged to cement alliances between rulers.[207] Agreements were made through common accords and sealed by a ritual drinking of beer, often made from maize or millet. One party drank half of the beer in a calabash and gave the remainder to the other side to drink. Once the calabash was emptied, the other side refilled it, drank half, and then passed it to the new partner to empty. Dancing and drumming followed the drinking to celebrate the forging of a new friendship.[208] The Ndau have sustained these practices over time, and the wider significance of beer is discussed further in chapter 6.

The Ndau shared common social and cultural traits over several centuries that contributed to the emergence of a sense of Ndauness. Social structures and cultural practices related to totems, marriages, births, and deaths served to bind the Ndau together across southeast Africa. Many of the conventions in place in the twentieth century, such as the burial and succession of chiefs, are similar to those practiced centuries earlier. While some of these "little traditions" have certainly changed with time, they have also retained a coherent relevance for the Ndau today. These traditions in Ndau history serve as cultural materials that define aspects of a scripted Ndau identity.

5

KEEPING UP APPEARANCES

IDENTITY AND ADORNMENT

At bathing places by the river, if you did not have *pika* and *nyora* you were laughed at and stalked by other girls and labeled as barbel, fish without scales.

—Chinungu Mtetwa

Meso haana muganho.

Eyes have no boundary.

—Shona proverb

The Ndau proclaimed their identity with cultural materials that were important to themselves and visible to others. They adorned their bodies and living spaces in a manner that signaled social and ethnic boundaries and accentuated gender and status distinctions. By marking their own appearances as Ndau, they presented a group identity to outsiders they encountered. Recognizable aspects of Ndau culture such as body art and ear piercing, as well as details of Ndau tastes in dress, jewelry, pottery, and houses, caught the attention of Europeans, who recorded various intricacies of Ndau culture to leave a rich written record of how the Ndau kept up appearances and maintained standards of beauty.

Body art was one important way to link people together as insiders and set them apart from others not in the social group. Tattoos, called *pika*, and scarification, known as *nyora*, were two observable expressions of female beauty and attractiveness.[1] Over several centuries, Ndau women shaped connections by sharing a body language of decorative markings, chains of beads, and metal jewelry such as anklets, bracelets, and earrings.[2] Performing identity with the body allowed the Ndau to shape, and indeed inscribe, a sense of being Ndau in both personal and communal ways.

Markings on the body allowed the Ndau, and particularly women, to claim an identity through beauty. Heidi Gengenbach discusses the "relational content"

70

of beauty from tattoos and scars in her work on women's history-making in southern Mozambique's Magude District.[3] Gengenbach notes how beauty becomes "constituted by standards held as normative or ideal by people with some sense of shared social location and identity."[4] In Magude, as in the Ndau region, a desire for female friendship and community helped to convince women to "cut" themselves. And in East Africa, beaded personal ornament among the Maasai and the Okiek is one way to shape "a common ground of understanding and identity through a set of signs with general similarities of both form and function, and yet simultaneously differentiate among those who use the common signs."[5] For the Ndau, tattoos and scarification were two common aspects of adornment that contributed to a shared cultural identity. This chapter focuses on how a process of adornment relates to meanings of Ndauness since the sixteenth century.

Clothing

Ornamentation and dress were popular topics of a Ndau material culture in the written record, and we can take many claims made by Europeans at face value. Dos Santos, for instance, noted in 1609 that weavers made cotton cloth, called *machira*, from thread spun by women.[6] Another observer reported that inhabitants south of the Zambezi River in the sixteenth century wore cotton clothing, including some finer clothes with gold threads.[7] There is evidence of cotton production in the Shona region since the era of Great Zimbabwe (1250–1450 CE).[8] At the end of the eighteenth century, the main cotton manufacturing regions of the Sofala hinterland were Danda and Teve, with production apparently rare in other Ndau-speaking areas.[9] Almost one hundred years later, in 1872, the explorer Erskine witnessed continued cotton manufacturing in Danda near the Save River.[10] He described the cloth as "strong and coarse, but clean and white."[11]

Inhabitants south of the Zambezi River in the sixteenth century, including probably the Ndau, wore cotton cloth from the northern side of the river that was woven on "low looms, very slowly."[12] Monclaro mentions in 1569 that this cloth, also referred to as *machira*, is worn by men around the body and crossed over the breast.[13] Both Monclaro and Barreto, writing almost one hundred years later, noted that the trade in cloth, often in exchange for beads, was flourishing.[14] Through dress and ornaments, the Ndau and their neighbors demonstrated their wealth and status in society. Pedro Machado's work points out how the exchange of textiles fostered "networks of ties between people" in the area.[15] The king of Teve and his nobles dressed in either fine cotton or imported silk that hung from the waist to the ankle. Dos Santos describes how elites displayed their status by throwing a larger cloth (again called *machira*) "over the shoulders like a cape, with which they cover and muffle themselves, always leaving the end of the cloth on the left side so long that it drags upon the ground, and the more it drags the greater their majesty and dignity."[16] Monclaro wrote that near the Zambezi River a black cloth known as "Bertangil" was unraveled and beaded in different patterns, as well as twisted into a cord that was worn around the neck.[17] Unfortunately, many documents, such as this one by Monclaro, do not specify if both men and women wore this cloth. According to dos Santos, only women spun cotton when he was writing in the 1580s.[18] This early practice of local manufacturing may have spread farther south to the Ndau area, for cloth continued to be produced locally despite a large and fairly steady volume of imports from India.

As part of their production, the Ndau harvested cotton, spun and dyed wide pieces of cloth and used spun sheep's wool as thread.[19] They added color with dyes made from crushed substances, boiled leaves, bark, roots, or mud from freshwater rivers.[20] Some cloth panels were dyed orange with saffron, brown or gray with dark clay, and red with blood.[21] Indigo and a plant referred to as "ambono" were common dyes in the Ndau region at the end of the eighteenth century.[22] Imported selections were limited in the interior. The first cloth in Zamchiya, for instance, was only red, black, or white.[23] People apparently first brought pieces of cloth to the Chikore area from the Portuguese trading base at Bwanyi on the coast.[24]

The Ndau also dressed in animal skins and bark from trees that differed little from cloth, according to an account from 1758.[25] A century later, Erskine described the use of baobab bark as large cloth coverings.[26] He described the coverings as "immensely heavy, but apparently of everlasting wear."[27] These coverings, known as *magudza*, were made out of woven strips or strings from baobab, musasa, and fig trees.[28] One cover was big enough for four or five children, who would sleep under it.[29] People wore *magudza* and wove strings from trees into cloth called *maswa* that was used as clothing.[30]

One account mentions locals south of the Zambezi River in the sixteenth century wearing sheepskins "because of the cold south winds."[31] The second skin, or membrane, of elephants was dried and used as a sheet, and leopard skins were particularly valued as clothing. Noting the prominent status of some women, one observer commented, "Only the most important among them wear cloth, according to their means, giving preference in this and other aspects to the women who are always highly respected and without whose opinion nothing is decided."[32] This reference most likely pertains to royal women, such as those of Teve, for the status of common women was below that of common men.

Although cloth was manufactured and acquired through trade in the Ndau region, many elders recall the prevalence of skins as well.[33] In the hinterland of Sofala, residents used a combination of cloth and skins and covered themselves from the waist down, according to an early sixteenth-century account.[34] One elder described the use of two small pieces of cloth called *foya* wrapped over the upper body as a covering.[35] Two straps of animal skin, one in front and one in back, were worn by men. The tanned skins, known as *njobo*, were from the *jangwa*, an animal in the mongoose family.[36] An inner skin was used as underwear.[37] At times a man covered only his penis with a *munyoto*.[38] Animal skins were also made into shoes to provide protection from thorns.[39] Women also wore skins in the front and back. Cowhide, called *dembe*, was mainly meant for women.[40] Skins wrapped around the waist were called *mukore*. Many women wore a short skirt called a *chikisa*, which is still used today for special occasions and certain ceremonies. Several elders proudly referred to the *chikisa* as one specific Ndau adornment that has lasted until today, and some were very pleased to show me a *chikisa*. On the upper body, a woman would sometimes wear two straps of cloth over each shoulder and tuck the straps into her *chikisa*.[41] Women did not cover their upper bodies at times, but an early account from 1518 notes that they cover their breasts once married.[42] Some elders preferred the tanned skins to clothes because they were very durable.[43] An elder from Chikore explained, "Some would marry using those skins if they were nicely and expertly done."[44] However, those that were not tanned properly were described as "laughing stocks."[45] So, skins were both admired and ridiculed as coverings, depending on the quality of the tanning.

Jewelry

To enhance their appearance, women—and some men—wore beads and very fine bracelets of copper, brass, and gold (*makosa*) on their arms and similar metal anklets on their legs, a practice that continued into the twentieth century.[46] In the sixteenth century the Mutapa leader sent eight of these metal bracelets to Francisco Barreto to honor him as one of his "wives."[47] Portuguese officials like Barreto were called the chief's wives as a symbolic sign of honor and affection. Beads, as described by Xavier, were "of various colors and kinds, the most appreciated being the ones that are mixed with small pieces of coral, and they also wear some made of tin."[48] On a journey from Inhambane to Sofala in the mid-1500s, one Portuguese priest admired women wearing "many strings of different colored beads twisted together in front, and arranged to fall one below the other at the back."[49] Locals wore copper bracelets (rather than iron) that were "much esteemed among them," according to this priest.[50] Women in the sixteenth century wore "all sorts of finery, such as crowns and circlets, on their heads, which are half shaved."[51] Elders in the twentieth century reported that Ndau women also wore headbands, or *makheyo*, and ornaments woven with beads.[52] Bracelets and anklets of metal, as well as bead necklaces, served as prominent marks of Ndau identity said to make women beautiful.[53]

The Ndau adorned themselves with other jewelry made from gold, copper, ivory, and imported glass beads. Men brought anklets from Bwanyi as gifts to their wives and girlfriends.[54] Ivory was cut into small pieces, which were soaked in cold water or buried in humid earth for some time.[55] The pieces were fashioned into combs, knife handles, and sheaths.[56] Other items were manufactured out of iron, copper, gold, cotton, and skins.[57] The coast near Sofala yielded amber and seed pearls for local use and export, such as a shipment in 1696 to Goa.[58] Iron also came from the regions of Danda and Teve. Iron ore, described as "dust like earth," was an abundant mineral that Ndau artisans smelted and worked into various implements such as knives, axes, arrows, and wire that was twisted around their legs and arms.[59] Blacksmiths made hoes from pieces of iron bars worked to perfection with hammers and files.[60] This technique may have been a recent development, since one writer claimed in 1796 that earlier peoples did not understand this method. Copper was worked in a similar manner to iron and fashioned into rings worn on the neck, legs, and arms.[61]

Ivory and gold—acquired in the hinterland of Teve, Manica, and Barwe—were traded at Sofala.[62] Monclaro could not explain the reluctance of local men and women to mine for gold in the sixteenth century, especially since he argued that "they have a great love of gold, and make different things of it which they wear round their necks like beads, and also use it in trading for cloth."[63] He concluded that people dug for gold only at certain times when they wanted to buy cloth.[64] Monclaro argued that locals valued gold even more than the Portuguese, using it to trade and to make jewels and ornaments.[65] The Ndau and their Shona neighbors also worked iron, copper, and pewter into ornaments and "other little things."[66] Blacksmiths made arrows, spears, hoes, hatchets, and a kind of half sword that they called a "lupanga."[67] Given the importance of jewelry and metalworking, mining was most likely carried out to meet the demand for metals, despite its inherent risks.

Among the elite, the *ndoro* shell is one enduring emblem that has lasted since at least the sixteenth century. Dos Santos noted that the Mutapa and his vassals all wore this white shell on their foreheads so that it hung from their hair. The Mutapa himself wore another white shell on his breast. The king of Teve despised these shells, according to dos Santos, since they were the insignia of his enemy.[68] The Teve leader was determined to set himself apart from his rival on the plateau. Soon after, Diogo Simões also gave the Mutapa a gold *ndoro* set with false stones "such as the Mokaranga kaffirs wear on their heads," according to a seventeenth-century chronicle.[69] The *ndoro* retained a religious significance into the twentieth century for the Ndau and their neighbors to the south, but it is worn "only by a person who is a medium for a Ndau spirit of very high rank," according to the missionary E. Dora Earthy.[70]

Although Ndau women have pierced their ears and worn earrings to decorate their bodies for centuries, men only began to pierce their ears in the nineteenth century after the invasion of the Gaza Nguni.[71] Ear piercing for men was a sign of subjugation under the Gaza Nguni, but the Ndau gave this practice a different cultural meaning after Gaza Nguni overrule ended in 1889. For the next thirty to forty years, a man's pierced ears, often very apparent with a large hole, were a sign of being Ndau. Men came to pierce their ears as a rite of passage, and this mark distinguished them from other migrant laborers in *Joni* (Johannesburg). The piercing of men's ears is discussed further in chapter 7 in the context of Gaza Nguni overrule. However, it is important to note here that Ndau men incorporated ear piercing as their own coming-of-age ritual and visible mark of identity to the public. Even after Gaza Nguni overrule ended, a man needed to pierce his ears in order to court a woman successfully, win her heart, and avoid being regarded as worthless.[72] Thus, during the nineteenth and twentieth centuries, ear piercing held important gendered and shifting meanings in Ndau society.

Pika and Nyora

Just as ear piercing became a right of passage for young men before they went to work in South Africa's mines, tattoos, or *pika*, marked the passage of young women into adulthood. Many elders, such as Philemon Khosa, explained that *pika* "was done as a symbol of identity, just like the piercing of ears so that people will be able to identify under whose chiefdom people belong."[73] If someone looked at a woman wearing *pika*, "you would know that this is a Ndau," said Allen Mundeta, echoing the remarks of others.[74] The beauty marks of *pika*, often placed on the cheeks, forehead, and stomach, were applied during puberty[75] "so that one would be attractive to boys."[76] But *pika* also demonstrated to the community that young women were now adults. "Without *pika* you were not considered a lady," noted one elder.[77] *Pika* was the quintessential sign of both beauty and womanhood in Ndau culture.[78]

Although *pika* was a matter of choice,[79] in the eyes of many, *pika* added beauty and made women look extraordinary among others.[80] It was common for *pika* to consist of three marks on each cheek, forehead, and stomach, but designs varied from this standard practice.[81] Some women, including many in Machaze, Mozambique, also had *pika* on their legs. In recent times, Ndau women used pins to make *pika* marks to beautify their faces.[82] There was much laughter from female elders surrounding private questions of *pika* and *nyora*, and most of those interviewed echoed Mucherechete Dhlakama's comment that both practices were "done for our men" and "done to attract our men."[83]

Nyora, or scarification, added beauty to women's bodies and pleased men.[84] The skin was cut, usually with a knife,[85] and keloids developed after a substance such as ash or clay was placed in the wound.[86] Women decorated their bodies with scarification patterns on their face, stomach, upper chest, and thighs. The European traveler Erskine noted in 1872 that the Ndau who lived in the low-lying region of Danda just north of the Save River "mark themselves with a V-shaped series of bumps" on their forehead, between the eyes, as well as sometimes on their cheeks.[87] On another journey in the same region the following year, he wrote that locals had "rows of skin-lumps between their eyes and at each corner of the mouth."[88] After proceeding to the Ndau highlands to visit the Gaza Nguni leader Mzila, Erskine did not remark on the practice of *nyora* there.[89] But elders interviewed throughout the Ndau region—in the highlands and the coastal plain—commented on the prevalence of *nyora* and *pika* as important marks of Ndau identity.[90]

The patterned scar tissue of *nyora* served not only to beautify women, but also to enhance sexual relations. This intimate sexual aspect created added pressure for women to have *nyora*. "Those without *nyora* are not that interesting," remarked one elder, since "it was done so that when caressing a woman you would feel the kind of 'bumpy' and rough surface, it is so pleasing."[91] *Nyora* was considered to be so important that a new bride would be inspected by her husband's aunts to make sure that she had *nyora*.[92] If the bride did not have *nyora*, she was ordered to have it done before she was accepted as a wife, according to an elder in Chikore.[93] *Nyora* decorated the body[94] and entertained the husband[95] as well. Even though many elders noted that *nyora* was pleasing to men, one male elder said that *nyora* was also "meant to arouse the woman when she was being caressed, just like fondling."[96]

Nyora, like *pika*, was a rite of passage for young women. "Without *nyora* one was not considered a full woman," explained Celani Mutigwe of Chikore.[97] Another elder recalled the atmosphere surrounding *nyora*: "It was meant to compete with other girls in having those designs. At bathing places by the river, if you did not have *pika* and *nyora* you were laughed at and stalked by other girls and labeled as barbel, fish without scales."[98] Thus, a woman without *nyora* was both ridiculed and frowned on by others as one who did not keep up appearances.[99]

Less information is available on the practice of teeth filing among the Ndau. One elder recalled her grandmothers sharpening their two upper teeth (incisors) to add to their beauty.[100] In 1872 and 1873 Erskine also observed Ndau in the Danda region near the lower Save River who "file their upper teeth to a point."[101] The European traveler H. P. Junod noticed in 1935 that the Ndau's neighbors just to the north of the Pungwe River, the Barwe and Manica, "file the inner side of their two upper incisive teeth in triangular shape."[102] And many Chopi women south of the Save River filed their upper teeth in the first half of the twentieth century as well.[103] Thus, it seems that some Ndau and their neighbors filed their teeth to enhance their appearance, but the practice is not viewed as an explicit Ndau custom.

Hairstyles

One of the earliest Portuguese accounts, from around 1518, noted that inhabitants in the hinterland of Sofala "adorn the head slightly."[104] This was an understatement, for details of intricate hairstyles and ornamentation appear in other documents from the sixteenth century. Women then, and some still today, wore bands of beads on their heads and used reddish rocks called *mukura*, probably ochre, to die their hair red.[105] The rocks were crushed into a powder and mixed with oil from *mupfuta* before being rubbed into hair.[106] Elders recall that people near the border, in the highlands, traded *mukura* with others to the west where it was in demand.[107] Erskine observed women farther east near the lower Save River "loaded with beads and red clay."[108] Women, including the wives of chiefs, were considered to be "very smart" with their reddish dye from *mukura*, according to one elder from the highlands.[109] A white settler recalled the fashion of long, straight, red hair among the Ndau in Melsetter District on the Rhodesian side of the border at the end of the nineteenth century.[110]

Men were also known for their creative hairstyles, and Monclaro provides a detailed account from the end of the sixteenth century:

> They wear horn-like headgear as an adornment, being made of their own hair turned back in a strange manner; these horns are in general use in Kaffraria, and provide a good shade. In the middle of the head they make one which draws the hair in most orderly and well-arranged fashion, first making the hair long by means of small pieces of copper or tin which they tie at the end of a few hairs brought together, so that the weight gradually makes them long and crisp, and thus they go about with their heads covered with these small pieces.[111]

Dos Santos describes a very similar procedure for making "horns" in hair, and notes that men cannot wear their horns in the same fashion as the king of Teve, who wears four horns in the following manner: "One a palm in length above his forehead like a unicorn, and three half a palm in length, one at the back of the head, and one over each ear; each horn standing very straight up in its place."[112] A man who did not wear horns faced ridicule and the insult "that he is like a woman."[113] Dos Santos continued his account by noting that locals do not use hats because of these horns. He also claimed that men did not cut their hair or beards.[114] Horns continue to be fashionable in recent times among some Ndau men and women, but alongside this continuity are the inevitable changing ideas about style.

Houses and Granaries

The Ndau did not adorn their homes in a decorative manner as they did their bodies. Round houses were made out of wooden poles and covered with thatch. They were often plastered with *dagga*, a clay mixture placed on either the inside or both sides of the dwelling. Men were the predominant builders of a house frame and the roof thatchers.[115] Women plastered the walls and treated the earth floors to prevent cracking and crumbling.[116] Today Ndau women decorate the outside walls of some houses with painted designs, but this appears to be a recent trend that may be an influence from the south.[117]

The size of a house was not uniform across the region or over time. There were very large houses at Great Zimbabwe in the sixteenth century, for instance, and large houses appeared again in Manica in the 1890s to avoid the Portuguese hut tax that accompanied formal colonial rule.[118] The entrances to houses in the highlands around Zamchiya were small, and people had to bend down to enter.[119] One elder in Zamchiya noted that some big houses were divided "into two compartments for two wives."[120] The Ndau in this region also built double-story dwellings called *dandara* where people would escape from lions.[121] Very small two-story houses called *zvitumba, zvitarahwi,* and *zvikurumbana* also existed farther north in Chief Mutema's region.[122] Possessions—such as a pot for cooking, two hoes for digging, and a bow with arrows for hunting—were stored upstairs in some of these houses, while people slept on the ground floor on woven mats.[123] Today the southeastern region of Machanga boasts the largest houses in the Ndau-speaking area.[124] At the end of the nineteenth century, there were "scattered" houses in parts of the highlands, prompting British officials to order the building of larger homesteads, or *kraals.*[125] Both the size of Ndau houses and their arrangement in a compound varied over time and space.

Grain was stored in some of the houses with a second floor, but the Ndau tended to construct separate granaries out of various materials to safeguard their food.[126] Common building materials were the same as those used in houses—pole and *dagga* with straw roofs—and these granaries are similar to those still in use today.[127] Numerous elders, when asked to describe houses long ago, pointed to a traditional round house or granary in their compound and noted that the construction methods and building materials had not changed over time. The houses that resembled those used by earlier generations often sat next to modern square houses made with cement blocks and corrugated iron roofs. Grain was also stored in pots underground, and elders recall this practice during the famine of *mwadiwa.*[128] When harvests were good, grain reserves lasted for two years to ensure food security.[129]

Like houses, granaries differed by region and personal preference. For instance, granaries in Mhakwe were not like those in Chikore. In Mhakwe, there were different granaries for each type of crop. The granary, or *dura,* was built like a double-story hut (*chitumba*), but the entrance at the top was smaller. A person needed a ladder to enter.[130] Yet, in Chikore only two-story huts were used as granaries. The Ndau wove bundles of grass or small poles and grass together to make granaries with small openings called *nyumbu.*[131] The grass weave permitted ventilation and discouraged weevils from damaging the grain.[132] A beer party would be an occasion for community members to gather and weave *nyumbu.*[133] Rapoko was stored in these large baskets or huts, where it was forced down using a pestle.[134] Some Ndau would also build granaries, plastered with *dagga*, in trees.[135] Residents from Zamchiya also recall using *magombana*, or thick musasa tree bark to store grain, and granaries in Zamchiya were made with only *dagga* or a combination of both *dagga* and small poles.[136] In all types of granaries, the important harvest of maize was stored with the husks.[137] Overall, the architectural similarities in houses and granaries overshadowed the differences, for common building methods and structures served to promote a wider sense of group identification among the Ndau.

Pots

Large woven baskets known as *nyumbu* are very impressive and still used by some Ndau, but female potters also made various kinds of clay pots (*hari*) for cooking and storage. Women would dig clay soil from valleys and the sides of rivers to mix it with sandy soil from a crushed piece of clay pot called a *mushapa*.[138] After sprinkling water over the clay soil, they would mix it the following day and add the sandy mixture before making their clay pots.[139] Once made, a pot would dry for five days inside a house before being burned in a fire until it was red-hot.[140]

Very large pots were surrounded by woven baskets to aid women in transporting them.[141] Each type of pot had a specific name. A large pot called *mabiya* was used for cooking a sauce of leaves or meat used as a relish.[142] Similar large pots were used to brew and store beer.[143] In the area around Mhakwe, a medium-sized *nhamba* was used for cooking the maize-meal staple of *sadza*. Women and girls carried water in *nhuvi*. A *chipfuko* was used for storing water, and a clay plate known as *mukheyo* was for serving relish.[144] *Zvikarairo* were used as water mugs during meals.[145] When asked about the kinds of pots that women made, Jona Mwaoneni Makuyana said, "They did not make those decorative ones that are made today for selling to whites. They made ordinary *hari* for cooking or *mukheyo* for drinking."[146] The size and function of pots mattered more to the Ndau than decorative aspects, but individual potters did make their mark on their own pots.

Conclusions about Identity and Adornment

The Ndau kept up appearances over time in ways that were both distinctive and similar to some of the cultural practices of their neighbors in southeast Africa. For instance, in the sixteenth century the Ndau shared a penchant for making horns in their hair with their neighbors to the south in the hinterland of Inhambane. Father André Fernandes observed people in this area wearing "two horns on their heads" with which they "stick in two pieces of wood" or decorate the points "with a little gold."[147] Even farther south around Delagoa

Bay (the site of Maputo today) in the early nineteenth century, residents wore brass rings on their arms "from their wrists to above their elbows," similar to those used by the Ndau and their Shona neighbors.[148] Despite the fact that others such as the Tsonga and the Valenge marked their bodies in a similar manner to the tattoos and scarification of Ndau women, elders in the Ndau region today consider tattoos and scarification to be specific, defining Ndau traits.[149] This sense of being Ndau through shared body markings is also gendered—women mark their bodies, while men (and women) enjoy the beauty of it. From the rich historical evidence about how Ndau speakers adorned themselves, it is clear that the Ndau adopted cultural practices as a result of internal dynamics as well as contact with others. Other chapters discuss these relations with outsiders that resulted from trade, incorporation, and resistance.

Although it is difficult to discern the exact motivations from the historical record, the living spaces, hairstyles, ornamentation, and body art of the Ndau were all examples of vehicles for expressing both individual and group identity. With *pika* and *nyora*, for instance, Ndauness was inscribed on women's bodies. By using *pika* and *nyora*, the Ndau made a statement about standards of female beauty and attractiveness while signaling an ethnic boundary. Hairstyles and jewelry served as both a status symbol and an aesthetic medium. As with the beaded ornaments of the Okiek and the Maasai, an ethnic identity among the Ndau was "claimed, advertised, and negotiated."[150] By expressing a distinct concept of the body and its adornment, as well as other material objects, the Ndau shaped a very public identity with a long historical continuity.

6

BREWING BEER, MAKING RAIN, AND HOLDING COURT

> The chief would tell people to go and instruct them that they would see a whirlwind. These people would not even reach their intended destination before rains fell.
>
> —Sarai Nyabanga Sithole

> *Ushe hahuzvitongi.*
>
> Chieftainship cannot rule itself.
>
> —Shona proverb

> *Mhosva haizvitongi.*
>
> A case cannot try itself.
>
> —Shona proverb

The Ndau have shared a mélange of beliefs reflected in the activities of brewing beer, making rain, and holding court. As important ingredients in the "mixed pot" of Ndauness, both the practical and symbolic aspects of these rituals were central to the development of a cultural identity among the Ndau. Beer drinking has a deep social significance, for as one proverb notes, "Where there is beer there is noise."[1] The noise may stem from a work party, a ceremony of thanksgiving, or a casual afternoon gathering of elders.[2] Beer drinks, both in the present and in the past, validate the position of each headman "as social dean and land manager."[3] Similarly, a chief whose ancestors continue to bring rain is viewed as "the rightful authority."[4] Legitimacy is also central to holding court, for chiefs relied on their communities to abide by decisions made at the *dare*, or court.[5] Leaders knew that "chieftainship cannot rule itself," but sufficient rain each year and a supply of beer made the affairs of the court run much smoother.[6]

A continuity of rituals based on shared cultural beliefs served to reinforce a collective sense of group identity in this corner of the world. Chiefs and their advisers led Ndau communities in distinct annual ceremonies that celebrated Ndau insiders and distinguished them from outsiders. Members of the community, in turn, followed cultural practices woven into the fabric of Ndau life. Both daily activities and special events contributed to a performance of identity that shaped Ndauness. Critical ties to ancestors and the spirit world fostered a continuous link with the past, present, and future.

Rain and the Spiritual World

In southeast Africa, life was not possible without ample rain and fertile soil. Therefore, chiefs and headmen took charge of rainmaking ceremonies, which gave thanks to both the chief and his ancestors for the crops harvested in the past.[7] Rainmaking ceremonies, called *makoto*, were "part and parcel of people's livelihood" in the chiefdom.[8] The Ndau held annual ceremonies in July and August under the guidance of the chief, or at other times of the year following a period of drought. Elders recall people celebrating at the residence of the chief when he asked them to prepare for rainmaking activities.[9] Women would ululate into the night at the chief's residence. "Even when the chief went to sleep, we would still dance and sing around his house," remarked one female elder from the highlands.[10] Meanwhile, men sat together and drank beer, and each family took care to reserve beer for the chief.[11]

Chiefs performed ceremonies at gravesites or other shrines to ensure rainfall and fertility, while people drank beer and sang praise songs to the ancestors.[12] One song repeated the phrase *Iri mubako mwemvura woye-e* (Going to the cave of water).[13] The Ndau also placed beer, the maize-meal staple known as *sadza*, and meat under a tree as an offering to the ancestors.[14] People passing by were permitted to help themselves to the food and beer under the tree, and after eating they thanked the ancestors and asked for a plentiful season.[15] The Ndau considered rainmaking ceremonies to be successful, and even if *makoto* failed to bring rain, people did not stop performing the ritual.[16]

The working relationship between Ndau chiefs and their subjects appears in an early Portuguese description of ceremonial rainmaking from the 1580s.

> When they suffer necessity or scarcity they have recourse to the king, firmly believing that he can give them all that they desire or have need of, and can obtain anything from his dead predecessors, with whom they believe that he holds converse. For this reason they ask the king to give them rain when it is required, and other favourable weather for their harvest, and in coming to ask for any of these things they bring him valuable presents, which the king accepts, bidding them return to their homes and he will be careful to grant their petitions.[17]

The author, dos Santos, went on to argue that the Teve king deceives his subjects and "does not give them what they ask for" until they make greater offerings.[18]

He lamented the many days spent "in these comings and goings" surrounding requests to the king, yet he noted the general satisfaction within the kingdom when it began to rain.[19] More than three hundred years later, when the rainy season approached in Nyabanga, Sarai Nyabanga Sithole recalled how her uncle, Magavhu, would "negotiate with the chief to plead on behalf of the people."[20] She explained that the chief, Mbonyeya, would then "tell people to go and instruct them that they would see a whirlwind. These people would not even reach their intended destination before rains fell. Women would then ululate for the people who would have gone to the chief's sacred place to bring rain."[21] It was also common for the Ndau to believe that a type of traditional medicine, *divisi*, caused crop failure by invisibly transferring one person's healthy crops into the targeted field of another.[22] If one farmer questioned his poor harvest compared to the abundant crop of a neighboring farmer, the chief usually intervened and ordered the beneficiary to stop relying on the charm of *divisi* at the expense of the harmed neighbor.[23] When insects such as caterpillars or worms posed problems for crops, people would collect the insects and bring them to the chief "pleading to have such creatures disappear to other places," according to Mubayi Mhlanga of Zamchiya.[24] This elder notes, "Normally after that things would become stable."[25] These requests for rain and crop protection stressed the central role of chiefs as a powerful stabilizing and unifying force in Ndau society.

In the seventeenth and eighteenth centuries, Shona speakers to the west from the Changamire dynasty of the Rozvi influenced the rainmaking of those to the east, including the Ndau and their Manyika neighbors.[26] Traditions claim that the founder of the Rozvi was expelled from the Mutapa state when he refused to drink a poison ordeal to confirm an oath.[27] In the late seventeenth century the Changamire ruler established his chiefdom in the southwestern Khami area of the Torwa kingdom where he adopted the local reliance on the Mwari rainmaking spirit.[28] The influence of this guardian spirit then spread eastward as the Rozvi kingdom expanded, and both the Ndau and the Manica arranged for delegates to visit the Mwari shrines in the Matopo Hills of southwestern Zimbabwe.[29] Research on the Manica just to the north of the Ndau region reveals that this Shona-speaking group sent tribute to the Rozvi kings for about one hundred years and then maintained important links after this tributary relationship ceased in the eighteenth century.[30] Thus, the power of the Mwari spirit extended over a large area and served to link the Ndau across political boundaries with others in the wider region.[31]

These connections, however, did not override local concerns. For instance, in the Sanga highlands to the east of the upper Save River, the *dziva* (pool totem) dynasties established in the seventeenth century had their own territorial cults that brought rain.[32] Despite conquest by *moyo* (heart totem) dynasties, these rain-bringing cults survived, and by the nineteenth century members of other lineages recognized the power of the leading chief, Musikavanhu, and brought presents for rain from as far away as the coast.[33] Even the Gaza Nguni leaders who ruled over much of the Ndau region in the nineteenth century sent payments to rainmaking chiefs such as Mafussi, according to the European traveler St. Vincent Erskine.[34] Rennie argues, however, that Musikavanhu's charismatic leaders impeded integration into the Sanga chieftaincy of Mutema.[35] The transformation of Musikavanhu into a secular chieftaincy would not take place until Rhodesian colonial authorities intervened in the twentieth century.[36]

As the case of the Rozvi demonstrates, Ndau chiefs were not the only figures who were believed to be able to bring rain. Even the explorer Erskine alleged, "I acquired quite a high reputation as a rain-maker, because it frequently happened that it rained upon my arrival at kraals [homesteads]."[37] On a journey through the Save River lowlands in the 1870s, Erskine claimed that an elderly chief named Sondaba asked him to make rain.[38] Sondaba offered Erskine "some corn and three fowls," but Erskine demanded a goat instead. Even though Sondaba did not fulfill Erskine's requirement, rain apparently fell for three days soon after the request.

Beer, Celebrations, and Spirits

Beer drinks, like rainmaking ceremonies, were important religious functions as well as popular social gatherings. A major annual feast with beer and dancing was called *bira*, a ceremony of thanksgiving for the care of the ancestors.[39] After a harvest, people presented a share of their crops to the local chief and offered a portion to their ancestors.[40] Relatives, friends, and neighbors brought beer and food to a ceremony that both praised and appeased the ancestors.[41] On the day of a special ceremony such as *bira*, nephews and nieces would lay by doors with tree branches and sing.[42] Beer was also brewed for *bira* to celebrate the homecoming of migrant laborers from South Africa in the nineteenth and twentieth centuries.[43] People would drink, sing, dance, and enjoy themselves. When men from the highland region returned home from Johannesburg, their communities participated in a traditional dance of the Ndau known as *muchongoyo*.[44] Across the wider Ndau region, women believed to be possessed by spirits performed another dance, the *chinyambera*.[45] Those possessed by spirits, known as *Mhongos*, had their own praise songs.[46] During a summer's full moon, children from the community gathered at homesteads to play and practice dancing *chinyambera*.[47] People would sing and beat drums, but not make any offerings.[48] *Doro rengoma* was a special beer brewed for occasions with drumming that led people to dance and play.[49] These ceremonies that brought Ndau speakers together to celebrate and drink beer reinforced notions of Ndauness.

For the Ndau, the power of the spiritual world is central to rainmaking and beer-brewing ceremonies. The Ndau have maintained beliefs in the power of ancestor spirits, healers, and spirit mediums over several centuries, as early evidence from dos Santos and other sources confirms. In 1758, for instance, Xavier described the religious beliefs of the Ndau in this manner:

They worship only one true God whom they call Mulungo [Murungo][50] and consider the prime cause of everything, and do not recognize any false gods, they worship almost to idolatry their dead and call them muzimos and at their festivals, which are carried out when they feel like it, without any established order, they make them offerings of food and drink and place them by a tree especially dedicated to their purpose and which they respect as sacred in the same way as they respect the graves.[51]

Despite the bias in this Portuguese description, it is mainly accurate. Gama noted in 1796 that the Ndau believe in a God called Murungo and have no word or concept for the "devil."[52] But for dos Santos, the spirit possession he described much earlier in the 1580s led him to draw a parallel with his own society and conclude that there was a "devil" present in Ndau society.[53] The Ndau, meanwhile, made offerings to their ancestors of beer and food at the sacred sites of graves, which they believed would appease the dead and prevent any malady from striking those still living.[54] On some occasions, clothing is left on a grave for two or three days before it is removed.[55] Burial places remain venerated sites of supplication, particularly the protected sites of chiefs. At the end of the seventeenth century, Manuel de Faria e Sousa argued that local inhabitants believe that their kings go to heaven and are called "muzimos."[56] This is a reference to the spirit elder of a family or the soul of a dead relative, called *mudzimu* (pl. *vadzimu*) by the Ndau. Sousa compared the belief in "muzimos" (*vadzimu*), called on in times of need, to the Catholic reliance on saints.[57] At the end of the sixteenth century, dos Santos thought that people in Teve observed days called "*musimos*," to honor the "souls of dead saints" (*vadzimu*).[58] Ancestral spirits continue to occupy a place of crucial importance to the living in the Ndau region today. For example, the ancestors from both families are informed of a pending marriage, and it is hoped that they will unite "and communicate well with both families."[59]

Many Ndau interpreted various incidents, such as their dreams or the songs of birds, as either good fortune or ominous signs.[60] Witchcraft was often an explanation for unfortunate events, and this preoccupation with fate gave witchcraft a prominent place in Ndau society.[61] Even though the Ndau viewed the sun, moon, stars, wind, and rain as natural creations, they considered thunder and lightning to be the result of witchcraft.[62] When the Ndau attributed deaths and misfortune to witchcraft, they would consult diviners to determine who brought about these calamities.[63] Negative associations with witchcraft led some Ndau to fear those associated with any magical powers.[64] Oracles, called *nhamussoros* or *pondos*, were both men and women. Diviners known as *cuchocucho* threw cowries on the floor and made their predictions based on how each shell landed.[65] Chiefs were responsible for resolving accusations of witchcraft that often involved domestic disputes. They consulted healers known as *n'angas* and spirit mediums, and then they ordered those held responsible for misdeeds to hand over cattle or goats as compensation.[66] Once again, Ndau leaders attempted to mediate social stresses and religious beliefs through accepted cultural practices.

Poison Rituals

The Ndau also turned to a centuries-old poison ritual to deal with questions arising over deaths. After a chief or other important person died, the surviving heir consulted a diviner to seek out the guilty party. Following a ceremony with dancing and drumming, the diviner reviewed the history of the deceased's grudges with his enemies and then used his brush or feathers to select one or more people as suspects. Some suspects were killed with knives while others had a chance to live if they survived a well-documented poison ritual to determine guilt or innocence. Dos Santos referred to this poison ritual, which he called *lucasse*, as one of the "most terrible and wonderful oaths" of three common practices used by the Ndau when someone's innocence is called into question.[67] The accused drank a cup of poison that was reported to kill the guilty but leave the innocent "safe and sound."[68] Once an accused man proved his innocence by surviving the ritual, the accuser was then punished for providing alleged false testimony. According to dos Santos, the accuser "becomes the slave of him whom he falsely accused, and forfeits all his property and his wife and children, half going to the king and the other half to him who was accused."[69] Gama, writing two hundred years later, described a similar poison ordeal with a substance called *moavi* that contained a mixture of bark, tree roots, and crocodile bile.[70] Those who vomited *moavi* were viewed as falsely accused, but those who did not expel the potion were forced to make a payment.

A second oath cited by dos Santos, called *xoca*, entailed licking a red-hot iron.[71] Those deemed innocent received no harm to their tongues. Another sixteenth-century truth-telling method used *calão*, a mixture of water and bitter herbs. A suspect proved his innocence by swallowing the liquid without vomiting afterward, but a guilty person was unable to swallow even "a single drop," according to dos Santos.[72] One Portuguese official insisted that these older practices continued under various guises as "Cush-Cush ceremonies" in the early twentieth century among the Ndau of the highlands.[73] A proverb "The one who pretends to be innocent is the evil-doer" reflected the desire of the Ndau and their Shona neighbors to test the claims of suspects and resolve the incident in question.[74]

Chiefs acted as important intermediaries between their constituencies and the spirit world. At the end of the sixteenth century, for example, the ruler of Teve ascended a mountain to perform a ceremony at the graves of his ancestors each September. Dos Santos described the excessive eating and drinking of the king and his entourage that characterized the first eight days of the ceremony.[75] According to dos Santos, after this prolonged feast, all mourned for the dead over several more days until an ancestral spirit, in this case the king's dead father, possessed a person present at the ceremony.[76] The spirit, according to dos Santos, "begins to cough and speak like the dead king whom he represents, in such a manner that it seems to be his very self, both in voice and movements."[77] All present "prostrate themselves before him" to demonstrate honor and recognition of the spirit. Then the people withdrew so that the living king could discuss forecasts of war or famine with the spirit. In the end, dos Santos claimed that "these blind men" continued to believe the answers of the spirit medium each year.[78]

A similar and more recent religious ceremony called *mandhlozi* centered on a *ndhlozi* spirit said to belong to a deceased warrior, who was usually a wandering Nguni warrior. These spirits could also inhabit the Ndau, but not other Shona speakers, because the Ndau and the Nguni "feel that they belonged to the same clan once upon a time," as one Chikore resident explained.[79] During a *mandhlozi* ceremony, a possessed participant became a "Zulu-speaking warrior" who might be angry or violent.[80] In addition to *mandhlozi*, spirits called *mazinda*, *madanda*, and *zvipunha* were also said to possess people, and still do during ceremonies today.[81]

Steven Feierman's argument that mediumship "constituted an entirely separate sphere of public authority," albeit an unstable one, helps explain why the history of healers in southern Africa and beyond has been invisible, for the most part.[82] Spirit mediums exerted a moral and religious authority in a realm separate from the expansive sociopolitical arena of chiefs. Religious figures concerned with the spirituality, health, security, and well-being of the community helped foster an intangible sense of a shared identity; whereas the rule of chiefs lends itself to visibility and stability—except for opportunistic succession struggles, as mentioned in chapter 4. An overall lack of firm religious backing weakened Ndau polities and added to their vulnerability. However, during both Zimbabwe's struggle against colonial rule and protracted anticolonial resistance in Mozambique, female spirit mediums such as Nehanda emerged as powerful actors to bridge the gap between the spirit world and the threatening situations at hand. In a similar postcolonial adaptation, Ndau chiefs rely on female spirit mediums "who act as power brokers between the different but overlapping worlds of chiefs and government" where men predominate.[83] Spirit mediums and other religious figures have occupied fluid spaces and worked within their communities to maintain the ties that bind the Ndau together.

The Power of the Court

The Ndau both feared and respected chiefs whose power was held in check by the *dare*, a council of village men who ruled over major court cases and served as state advisers.[84] The decisions of the *dare* were firm; even people of authority involved in a case abided by the judgment of the court. In each village, from at least the sixteenth to the twentieth century, a chief or headman presided over small cases and attempted to reconcile parties involved in minor disputes.[85] Serious offenses, however, were reserved for the court of paramount chiefs, where leaders made decisions related to cases of witchcraft accusation and advised parties to consult with a *n'anga*, or healer, at times.[86] "If found guilty a person would be humiliated. They were then made to pay by a human being," noted one elder.[87] In the seventeenth century, Sousa also wrote about severe punishments for witchcraft, theft, and adultery.[88] Leaders turned to fratricide and banishment to settle all-to-frequent succession disputes.[89] These practices have remained fairly constant since the end of the sixteenth century, so holding court over time is one more commonality shared by the Ndau.

Respected men from the community assisted with proceedings at each chief's court, the *dare* proper.[90] Plaintiffs would relate their accusations and then defendants would respond to the allegations. The chief and his council of elders would deliberate and decide the guilt or innocence of those accused. Common crimes before the court included adultery, murder, and theft.[91] Depending on the nature of the offense, guilty parties were made to pay for their crimes by providing compensation such as hoes, chains of beads, livestock, money, or even a human being.[92] One elder from Chikore noted that in some cases, guilty parties "were made to pay with their own child, pledging out a son, daughter or sister as a form of payment."[93] But if a man courted another's wife, for instance, the adulterer could be forced to provide the husband with cattle.[94] If a woman was unable to make a payment, she could pledge herself in lieu of a fine.[95] Or, if a guilty party was unable to provide goods toward restitution for a death, "they would give a little girl to the deceased and say, 'this is your wife,' and that would be the end of the topic."[96] Many of these practices, such as giving a daughter to the spirit of the deceased (and thus to his family), occurred both before and during the nineteenth-century occupation by the Gaza Nguni.[97]

Chiefs also relied on their court messengers to act as a liaison with the community.[98] People would report offenses to a messenger who would then relate the complaint to his leader. The chief would then instruct his messengers to summon the offender to the *dare*, where the chief and his councilors would preside over the case. These agents who enforced the law were well respected for the most part, but sixteenth-century documents reveal that the ruler of Teve had a bodyguard of two hundred to three hundred men called *inficis* who also acted as bloodthirsty executioners.[99] In this case, dos Santos notes that the *inficis* encircled the king's enclosure shouting "Inhama, Inhama" (signifying "flesh") to call on the king to issue a death sentence so "that they may exercise their office of executioner."[100] Another group, known as *marombes*, acted as court jesters to relieve some of the pressures at court.[101] *Marombes* recited praises of the chiefs and performed with a group of dancers and musicians who played many-keyed instruments known as *ambira* made with iron, wood, and gourds.[102] Some of these attendants also accompanied ambassadors on their missions, and the threatening nature of the *inficis* surely helped make the early missions successful.[103]

Although plaintiffs normally sought justice from a chief, there are claims from a late eighteenth-century report that laws once enforced by the leaders were altered so that almost anyone judged crimes and meted out punishments.[104] This form of vigilante justice, echoed much later during the war in Mozambique after independence, included the killing of a suspect, or the removal of eyes, hands, or ears. Thus, a large population of blind and maimed subjects stationed themselves at the doors of their "kings and princes," according to the report, where they sang, danced, and played instruments in exchange for sustenance from a gracious king.[105] Some of these casualties were even elevated in status and permitted to join royal entourages.[106] This lack of deference to rulers that is cited in the written record indicates faults in the political authority of Ndau leaders. However, most chiefs certainly ruled with an iron fist, and documentary evidence describes how they failed to exhibit graciousness in matters related to their own families. For instance, any man who was caught looking at one of the king's wives lost his eyes as a punishment, and the ogler was then forced to rely on alms for sustenance along with other blind subjects.[107] Custom and tradition were central to Ndau societies, but chiefs adapted to changes and created new rules of conduct as demanded by the situation at hand. Overall, peace was maintained by the decisions of leaders who presided over their courts and acted as judges.[108]

Pomp and Circumstance

Consultations with any local Ndau chief were ceremonial in their own right. Outsiders who wished to speak with a chief had to make their requests through others so that "the word is passed through three or four before it reaches the *fumo* [chief], even though he understands it."[109] The chief sat on a small stool while those in attendance remained on mats. In the written record, European observers refer to the elaborate clapping used to open and close each meeting—a formality similar to the greetings discussed in chapter 4.[110] This practice remains firmly entrenched in Ndau society today and occurs before and after a meeting with local variations in pattern and rhythm. Meeting and greeting in this manner, although also practiced by neighbors of the Ndau, is viewed as something specific to the Ndau.

Commenting on the authority of leaders in southeast Africa, Monclaro observed, "They have great ceremonies among themselves, and no council is held without the *fumo*, who is often kept rather for ceremony than for any substantial obedience shown to him."[111] Today the custom of ululating for a chief also continues. Chinungu Mtetwa describes the protection that chiefs provided when she explains, "Long back such ululation and dancing for the chief was done as a token of thanking him for taking care of their welfare in the jungle infested by lions."[112] At the village level, sociopolitical structures relied on the authority of local chiefs. In a description that holds true throughout the Ndau region, Monclaro noted, "The greater part of this Kaffraria is governed by *fumos* and petty rulers, and though it has powerful kings whom it obeys, it has nevertheless these *fumos* and headmen by whom people are governed."[113] Despite an official Portuguese focus on paramount chiefs and the Mutapa leader, Monclaro recognized the hidden authority of the little society—local chiefs and their ancestors. This small-scale power at the grassroots level was instrumental in the fostering of a sense of belonging, and being Ndau, within each community.

Conclusions about Rituals and Beliefs

The practices and ideas surrounding beer brewing, rainmaking, and affairs of the court are major contributors to what it means to be Ndau. People followed the customs of their ancestors that stretched back over several centuries, and they sought justice from their chiefs for any redress.[114] There was an important connection between the authority of ruling chiefs and the power of the ancestors. Chiefs and headmen made offerings to ancestral spirits, usually at graves in sacred forests, as a legitimating part of their duties.[115] Traditional religious ceremonies, or *mabira*, were important gatherings that emphasized shared beliefs and demonstrated an investment in the power of both political leaders and ancestor spirits. Social and religious customs revolved around brewing beer and making rain within the greater Ndau region. While beer drew people together for religious ceremonies, it could also attract a husband's love or satiate a work party.[116] The three activities of brewing beer, making rain, and holding court are common strands of a web of shared beliefs maintained by the Ndau over centuries. The arrival of the Gaza Nguni in the nineteenth century, discussed in the next chapter, threatened the sociopolitical fabric of Ndau life in ways both large and small.

7

MEMORIES AND IDENTITIES IN THE SHADOW OF NGUNGUNYANA

> Ngungunyana was a problem. . . . We are called Ngungunyana's people
> yet we are Ndau. We were changed into Changana (Shangani).
> —Jona Mwaoneni Makuyana

> People who were staying here were called Machangana (Shangani), but
> they were Ndau. Their leader was Ngungunyana.
> —John Kunjenjema

When speaking about history long ago (*kare kare*), many Ndau in central
Mozambique and eastern Zimbabwe recall a past marked by a shifting political and cultural terrain of invasion and domination in the nineteenth century. This turbulent period, known by many as a time of terror, began with the
migrations of several northern Nguni peoples, most notably the Gaza Nguni,
who first settled in the Ndau heartland in the 1830s and returned later for an
extended occupation from 1862 to 1889. Most of the population in this corner of southeast Africa submitted to Gaza Nguni overrule and came to be
known as Ndau partly in response to the presence of these outsiders. This conquest by the Gaza Nguni in the nineteenth century acted as a foil for the Ndau
to re-create their identity and assume a sense of Ndauness with a powerful
salience that reverberated into the twentieth century.

The previous chapters argue that Ndau speakers shared a collective identity
long before these more recent events. However, this nineteenth-century
episode of common suffering at the hands of others reinforced a sense of
being Ndau as earlier relationships had not. The "other" came to rule over the
Ndau in a more direct manner in the nineteenth century, and this harsh reality continued into the period of formal colonialism under the Portuguese and
the British. Indeed, some would say that aspects of overrule lasted beyond
independence, when others who were not Ndau, such as Shona in Zimbabwe
and members of ethnic groups from other areas in Mozambique, prevailed
over the Ndau living in two independent nations. There were few Ndau in the

national leadership of either Mozambique or Zimbabwe after independence. Instead, Ndau speakers were more likely to be prominent members of the political opposition in Zimbabwe or leaders of the rebel movement Renamo that waged a war against the Mozambican government. In the conclusion, I discuss the lingering effects of this domination over the Ndau in the twentieth century.

This chapter examines the shaping of memories and identities amid a nineteenth-century culture of terror to show how a Ndau identity became very powerful over a short period. Michael Taussig's work on the "space of death" in South American societies "where torture is endemic and where the culture of terror flourishes" informs my focus on overrule here.[1] Just as Taussig argues that terror is a social state that can "serve as a mediator *par excellence* of colonial hegemony," the fear and tyranny spread by the Gaza Nguni cast a hegemonic shadow over the Ndau region just before the coming of European colonial rule.[2] The relatively recent and heightened sense of a common Ndau identity is similar to the awareness developed by the Igbo people of a collective Igbo identity during the Biafran War that followed independence in Nigeria. Chinua Achebe explains how the invention and declaration of Biafra led to the emergence of a complex identity where "[y]ou can suddenly become aware of an identity which you have been suffering from for a long time without knowing."[3] Achebe notes that being Igbo "became a very powerful consciousness" that arose amid the horror of war.[4] "But it was *real* all the time," he insists.[5] In addition to the case of the Igbo, Kwame Anthony Appiah points to how the "tribe" in various African settings "is invested with new uses and meanings" precisely because people believe in it and give it meaning.[6] These complicated identities arise out of a response to forces, both internal and external, and are "almost always in opposition to other identities."[7] For the Ndau, the Gaza Nguni presence in the nineteenth century triggered a new belief in and a new meaning of being Ndau.

Memories and identities are as much about the present as the past. The present influences aspects of memory and identity such as recollection, selection, and presentation. Indeed, memory and history can be in fundamental opposition, as Pierre Nora has articulated so well for the case of France.[8] Recent events, moreover, often shape the discourse surrounding the writing and telling of history, as Alessandro Portelli demonstrates in his work on the errors surrounding the retelling of episodes in Italian history.[9] This interconnectedness between memory and identity prompts historians who use oral evidence to consider how aspects of identity play out in the memories of elders and how identities are gendered and flexible for both men and women. Studies of the social construction of identities are also inextricably linked to gendered histories over the *longue durée*. In the Ndau region, evidence uncovered about shifting identities in the past pertains more to men's experiences than those of women. Even though men and women in Ndau societies actively defined and redefined their own identities, we know much more about the activities of men. Thus, this chapter grapples with these gaps as it considers the gendered meanings that surround memory and identity among the Ndau.

The Coming of the Nguni

The difficult time and "problem" that the Ndau attribute to Ngungunyana actually began two generations before his time with the arrival of Ngungunyana's grandfather, Soshangane (also known as Manukosi).[10] He was one leader among several groups of Nguni-speaking migrants fleeing disturbances in Natal associated with the rise of the Zulu state in South Africa. These Nguni speakers first reached the area of central Mozambique and eastern Zimbabwe inhabited by the Ndau in the 1820s. Raids, battles, and retreats occurred along the routes of these migrations—the result of a complex interaction of environmental, political, and economic factors.[11] At this time populations in weaker positions sought security through incorporation into stronger societies ruled by powerful leaders. Violent and chaotic episodes led vulnerable groups to submit both voluntarily and involuntarily to "great men" such as Shaka, Moshoeshoe, and Soshangane, the founder of the Gaza Nguni state in southern Mozambique.

A handful of Nguni-speaking groups under several leaders cultivated a culture of terror in the wider Shona-speaking area that spread beyond the world of the Ndau. However, many Nguni stayed only briefly before moving northward into the lakes region of East Africa.[12] For instance, the leader Nxaba remained in the eastern highlands near the modern border and around the Ndau states of Sanga and Danda for almost a decade, from about 1827 to 1836, before Soshangane drove him and his followers north of the Zambezi River.[13] Nguni warriors also raided heavily populated areas such as Teve and Sofala for food until the Gaza Nguni under Soshangane gained control.[14] These Nguni-speaking groups rocked the balance of power in the wider region through raids, conquest, and the imposition of overrule. An assortment of recollections and connections arose out of the nineteenth-century relationship between the Gaza Nguni and the Ndau of central Mozambique and eastern Zimbabwe. And for many Ndau elders today, the name Ngungunyana is synonymous with all the memories associated with distinct, and at times short-lived, periods of overrule clouded by terror. The Ndau have condensed their memories of Nguni dominance like a telescope to focus mainly on Ngungunyana.

Soshangane and his Nguni followers established the Gaza state in the lower Limpopo Valley to the south of the Ndau region (as shown in map 7.1). Following the pattern of strong leaders of the time, Soshangane incorporated both refugees and local populations under his control to gain strength

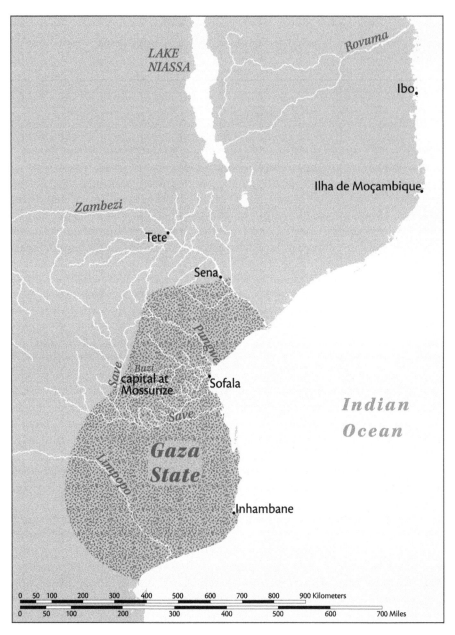

Map 7.1. Extent of the Gaza state.

in numbers. Like his contemporary Mzilikazi of the Ndebele in southwest Zimbabwe, Soshangane ruled over a military state with age regiments for male warriors based on the Zulu model in South Africa. Several centuries earlier, Shona-speaking (Karanga) chieftaincies had dominated over some of the same Tsonga-speaking groups that came to live under Soshangane.[15] However, by the beginning of the nineteenth century these Tsonga chieftaincies had asserted their autonomy to establish themselves as culturally distinct from their Ndau neighbors.[16] This population came to be called Shangani (alternately Shangaan or Changana) after Soshangane, the first Gaza Nguni leader who settled in their midst.

In about 1836 Soshangane moved his capital northward to the fertile highlands of the Ndau heartland at Mossurize near the middle Save River. He remained in this area of Sanga only briefly until 1839 when he returned to his previous southern location by the Limpopo River.[17] After Soshangane died in the late 1850s, a son named Mzila emerged as his successor.[18] Mzila promptly moved the capital back among the Ndau in the highlands near the headwaters of the Buzi River in 1862. Later, under the leader Ngungunyana, the court eventually returned to the south near the Limpopo in 1889.[19] Map 7.1 shows the extent of the Gaza state. The shifting capital, called Mandhlakazi regardless of its location, remained in the south at Bilene until the state was conquered by the Portuguese in 1895.

The Influence of Overrule

The lengthy Gaza Nguni presence amid the Ndau, centered at the headwaters of the Buzi and Mossurize Rivers, affected Ndau polities in different ways. Some Ndau leaders submitted to the invaders while others refused to accept Gaza Nguni rule and were killed.[20] Mzila's conquest of many of the Ndau people, particularly those living in the highlands, and the subsequent rule of his son Ngungunyana appear to have been especially harsh, according to the memories of Ndau elders—both men and women. While elders interviewed in the late twentieth century attribute much of the terror that people faced at the hands of the Gaza Nguni to the more renowned (and recent) Ngungunyana, elders also cite the earlier rule of Mzila from 1861 until 1884 as repressive. Ngungunyana's relocation of the capital to Bilene in the south was accompanied by an exodus of many Ndau forced to demonstrate their loyalty to him. After the Portuguese defeated the Gaza Nguni in the late nineteenth-century European scramble for African territories, many Ndau left Bilene to return to their homeland north of the Save River. Others, however, stayed behind and settled in the south outside of the Ndau heartland, contributing to the overlapping and fluid nature of ethnic identities in the wider region.

The influence of the Gaza Nguni on the Ndau was significant in several ways, and perhaps most symbolically in the naming of this widespread group as Ndau. Most likely the phrase *Ndau-we, Ndau-we,* used by Ndau speakers in their act of supplication to greet the invading Nguni, led the Nguni to select the term Ndau as a label for their subjects.[21] Even though Ndau was initially a derogatory nickname used by the Gaza Nguni, it endured through overrule as a lasting label. Most elders in interviews, with no apparent embarrassment or shame, traced the origin back to the deferential greeting *Ndau-we, Ndau-we.*[22] The Ndau, in turn, referred to the language of the Gaza Nguni with their own pejorative term, *xibitzi,* and called Nguni warriors *mabziti.*[23] In the case of the Ndau, as in the Igbo region and elsewhere, naming practices employed to describe the "other" are often of a derogatory origin.[24] However, these given labels tend to stick as identifiers that come to be appropriated by the group in question to reflect a powerful identity.

Social and Political Identities

To secure loyalty from the Ndau, the Gaza Nguni successfully defined political identity in terms of a state culture.[25] The state apparatus drew people into a systematic web through a combination of incorporation and conquest. Ndau men who lived with Ngungunyana, for instance, became Nguni warriors.[26] However, subject populations on the periphery, including some Ndau and their neighbors to the north (Manica) and south (Tsonga), also managed to influence the language and culture of the Gaza Nguni while submitting to overrule. One male elder, drawing comparisons between the Gaza Nguni and the Ndau, insisted that the mother of Ngungunyana was a Ndau woman.[27] This historical memory, consistent with the written record, reflects the important presence of Ndau women as wives and mothers among the Nguni elite.[28] In this position Ndau women served as transmitters of various aspects of a Ndau cultural identity to children of the next generation. This social reality reveals one method the Ndau relied on to maintain a continuity of cultural traits amid political overrule.

A single Gaza Nguni culture never emerged among the diverse groups living in south-central Mozambique and eastern Zimbabwe under Gaza Nguni rule.[29] Instead, conquered populations such as the Ndau influenced the small Nguni nucleus, perhaps originally only about one hundred people.[30] Cross-cultural exchanges occurred throughout this period, such as the Gaza Nguni use of an indigenous Tsonga-based language from the Ndau's southern neighbors. The northern Nguni language of the elite scarcely remained in use, but loanwords infiltrated other languages such as Ndau. By the end of the nineteenth century, most Gaza Nguni also spoke Shangaan, a subgroup of the local Tsonga language in southern Mozambique. The Gaza Nguni assumed certain aspects of a Tsonga identity to the south and a Ndau identity to the north. Nguni clan names, songs, dances, and a certain pride in a glorious military past—emphasized alongside resistance to the coming of colonial rule—all survived. Two-way acculturation carried over into the colonial period as the Gaza Nguni came to be Shangaan.

There was an element of reciprocity between Nguni ways and Ndau culture. The Gaza Nguni used Ndau drums and pots, as well as Ndau methods of healing and the Ndau word for healer, *nhamussoro*.[31] In southeast Africa today, Ndau healers continue to enjoy a reputation as the most powerful practitioners in the region. In the large and mobile Gaza Nguni state, both the rulers and the ruled inevitably shaped identities that combined characteristics from the small Nguni elite and their incorporated followers. Soshangane, for instance, based his government structures in south-central Mozambique on Tsonga and Ndau chiefly lineages. Meanwhile, populations far from Mandhlakazi, the mobile capital, maintained their own sense of identity since they faced little pressure to assimilate on the periphery.

Throughout the Ndau region, elders at the end of the twentieth century express a resilient and proud sense of being Ndau, while some also acknowledge the "mixed pot" of blended cultural influences that make up current notions of Ndauness.[32] As the Ndau re-created their identity over time, conquest led to "a common pool of key signifiers binding the transforming culture of the conqueror with that of the conquered," just as Taussig argues for South America.[33] However, he notes that signifiers can be "strategically out of joint with what they signify," leading to "rupture and revenge of signification."[34]

In interviews, Ndau speakers described the presence of the Gaza Nguni in their region as an intense period of rupture that was full of difficult memories. This recollection was in contrast to a more nostalgic view of the earlier past without the misdeeds that accompanied the invaders. Before these outsiders arrived, one elder noted, "Our fathers told us that people here were living harmoniously."[35] Some regions practiced politics by consensus.[36] These political realities changed with the coming of the Gaza Nguni and their transgressions. Out of this overrule and its violence came new meanings of identity.

Frequently, the Ndau today refer to the Gaza Nguni as "the Zulu," even though nineteenth-century conceptions about what it meant to be Zulu were shifting and often in flux. In the beginning of the nineteenth century, for instance, the Zulu chiefdom in South Africa was quite small in relation to larger Nguni states such as the Ndwandwe, Mthethwa, and Ngwane. After the death of Dingiswayo of the Mthethwa, the Zulu kingdom under Shaka's leadership grew. As Shaka conquered surrounding chiefdoms, the "Zulu" gained fame and emerged as a powerful state in southeast Africa. Ndau elders in the twentieth century then transferred the powerful image of the fierce Zulu warrior—reputed to be prone to violent and ruthless action—to a similar oppressor, the Gaza Nguni. In addition to this conflation, Ngungunyana gained a reputation in the narrative as an anticolonial hero for his stance against the

Portuguese. According to one Ndau elder living in Chikore, Zimbabwe, the Ndau say that "Shangani, Zulu, and Ndebele are one and the same thing."[37] Soon after the Gaza Nguni conquest, Ndau clan names in the region were transformed into their Nguni equivalents.[38] When these "Zulu" arrived, "everything changed because the Zulus would marry the most beautiful Ndau women."[39] Thus, the Gaza Nguni presence disrupted Ndau social structures, significantly altered the names of clans, and called existing identities into question.

The Gaza Nguni leaders appointed political and military deputies known as *ndunas* to control the far reaches of their state, including the Ndau region. Ndau men, if "found fit," could be *ndunas* as well.[40] These deputies acted as governors and supervised Ndau chiefs who pledged allegiance to the Gaza Nguni rulers. Some elders described the despotic nature of Gaza Nguni rule, and they claimed that the conquerors were reluctant to trust Ndau chiefs. For instance, one elder recalled, "The likes of Musikavanhu were not allowed to rule because Ngungunyana was the only chief without subordinate or cochiefs. Wherever Ngungunyana conquered, he would not respect any of his subordinates."[41] Elders repeatedly relayed perceptions of Ngungunyana's rule as harsh. The majority of Ndau chiefs, such as Mafussi for example, submitted to the system of overrule.[42] Many had little choice, since the military might of the Gaza Nguni was formidable. The Gaza Nguni used tactics of intimidation to assert control over Ndau populations. When Chief Ngorima resisted incorporation by the Gaza Nguni, he faced repeated raids from their army. His subjects fled into the Chimanimani mountains, and he sought safety farther west in Gutu.[43] The Gaza Nguni captured many of Ngorima's followers and incorporated them into their regiments. This created a dual identity for these men, as one Ndau elder from Melsetter explained: "This is why we are Ndau and Shangaans at the same time."[44] When Gaza Nguni leaders did not take matters into their own hands, the deputies (*ndunas*) served as the link between the Ndau and the state apparatus ruling over them.

The Gaza Nguni failed to develop an apparent connection with Ndau ancestral spirits tied to the land, an important relationship for successful rule.[45] As old territorial loyalties clashed with new political realities of conquest, ritual opposition to the Nguni presence grew. The Gaza Nguni harassed and exiled many Ndau chiefs from the highlands, but groups such as the Musikavanhu territorial cult survived to unite the Ndau.[46] As Rennie notes, "[T]he Nguni never managed to reach accommodation with the territorial cult leaders, the 'owners of the soil,' and to create ideological consensus in the same way that the rulers of Sanga, Teve, and Danda seem to have done."[47] Despite the power held by rain shrines of Ndau territorial cults, Mzila rejected their legitimacy under his leadership and chose not to incorporate them into the Gaza Nguni political realm. This division between Ndau beliefs and Gaza Nguni overrule served to reinforce cultural and political differences between the two groups.

One of the most dramatic shifts for Ndau society in the nineteenth century was the arrival of Gaza Nguni warriors who became a "military aristocracy of non-producers."[48] These conquerors (depicted in fig. 7.1) appropriated surplus food and cattle from surrounding populations.[49] They regulated hunting, collected tax, monopolized the export of ivory, and controlled cattle movements.[50] The Gaza Nguni relied on personal subordination and clients to maintain control over their vast state. Local populations were forced to pay tribute to the state and support military raids of nearby communities. Some men and women pledged themselves to Nguni deputies, and Patrick Harries even argues that scholars have overlooked the existence of internal slavery within the Gaza Nguni state.[51] Captives from raids, orphans, and destitute people all served as clients. Various forms of subservience, known as *kukhonza*—either allegiance, capture, pawning, or bride service—constrained many Ndau in both their daily labor and wider life.[52] Cattle, animal skins, cloth, food, and brass beads were all items of tribute.[53] Women sought protection and support as the wives of either Ngungunyana, his deputies, or Ndau chiefs loyal to the Gaza Nguni. Ngungunyana's children from marriages with Ndau women were given to the elite—Nguni or acculturated Nguni—as wives and laborers.[54] Ndau speakers were forced to act as soldiers, porters, concubines, and wives as the Gaza Nguni capitalized on their wealth in the Ndau people.[55]

Gendered Identities

Both Ndau and Nguni women played an important role in the shaping of nineteenth-century culture and society in southeast Africa. Their contributions were most notable when marriage alliances or arrangements provided women with the opportunity to produce and reproduce the regional political order. Women played an integral part in maintaining a common language and culture over a wide geographic area, yet scholars often overlook their activities. In *The Creation of Tribalism in Southern Africa*, Leroy Vail repeats the Tswana proverb that "women have no tribe" and argues that the appeal of ethnicity "was strongest for men."[56] But in the Ndau region, women were active in the crafting of identities within communities, clans, and lineages. Ndau women raised their children within a certain cultural and linguistic framework that shaped identity formation. And although men usually held positions of political power among the Ndau, female chiefs were appointed at times.[57] Women tended to assert their power overtly in Ndau society as influential healers and spirit mediums.

Among the Nguni elite, some women of the ruling family held both political and social power.[58] Ngungunyana's mother, the Ndau woman Empiumbecasane, exerted control over her son's decisions and over the affairs of a village.[59] Empiumbecasane was also the head priestess at the shrine where

GRUPO DE LANDINS DO GUNGUNHANA

(Seg. phot. do cap. Sousa Machado)

Figure 7.1. Ngungunyana's warriors. *Source*: Baptista 1892.

Ngungunyana worshipped the grave of his grandfather, Soshangane.[60] Some of the wives of the ruler lived in distant parts of the region and helped the Gaza Nguni king to maintain relations over a wide area.[61] These women most likely supervised agricultural production in the royal gardens of outlying areas. Thus, women served symbolically and practically as stewards of the state.

When I raised the subject of Ngungunyana in interviews, most Ndau women initially claimed that they knew "nothing" about the time of Ngungunyana and the affairs of men in the political realm. This is not really the case, however, for harsh details of terror and intimidation emerge in interviews with women (and men) about the rule of the Gaza Nguni leader. The reluctance of women (as opposed to men) to identify with Ngungunyana's reign is telling of the gendered political spaces in southeast Africa. Other studies, however, have shown how men and women on the margins participate in the shaping of their cultural identities.[62] Diana Jeater's work in the Gwelo District of Zimbabwe demonstrates how the transfer of women between lineages created "gender difference and separate social identities between men and women in bridewealth societies."[63] This was surely the case for Ndau men and women as well. Disadvantaged Ndau speakers who actively challenged their social definitions as the "other," as well as groups who came from the fringes of society, were able to alter their identities to "fit" into an acceptable community within a centralized state. A consideration of this turbulent time in the Ndau region reveals interwoven connections between ethnicity and gender across the social field.

Assimilation among Men

The Gaza Nguni conquest followed earlier migratory patterns that ushered in new inhabitants to the Zimbabwe Plateau and central Mozambican coastal plain. Emerging male leaders broke with patriarchs and migrated to new territories where they secured their own power over people. Even the breakup of the famous Mutapa state in earlier Shona history is explained by a myth that follows this pattern. The Nguni, however, invaded more territory over a shorter length of time than earlier migrants to the area. The Gaza Nguni widened their cultural identity to incorporate some conquered subjects, but outward signs of assimilation were more common among Ndau men than women.[64] Men learned the language of the rulers, pierced their ears in the Nguni fashion, served in the army, and renamed their clan using the nearest Nguni equivalent to the Ndau term.[65] Some Ndau men even adopted the Nguni language as their own and wore a distinctive Nguni head ring.[66] Through assimilation, however, local men also came to be Ndau.

Ndau men who served in the army were assigned to Gaza Nguni age regiments that broke down existing group identities tied to political loyalties.[67] Regiments raided frontier areas and worked in the royal homesteads of the king's wives.[68] Unmarried Ndau men were dispersed to other areas of the state, in order to sever their local ties and loyalties. The Nguni state system helped foster a sense of "national" identity when the ruler's position as head of the army and the agricultural cycle was reinforced during state ceremonies.[69] Military service was another form of labor tribute. Even though Ndau speakers, particularly large numbers of men, adopted Nguni traits and cultural practices, many elders interviewed in 1998–99 considered Ngungunyana and his warriors to be the only true Nguni. Thus, in the present memory, elders reject a historical process of ethnic integration and assimilation.

The piercing of men's ears was one very obvious mark of identity that symbolized Gaza Nguni dominance over the Ndau. The Ndau say that men only started to pierce their ears after the Gaza Nguni invasion when Ngungunyana relied on ear piercing to identify those who had submitted to his overrule.[70] A similar identifying body mark does not exist for women, but Gaza Nguni control over women's bodies (particularly those deemed beautiful) was a very public sign of subjugation.[71] Idah Manyuni of Chikore described the piercing of men's ears as "a form of identity" that was Ngungunyana's directive.[72] "He is the one who did this," she said, referring to Ngungunyana; "The piercing of ears was a sign of identity to show that we are warriors, Ndaus," she explained.[73] This act demonstrated that Ndau men "were warriors, *madzviti*," according to Phillip Mutigwe.[74] The Ndau called Ngungunyana's order to pierce ears *chidzviti*, after *dzviti*, meaning invader or warrior.[75] Mubayi Mhlanga of Zamchiya explained, "It was a mark of identity. My ears are pierced to show that I belong to Ngungunyana."[76] Other elders echoed this sense of belonging to an identity. Phillip Mutigwe recalled that the Gaza Nguni "upheld their custom by claiming that those with unpierced ears did not belong to them."[77] Subjects without pierced ears who were "not part of them" were killed, "but those with pierced ears were spared because they shared a common identity," he explained.[78] Freddy Sithole concluded, "So we from Bilene, as followers of Ngungunyana, we had this distinct identity, of pierced ears."[79]

After the defeat of the Gaza Nguni by the Portuguese, ear piercing became a rite of passage for all young Ndau men in the late nineteenth and early twentieth century before they served their time in the mines of South Africa. Most young men pierced their ears when they reached puberty. This "form of tribal identity," as one former headman described it, was necessary for all of the men who went to Johannesburg.[80] Men used a knife to pierce their ears and some created large holes that could hold a snuff container or a peeled maize stalk staff.[81] This practice made a man more attractive and maintained standards of beauty.[82] One woman from Chikore in Zimbabwe saw men from the east in Mozambique actually wearing earrings, an uncommon sight among most Ndau men.[83] Among male Shona speakers, only the Ndau pierced their ears, and this mark proclaimed an identity that was visible to all.[84] One elder from Chikore explained that Ngungunyana's warriors first forced Ndau men to pierce their ears "because it was a Zulu custom that every adult should have pierced ears."[85] "It all started with Ngungunyana who distinguished people as Ndaus and Tongas," according to an elder of Zamchiya.[86] Ear piercing "was a sign of identity for people under Ngungunyana"[87] that "served to differentiate tribal identities."[88] Ndau men pierced their ears to show that they were subordinates of Ngungunyana, as another elder explained, "If you did not have pierced ears you were not on Ngungunyana's side."[89] Ngungunyana's order to pierce men's ears was one lasting mark of the Gaza Nguni occupation in the Ndau region.

In the highlands, men also pierced their ears, according to one elder, "to show that we are not vaDuma."[90] Ear piercing was used by Ndau men in the highlands to set them apart from *masvina*, others who did not pierce their ears, such as the Duma who live farther west across the Save or Malawians known as *mabhurataya*.[91] Ndau men pierced their ears initially because of a Gaza Nguni directive, but later they continued the practice by choice to mark ethnic boundaries and demonstrate to others that they were Ndau. The piercing of men's ears is one distinct example of a gendered sense of Ndauness that the Ndau manipulated themselves following Gaza Nguni overrule. What was once a practice of the Gaza Nguni became a distinct Ndau act.

Living with a Tyrant

Political and cultural conditions give rise to social identities in an assortment of ways. We know from studies such as Terence Ranger's work on Manica identity in Zimbabwe that Africans across the continent were not duped into accepting any random "tribal" affiliation during the colonial period.[92] Rather, at times people were able to embrace aspects of identities that suited them, and ethnic identification played an instrumental role in what always remains a complicated process of defining "us" and "them." However, the repression, intimidation, and very real threat of violence from the Gaza Nguni constrained the Ndau and limited their opportunity to express and adopt cultural identities in the nineteenth century. For the Ndau in the twentieth and twenty-first centuries, this legacy led to a powerful sense of being Ndau in contrast to the Gaza Nguni presence. The psychological effects of overrule amid a culture of terror remain unclear, but recent violent transgressions in Mozambique during the war with Renamo may be intricately tied to the cultural history of the region.[93]

The Gaza Nguni controlled many facets of Ndau life and had the power to order the death of their subjects. Evidence from interviews with elders reveals a historical memory of incredible atrocities attributed to Ngungunyana.[94] The Ndau remember Ngungunyana as an oppressive leader who ordered harsh penalties for his subjects. One elder recalled Ngungunyana's distaste for the sight of animal bones and his threat to kill people who left their bones in full view.[95] Another noted that Ngungunyana tore out the eyes of anyone who looked at one of his wives, echoing a similar eighteenth-century practice in the hinterland of Sofala.[96] Ngungunyana was infamous for killing men indiscriminately and seizing their daughters for distribution as offerings to his warriors. Informants assert that he would order the massacre of an entire village when one person was suspected of witchcraft or of displaying excessive sympathy for a local leader.[97] Men and women who committed adultery were assaulted—sometimes their eyes were removed and their hands cut off[98]—and murderers were executed.[99] People suspected of witchcraft or a crime such as the theft of a cow were impaled on wooden sticks and left on display at the junction of two paths.[100] These corpses were left to rot without a burial to serve as a deterrent to potential offenders.[101] A person found guilty of almost any crime was most likely killed during Ngungunyana's time, according to many elders.[102] As one man gravely noted, "He did what he wanted at will."[103] This culture of violence is an eerie foreshadowing of what was to come during the colonial period, the struggle for independence, and the war with Renamo.

Exodus to Bilene

Ngungunyana's mass exodus from his capital at Mossurize to Bilene in southern Mozambique was a grave collective hardship for the Ndau. The Gaza Nguni leader most likely ordered this migration to benefit from the fertile lower Limpopo Valley near Bilene and return to the land inhabited by his grandfather. Ndau elders recall this forced march in 1889 as a "death march" where many Ndau died from lack of food and water during a trip that lasted about one month.[104] Anywhere from sixty thousand to one hundred thousand Ndau migrated, with Gaza Nguni guards punishing deserters by killing them.[105] Some managed to escape during the journey and return to their communities, but many more Ndau had to wait until after Ngungunyana's defeat at the hands of the Portuguese before they could return to their homeland.[106] Others remained permanently in the south to form a contingent of Ndau in the population around Bilene.[107] Despite the death and suffering associated with this involuntary migration, Ndau elders today credit Ngungunyana for bringing "civilization" to their region. Perhaps this is how the Ndau have come to interpret military prowess and strong-armed overrule. This is one of the interesting repercussions of Ngungunyana's presence that lingers alongside his legacy of despotism and terror.

After Ngungunyana's departure from the Ndau region, other Ndau chiefs resumed their rule with headmen as their aides and juniors.[108] Some of Ngungunyana's warriors stayed behind or decided to return later.[109]

Presumably, members of this group of warriors were reluctant to leave their Ndau wives (said to be some of the most beautiful Ndau women) and start a new life in Bilene. Yet, those who remained were considered outsiders.[110] But the Ndau accepted their presence, and they assumed political roles, as one elder explained: "The likes of chief Mpungu are Ngungunyana's warriors who remained here. That is where you can find most of the returnees from Bilene."[111] This example illustrates how the Ndau region bears the marks of Gaza Nguni overrule today in ways both subtle and conspicuous. It is said that Ndau spirit mediums warned about the coming of Nguni warriors, declaring that these "warriors would dominate the land but were destined to move south and return no more."[112]

The Legacy of Ngungunyana's Shadow

The Ndau recall an incredible assortment of memories surrounding their experience of living under a tyrant at the end of the nineteenth century. Ngungunyana's legacy casts a large shadow that dwarfs the presence of his predecessors, Mzila and Soshangane. This exploration of the relationship between memory and identity in southeast Africa reveals that the Gaza Nguni influence is one aspect of the constant reworking of identities within the Ndau context. Although a sense of being Ndau was apparent much earlier, as this study demonstrates, some Ndau elders actually give Ngungunyana credit for forging a sense of identity among the Ndau, particularly a sense of being Ndau for men before he "left" them to head south.[113] Others refer to the practice of assuming male identities that were Shangaan or Zulu during Gaza Nguni overrule as a transformative event for the Ndau. One elder summed up the uncertainty of the Gaza Nguni experience when he said, "We do not know where we would have ended up had Ngungunyana not died."[114]

The history of Ndau subjugation at the hands of the Gaza Nguni demonstrates how ethnicity is shaped by cultural practices and often used to further political aims. Although ethnic identities may arise under a host of conditions, they are most famous for leading to violence when they are used to satisfy one group's aspirations at the expense of others'. Edwin Wilmsen and Patrick McAllister argue that ethnicity holds the key to structures of inequality and is frequently the object of manipulation in the exercise of power.[115] The dominant use group identities to define the subordinate, but the subordinate can "adopt the terms of their definition" to organize and assert their own collective identity.[116] This is what the Ndau managed to do as they faced a harsh episode of Gaza Nguni overrule in the nineteenth century. Their experience illustrates how the powerful and the weak, men as well as women, reproduced an ethnically ordered world under the shadow of a tyrant.[117]

8

PAST AND PRESENT IN THE NDAU REGION

> You also became Ndau because you speak the Ndau language, are born of Ndau parents, so you are Ndau.
>
> —Ellen Gapara

> We are now a mixed pot, it is no longer Ndaus only.
>
> —Idah Manyuni

Over a four-hundred-year period in central Mozambique and eastern Zimbabwe, the Ndau actively crafted their own identity and gave it meaning. Amid the continuities and changes of centuries, the Ndau forged a sense of identity that has come to resemble a mixed pot.[1] Today Ndauness is present throughout the region, but it is neither prominent nor particularly striking to the casual observer. A closer look at the present reveals influential legacies from the past that linger in this corner of southeast Africa. The multiple meanings inherent in cultural rememberings of Ndau history demonstrate the intricate nature of histories and identities. Elders preserve historical memories and use them either to support or to suppress ethnic identification. The Ndau have reconstructed memories and oral traditions to address contemporary realities, and the recent war between Renamo and the government in Mozambique has strongly influenced histories and relationships on both sides of the border. My investigation of Ndau history since the sixteenth century reveals that neither the pressures of colonialism nor the politics of nationalism created a sense of being Ndau. Evidence shows that Ndauness, while not reflecting a deep primordial allegiance, was shaped as an ongoing practice in the precolonial period.

Coming to Be Ndau

An enduring sense of being Ndau is the hallmark of this cultural identity that has persisted over the *longue durée*. Although it is not always easy to glean Ndauness from the historical record (or from current inhabitants of the region), the presence of Ndau speakers in the hinterland of Sofala since the era of dos Santos and other early Portuguese writers offers a fascinating yet incomplete picture of a lasting *and* changing identity. The history of Ndau speakers is rooted in a common group of people who have endured various hegemonies while maintaining their own local traditions. Despite facing exclusion and incorporation during periods of intense domination, the Ndau have demonstrated an ability to alter their identities, both temporarily and permanently, in creative ways. This examination of such a long period of transformation allows us to see the continuity of some identity markers as well as the emergence of newer ones, particularly in the nineteenth century, during the short history of the recent past.

Elders at the end of the twentieth century expressed various opinions about Ndauness, reflecting the twists and turns of identity formation. For Jona Mwaoneni Makuyana, being Ndau is "a tribal identity."[2] He explained, "We were called VaShangani before Ngungunyana changed us into Ndaus."[3] Similarly, Mateus Simango claimed, "Long back we were not called Ndaus; we were called Shangani."[4] Other Ndau elders also linked a Ndau identity with an earlier Shangaan one rooted in the Gaza Nguni presence. "We are called Ndau, but we are Shangani," said John Kunjenjema.[5] The Ndau became Shangani and the "original Shangani went to Bilene with Ngungunyana," he explained, referring to Ngungunyana's forced march in 1889 to Bilene in the south.[6] Speaking to his young son, Freddy Sithole said, "The Ndaus are your generation, but those of our generation are Shangani, *madzviti*."[7] For the elder Sithole, the act of becoming Ndau occurred *after* the Gaza Nguni occupation. His use of a temporal marker to make a distinction about being Ndau was common among male elders interviewed.

When women were asked what it meant to be Ndau, they often took a longer view and referred to language, place of birth, and "tribe." Idah Manyuni, for instance, replied, "I can say it is just a name which has been there since time immemorial."[8] Bertha Munedzi responded, "It means I was born among the Ndau,"[9] and Mbuya Dhliwayo explained, "It means I speak Ndau."[10] For some elders, being Ndau has a "tribal" connotation. "To say I am Ndau, Zezuru, or Zulu, it means my tribe," commented Celani Mutigwe of Chikore.[11] Being Ndau *is* a matter of identity for many Ndau elders. "I am Ndau because that is my tribal identity," remarked Phoebe Mukokota of Chikore.[12] Among men, Philemon Khosa echoed these sentiments with his explanation that "to be Ndau simply means your tribe or dialect."[13] Another female elder, Ellen Gapara, remarked matter-of-factly: "You also became Ndau because you speak the Ndau language, are born of Ndau parents, so you are Ndau. Hlengwes are called Hlengwes because they speak their own language, so they are Hlengwe. The same applies to Zezuru and Ndebele people."[14] The Ndau are also conscious of their totems, but they do not draw on their totems for "an actively operational ethnic identification."[15] The different answers of elders, men and women, reflect the confusing and complex nature of explaining a sense of being something that is often maintained in part by local traditions.

Ndau speakers crafted identities in the nineteenth century and into the twentieth century in especially powerful ways. During this time, ethnicity was often manipulated away from home in sites such as the mines. As many Ndau men traveled to *Joni* (Johannesburg) in search of the best opportunities for migrant laborers, the journey became a "cultural necessity" for males throughout much of the Ndau-speaking region.[16] As a rite of passage for young men, with earnings that enabled them to accumulate wives, "mining became associated with manhood itself."[17] Laborers who remained in Mozambique usually failed to earn enough wages to secure wives.[18] In South Africa, Ndau speakers would adopt a Shangaan identity to receive better pay as mineworkers. These laborers experienced a multicultural milieu that included other languages such as Shangaan, Zulu, and Sotho. Ndau men continued to manipulate their identity by piercing their ears, a practice first introduced by the Gaza Nguni, as one gendered sense of Ndauness.

People call on various identities in the midst of ethno-political conflicts. Some elders remembering history reflected the views of a rural community alienated by the central government in a distant capital. Even though elderly Ndau men have pierced their ears because of the Gaza Nguni presence, those in Mozambique feel isolated from the "South" and the Mozambican capital in Maputo, where they consider the government to be dominated by Shangaan interests. Similarly, in Zimbabwe the Ndau feel ignored by the government and passed over for powerful positions. To complicate matters, the Ndau in each country have a reputation as confused troublemakers. "Confusion" (*confusão*) was a common term I often heard used by other Mozambicans and Zimbabweans to describe Ndau speakers and the Ndau region. Some Ndau even employed this term as a self-identifying characteristic. This reflects some uncertainty about who the Ndau are and what it means to be Ndau.

The Meanings of Identity

The many divisions and differences among those who speak what has come to be called Ndau suggest a lengthy presence of Ndau speakers in the area as time allowed for the development of diversity.[19] The Ndau set themselves apart from outsiders, and even from each other, when they speak. John Kunjenjema, a Zimbabwean who was born in Mutema and then moved to Chikore when he was about forty years old, noted, "In Mozambique they speak Ndau although there is a small difference in that those in Mozambique have an accent or intonation that sounds like a child."[20] For Kunjenjema, "real Ndau" is found in the highlands of Chimanimani, and "moderate Ndau" is spoken in neighboring Chikore.[21] Celani Mutigwe also distinguished "real Ndau" from the Hlengwe language spoken farther south.[22] Her husband, Phillip Mutigwe, insisted that "real Ndau speakers" who speak "pure Ndau" are found on the Zimbabwean side of the border in Chirinda and Chikore, near Espungabera. He argued, "If you go down into the valley the tone is different. Again beyond Espungabera we do not understand each other because of tonal differences."[23] Yet many consider this area east of Espungabera to be part of the Ndau region.

On the other hand, Idah Manyuni, living in Chikore but born in Mount Selinda, described the Ndau spoken near Espungabera as "no longer Ndau but a mixture of its bits and pieces."[24] She added, "Going further down across and along the border with Mozambique up to Zamchiya and Mahenye, people there do not speak like we do here. For example, instead of labelling a clay pot as *hari* they call it *mbende*."[25] Freddy Sithole, also from Chikore, noted that in Chimanimani just to the north the tone of spoken Ndau was different.[26] He observed, "If we cross into Mozambique there are fluent Ndaus, but further into Mozambique the tone changes into Danda."[27] Allen Mundeta, a resident of Chikore and member of a younger generation, observed that even though the Ndau dialect changes as one travels farther east, "basically it is still the same."[28] He explained that Ndau speakers farther to the east "speak a different language," but "they are Ndaus."[29] They are often referred to as Danda, which some consider to be a derogatory term. According to Mundeta, "It means people who are not really smart, just like the British talk about the Irish as not being very smart."[30] One elder argued that, over time, the Ndau language came to be "mixed up with the other people" in the region.[31]

Straddling an international border, the Ndau region challenges the hard boundary separating Mozambique and Zimbabwe.[32] Many Ndau elders in both countries do not cite any firm boundaries for the Ndau region, perhaps because their sense is that they are *between borders* with an unbounded sense of Ndau territory. Often elders did not supply answers to questions about the extent of the area inhabited by Ndau speakers in terms of borders or frontiers. Most people interviewed in Zimbabwe did note that the Ndau region extended across the border into Mozambique, although they differed over the extent of the Ndau region within Mozambique. And Mozambicans acknowledged that Ndau speakers stretched into Zimbabwe as well. For one former headman in Chikore, Zimbabwe, the Ndau region spread into Mozambique and northward to Mutema's area of control.[33] But he noted that in Johannesburg, Ndau speakers are easily identifiable, even though "those from Mozambique have their own accent."[34] Thus, national distinctions between Zimbabwe and Mozambique were apparent in a third country, South Africa.

In addition to differences in language, there are other observable markers, or local traditions, that make the Ndau distinct. The Ndau proclaim an identity visible to others through body art such as tattoos (*pika*) and scarification (*nyora*) on women's bodies. This shared body language of decorative markings and adornment shaped connections among Ndau women over several centuries. Elders such as Mubayi Mhlanga argue that the Ndau have their own greetings that set them apart from their Hlengwe neighbors to the south and Manyika neighbors to the north.[35] Despite differences such as these that shape a public identity, there is also movement across ethnic boundaries. For instance, Mateus Simango of Zamchiya recalled that outsiders, referred to as "vaShangana," arrived from the Hlengwe region while Ndau speakers from Zamchiya also went to stay among the Hlengwe.[36] Being Ndau meant noticing outsiders as different when ethnic boundaries were crossed, thus reiterating the fluid nature of ethnic identities.

Even though many Ndau see themselves as a distinct group, it is misleading to envision an "archipelago of cultures" in this region of southeast Africa, for as Eric Wolf argues, seemingly discrete societies have always been partly maintained by virtue of their mutual contacts.[37] This is indeed the case with the Ndau. While groups emerged among the Ndau with separate genealogies considered culturally distinct, Ndau speakers as a whole shared a common cultural identity. These communities of Ndau speakers—families, clans, villages, and chieftaincies—experienced contact and interconnectedness through sexual politics, regional links of trade, warfare against common enemies, and migration together to the mines and fields of South Africa. In both the past and the present, being Ndau does not correlate neatly with any single political system or process. Rather, in the dynamic political history of the region, local political identities and traditions stand out amid an overarching Ndau cultural identity.

Negotiating the Past and the Present

In the postindependence period, a sense of being Ndau continues to transcend the arbitrarily drawn border between Zimbabwe and Mozambique. However, the Ndau have formed distinctions on each side of the international border. For example, many Ndau speakers in eastern Zimbabwe will cross into Mozambique to consult with a traditional healer, or *n'anga*, since Ndau spirits in Mozambique are perceived as having more power than their Zimbabwean counterparts. Even the term Ndau carries different connotations in each country. For most Zimbabweans, a Ndau speaker belongs to one of the six main subgroups of the Shona language. In Mozambique, however, Ndau can be a very separate and distinct label with tenuous connections to a sense of Shonaness and the wider Shona language spoken in other parts of central Mozambique and Zimbabwe.[38]

Perhaps even more telling, the Ndau in both Zimbabwe and Mozambique remain marginalized in the political realm, and others use the Ndau as convenient scapegoats for economic and security problems in the southern African region. Some of these accusations stem from the heavy Ndau participation in Renamo, the rebel movement in Mozambique's war.[39] Ndau became the lingua franca of Renamo since many of Renamo's leaders were Ndau.[40] On the Zimbabwean side of the border, Ndau speakers in the Chipinge constituency have always voted in "their" candidate from the small "Ndau" opposition party, Zimbabwe African National Union (ZANU) Ndonga, led by Ndabaningi Sithole.[41] Even though "it is rare for politicians to campaign along ethnic lines" in Zimbabwe, Masipula Sithole points out that "the electorate votes along ethnic lines."[42] Calls for inclusion in government power structures and the absence of outright ethnic campaigning by political leaders may be linked to the stalled democratic process in Zimbabwe.[43] The minor presence of ZANU (Ndonga) in the seat for Chipinge is most likely a mere thorn in the side of the ruling party, ZANU Patriotic Front (PF). Another thorn, perhaps more dangerous, exists in the form of the *chimwenjes*, an armed group based in western Mozambique that operated on both sides of the border in the 1990s. Understanding more about the negotiations between past and present shifts in identity will help scholars analyze the motivations of violent groups such as the *chimwenjes* that take advantage of the relatively porous border that exists today.

As countries such as Mozambique and Zimbabwe struggle to reconcile cultural pluralism with nationalist fervor, cultural identities that cross borders present a challenge to postcolonial states.[44] At the end of the millennium, UNESCO's World Culture Report for 2000 noted that culture may be "threatened by globalization and exploited in situations of conflict."[45] The presence of the former rebel group Renamo, now the major official opposition in Mozambique, complicates the picture.[46] Renamo's leader, Afonso Dhlakama, speaks Ndau and draws on his identity as a Ndau from the center of the country to increase his power base and fuel a long-standing rivalry with Frelimo, the ruling party since independence in 1975. Thus, a new ethno-political situation emerged in Mozambique in the 1990s alongside Dhlakama's rise from the leader of an armed organization to a very important political player since the end of the war.[47] But in Mozambique's 2004 presidential elections, Dhlakama's support declined to below 32 percent from 34 percent in 1994, and Renamo received almost 1 million fewer votes than in 1994 to hold nearly 30 percent of the parliamentary seats. Although Dhlakama continues to make references to ethnicity and those on the margins, as he did frequently during the 1994 campaign, it remains to be seen if a Mozambican electorate will develop strength along ethnic lines.[48]

Ethnicity and regionalism, as powerful political resources, certainly have the potential to wreak havoc with nationalism and modernism. During fieldwork in Rogo, Nigeria, Abdul Raufu Mustapha found complex and multilayered ethnic identifications that revealed "principles of inclusion and exclusion in the process of community formation."[49] He also noted "a preserved historical consciousness, rather than an actively operational ethnic identification."[50] This is similar to the awareness of Ndau totemism among most Ndau, or feelings of Ndauness among Mozambicans in the east who also consider themselves to be Danda. Mustapha calls for an examination of the "possibilities and constraints offered by the actual historical dynamics of the sub-nation groups and formations whose integration lie at the heart of 'nation-building.' "[51] He cautions against following a "state-centered" approach to nation building that ignores the relevance of "processes of identity formation in the pre-colonial period."[52] For Mustapha, an emphasis on "universalistic concepts of state and citizenship" has "little regard to pre-colonial cultures of exclusion which impede the access of castes, women and some linguistic and social groups to full citizenship in the 'nation-state.' "[53] Processes of incorporation, rather than exclusion, emerge as the dominant historical pattern in the Ndau region, and indeed in the underlying cultural history of Mozambique and Zimbabwe.

Why all of this concern about ethnicity? Put simply, the implications of history and identity for present concerns, and for future national integration, must be considered. Whether it is "real or imagined," "ethno-regional domination" can have divisive and deadly consequences.[54] On the one hand, in Mozambique, Michel Cahen has noted how "a fierce denial of the relevance, even of the existence of all the different communities" in a nation leads to resentment.[55] When Mozambique's first president, Samora Machel, proclaimed, "There are no more whites or blacks, only Mozambicans," he was hard at work constructing a socialist program that considered ethnic appeals to be reactionary and opposed to a modern, nation building process.[56] As the sole party after independence, Frelimo "had the function of hindering any expression of different identities or regional social trajectories," according to Cahen.[57] In this instance, rejecting ethnicity rendered invisible the social hierarchies intricately tied to ethnicity.

In Zimbabwe, on the other hand, an "ethnic electorate" has silently yet consciously supported the "ethnic leader."[58] And yet, the multiethnic nature of Zimbabwe's society may "be a facilitating factor for democracy."[59] Sithole suggests that ethnic conflict be managed "by deliberately creating political structures and other social institutions and processes that are calculated to moderate and diffuse ethnic tensions."[60] This allows ethnicity and regionalism to "become the legitimate social pressures and concerns that they are."[61] Similarly, John Comaroff, writing of identity politics, warns of "our continuing inability to grasp the historical character of the beast in its full, unpredictable complexity."[62]

Ethnic identities must no longer be dismissed as mere creations or inventions. This explaining away is wishful thinking, for these same identities persist or resurface in various guises to rear their ugly heads. Past leaders, both before and after colonial rule, drew on inventions of ideology and tradition to gain and maintain loyalty from their subjects.[63] Even today rural supporters of Renamo in Mozambique express a desire to return to the past, to an earlier time before Frelimo, before the modern state and before the Portuguese, according to Cahen.[64] Mozambicans recall this as the place of the ancestors, and it is the place of this book. What, then, is in store for the future?

This study, by showing how local history is embedded in the cultural landscape where identities flourish as "fictions in our lives," is one contribution to a desperately needed disruption of the discourse of difference.[65] Ndau identity is real because Mozambicans and Zimbabweans have given it meaning "based on an idealizing fiction" of social identities.[66] These meanings need to be taken seriously. But it is also time to lay bare these ethnic assertions and put them on the table as part of an interrogation that disrupts an existing "discourse of 'racial' and 'tribal' differences."[67] For as Kwame Anthony Appiah observes, "the inscription of difference in Africa today plays into the hands of the very exploiters whose shackles we are trying to escape."[68]

The Past Will Never Remain the Past

This examination of the historical processes of identity formation among the Ndau reveals patterns of social, political, and economic integration, as well as periods of domination, among communities in southeast Africa. Shifts in identities at various periods in Ndau history occurred because of changes from within Ndau society as well as from outside influences. Both written and oral sources reveal common themes and continuity over the *longue durée*. By weaving strands of Ndau history into an analysis of a collective identity, I have enhanced our understanding of continuity and change in this corner of the world. It is clear that studying history and identity from 1500 to 1900 in this setting prompts questions about more recent processes of identity formation in the twentieth century. Fortunately, the written record and the knowledge of gracious elders allows for future investigations to be informed by rich historical sources. By continuing to historicize ethnic and national identities, we can revisit the trying problems of "tribalism" that are with us today and address contemporary definitions of what it means to claim an identity such as Ndau. According to local wisdom, "The past will never remain the past," as histories and identities are reinterpreted over time.[69]

NOTES

Acknowledgments

Epigraph. Mordikai A. Hamutyinei and Albert B. Plangger, *Tsumo-Shumo: Shona Proverbial Lore and Wisdom* (Gweru, Zimbabwe: Mambo Press, 1987), 422.

1. Ibid., 291.

Chapter 1

Epigraph One. Interview with Sarai Nyabanga Sithole, Zamchiya, Zimbabwe, 13 July 1999. (All interviews are hereafter cited with the name of the elder interviewed, location, and date.) The prefix "Va-" in *VaNdau* denotes the plural.
Epigraph Two. Jona Mwaoneni Makuyana, Zamchiya, Zimbabwe, 14 July 1999. Makuyana was commenting on the limits of the Ndau region.

1. *Tribe* is a term that lacks a consistent meaning. A tribe can be a social group of families, clans, or generations united by common descent, or the term can describe a group of people with similar characteristics or interests. In African contexts, a tribe is often described as an ethnic group with a shared language or culture. However, given the millions of people that speak the same African languages and share the same cultures, the term tribe is often an inappropriate description that obscures realities. *Tribe* is used to describe many different groups, from the more than 9 million Zulu speakers in South Africa to a small band of Americans competing in a remote setting on the popular television show *Survivor*. There can be smaller tribes inside of larger tribes, or tribes that run across vast regions. Therefore, if a tribe can be just about anything, it serves as an unsatisfactory and contradictory label. Speakers of the Shona language in Zimbabwe, for instance, might use the term *rudzi* instead among themselves to denote a type or kind of group. One main problem with the term tribe is that it fails to be specific and descriptive of the subtleties of many situations. The term also carries many negative connotations by reinforcing an image of the primitive and conveying a static sense of timelessness. Despite the relatively useless meaning behind the term tribe, the phenomenon of "tribalism" continues to haunt postcolonial Africa. See Chris Lowe, "Talking about 'Tribe': Moving from Stereotypes to Analysis," *Africa Action Background Paper* (November 1997), http://www.africaaction.org/bp/ethall.htm.

2. Frederick Cooper and Rogers Brubaker discuss these options in *Colonialism in Question: Theory, Knowledge, History* (Berkeley: University of California Press, 2005), 70–77.

115

3. As Cooper and Brubaker contend in *Colonialism in Question*, 59.

4. Ibid., 67.

5. Ibid., 90.

6. Elizabeth Tonkin, Maryon McDonald, and Malcolm Chapman, eds., *History and Ethnicity* (New York: Routledge, 1989), 16.

7. Cooper and Brubaker, *Colonialism in Question*, 65.

8. John Comaroff and Jean Comaroff, *Ethnography and the Historical Imagination* (Boulder: Westview Press, 1992), 66.

9. Kwame Anthony Appiah, "The Case for Contamination," *New York Times Magazine*, 1 January 2006. Appiah goes on to conclude, "Societies without change aren't authentic; they're just dead." See also his book *Cosmopolitanism: Ethics in a World of Strangers* (New York: W. W. Norton, 2006).

10. Gerhard Liesegang, "Archaeological Sites on the Bay of Sofala," *Azania* 7 (1972); T. H. Elkiss, *The Quest for an African Eldorado: Sofala, Southern Zambezia, and the Portuguese, 1500–1865* (Waltham, MA: Crossroads Press, 1981), 72. Erosion has changed the shoreline of Sofala and destroyed the Portuguese fortress. The modern port is twenty miles to the north at Beira, Mozambique's second-largest city.

11. Over the first two centuries of the Portuguese presence, exports of ivory rose to overshadow a declining gold trade. As Malyn Newitt notes, "By the eighteenth century the rest of the world thought of east Africa, if it did so at all, as the producer not of gold but of ivory." *A History of Mozambique* (Bloomington: Indiana University Press, 1995), 176.

12. The main Manica fair was at Chipangura, later named Masekesa, and Bandire was an important *feira* in Teve. The names and exact locations of other fairs farther south are not known. See Newitt, *History of Mozambique*, 194–202, 211–16; H. H. K. Bhila, *Trade and Politics in a Shona Kingdom* (Harlow, Essex, UK: Longman, 1982); "Senhor" Ferão, "Account of the Portuguese Possessions within the Captaincy of Rios de Sena," in George McCall Theal, ed., *Records of South-Eastern Africa* (Cape Town: C. Struik, 1964; hereafter cited as *RSEA*), 7:380.

13. In subsequent Portuguese texts, the terms "Mocaranga" and "Makalanga" appear. See, for example, Joseph da Fonseca Coutinho, "Report on the Present Situation of the Conquistas of the Rivers of Soffalla" (1699), in D. N. Beach and H. de Noronha, eds., "The Shona and the Portuguese, 1575–1890" (Harare, 1980), vol. 1; Newitt, *History of Mozambique*, 196.

14. The Mutapa state—ruled by a leader known as the "Mutapa," "Monomotapa," or "Benomotapa"—was linked to several dynastic territories farther east under changing conditions from the 1400s to the 1880s.

15. Gerhard Liesgang, "Sofala, Beira, e a sua Zona," *Arquivo* 6 (October 1989): 31.

16. H. A. Wieschhoff, *The Zimbabwe-Monomotapa Culture in Southeast Africa* (Menasha, WI: George Banta, 1941); Octávio Roza de Oliveira, *Amuralhados da Cultura Zimbáuè-Monomotapa de Manica e Sofala* (Lourenço Marques, Mozambique: Artes Gráficas, 1963); James H. Bannerman, "Notes and Questions Regarding the Archaeology, Language, and Ethno-History of Central Mozambique between the Zambezi and Save Rivers" (Paper presented at the Tenth Pan African Archaeological Congress, Harare, Zimbabwe, June 1995); Graham Connah, *African Civilizations: An Archaeological Perspective* (Cambridge: Cambridge University Press, 2001); and Martin Hall, *The Changing Past: Farmers, Kings, and Traders in Southern Africa, 200–1860* (Cape Town: David Philip, 1987).

17. Damião de Goes (Góis), "Chronicle of the Most Fortunate King Dom Emanuel of Glorious Memory" (1566), in *RSEA*, 1:128–31; Newitt, *History of Mozambique*, 37–38; John Keith Rennie, "Ideology and State Formation: Political and Communal Ideologies among the South-Eastern Shona, 1500–1890," in *State Formation in Eastern Africa*, ed. Ahmed Idho Salim (Nairobi: Heinemann Educational Books, 1984), 166.

18. Goes, "Chronicle of King Dom Emanuel," in *RSEA*, 3:130.

19. *Zimbabwe* or *dzimbahwe* refers to the court, home, or grave of a chief. It is thought that *zimbabwe* (pl. *madzimbabwe*) evolved from one of two contractions: *dzimba dzamabwe:* houses of stone, or *dzimba woye:* venerated houses. Connah, *African Civilizations*, 232; Goes, "Chronicle of King Dom Emanuel," in *RSEA*, 3:129; Rennie, "Ideology and State Formation," 166–67; For evidence of an elite population living inside the stone enclosure at the *zimbabwe* Manyikeni farther south, see Peter Garlake, "Excavation of a *Zimbabwe* in Mozambique," *Antiquity* 50, no. 198 (June 1976): 146; and "An Investigation of Manekweni, Mozambique," *Azania* 11 (1976): 25–47; Graeme Barker, "Economic Models for the Manekweni Zimbabwe, Mozambique," *Azania* 13 (1978); Berit Sigvallius, "The Faunal Remains from Manyikeni," in Paul J. J. Sinclair, ed., *Analyses of Slag, Iron, Ceramics, and Animal Bones from Excavations in Mozambique* (Maputo, Universidade Eduardo Mondlane, 1988), 27; and Paul J. J. Sinclair, *Space, Time, and Social Formation: A Territorial Approach to the Archaeology and Anthropology of Zimbabwe and Mozambique, c. 0–1700 A.D.* (Uppsala: Department of Archaeology, Uppsala University, 1987), 96.

20. André Fernandes, "Letter from the Father André Fernandes to the Father Provincial in India" (1560), in *RSEA*, 2:66. The term Tonga (also Thonga, Bonga, and Bitonga) was a derogatory one that implied chiefless or subject people. Various groups used the term to describe different groups between Lake Malawi and Delagoa Bay in southern Mozambique. Today BiTonga speakers and Tsonga speakers live south of the Save River in southern Mozambique. D. N. Beach, *The Shona and Zimbabwe, 900–1850: An Outline of Shona History* (Gweru, Zimbabwe: Mambo Press, 1980), 158; Rennie, "Ideology and State Formation," 166.

21. João dos Santos, *Ethiopia Oriental*, in *RSEA*, 7:273, 285–86; Newitt, *History of Mozambique*, 42–43; Rennie, "Ideology and State Formation," 166–67.

22. These competing paternal claims were a legitimating device. See Beach, *Shona and Zimbabwe*, 162–63; dos Santos, *Ethiopia Oriental*, in *RSEA*, 7:273; Manuel de Faria e Sousa, *Asia Portuguesa* (1674), in *RSEA*, 1:23; Rennie also discusses several examples of legitimation and external political authority in "Ideology and State Formation," 172–73.

23. Two detailed studies of the Mutapa state are by W. G. L. Randles, *L'empire du Monomotapa du XVe au XIXe siècle* (Paris: Mouton, 1975); and S. I. G. Mudenge, *A Political History of Munhumutapa, c. 1400–1902* (Harare: Zimbabwe Publishing House, 1988). Most Portuguese writers expressed a fascination with and penchant for exaggeration about the Mutapa's control over the region they referred to as "Karanga." Early maps supported this view of a far-reaching Mutapa as well. For exaggerated accounts of the Mutapa's power, including the claim that his overrule reached to the Cape of Good Hope, see, for example, Franciso Monclaro, "Relaçaõ da Viagem que Fizeram os Padres da Companhia de Jesus com Francisco Barreto na Conquista de Monomotapa no Anno de 1569, Feita Pelo Padre Monclaro, da Mesma Companhia" (post-1573), in *RSEA*, 3:227; and Manuel Barreto, "Informação do Estado e Conquista

dos Rios de Cuama" (1667), in *RSEA*, 3:482. The works of both Barreto and Monclaro appeared in other publications before Theal's *RSEA*. Although I consulted earlier versions of each work, I cite Theal's translations here.

24. Rennie, "Ideology and State Formation," 167.

25. Ibid.

26. Ibid.; Arquivo Histórico de Moçambique (AHM), *Revista de Manica e Sofala* (1a. Serie, no. 2, Abril de 1904).

27. The Ndebele under Mzilikazi migrated from South Africa in the early nineteenth century into the Changamire region ruled by a power that originated in the late seventeenth century. The term Shona first appeared in writing in 1835, according to David Beach, "The Zimbabwe Plateau and Its Peoples," in *History of Central Africa*, vol. 1, ed. David Birmingham and Phyllis M. Martin (New York: Longman, 1983), 268. See also Beach, *Shona and Zimbabwe*, 163.

28. This coincides with the onset of formal colonialism in Zimbabwe and Mozambique. Beach, "Zimbabwe Plateau," 268; Terence Ranger, *The Invention of Tribalism in Zimbabwe* (Gweru, Zimbabwe: Mambo Press, 1985), 4.

29. Ranger, *Invention of Tribalism*, 4.

30. Zezuru is a dialect of Shona spoken in the region around Harare. Sanga is spoken in the Ndau highland region. This map is titled "Map of Zambezia and adjacent regions by the Marquis Sá de Bandeira." Randles, in *L'empire du Monomotapa*, notes that the map is a second edition from Lisbon in 1867.

31. This map is titled "Map of Mozambique" (1889), according to Randles, *L'empire du Monomotapa*.

32. Clement M. Doke, *Report on the Unification of the Shona Dialects* (Hertford, England: Printed for the Government of Southern Rhodesia by S. Austin and Sons, 1931), 78–80.

33. Ibid., 78.

34. Ranger, *Invention of Tribalism*, 14–15.

35. National Archives of Zimbabwe (NAZ), "Chindau-English and English-Chindau Vocabulary" (Binghamton, NY: Rhodesian Branch of American Board Mission in South Africa, 1915), GEN, AME; NAZ, "Brief Notes on the History of the Mission on Its 60th Anniversary" (1953?), Historical Manuscripts, United Church Board for World Ministries (UCBWM), UN 3/8/5; NAZ, "Stations: Location and Special Work of Missionaries" (1916?), Historical Manuscripts, UCBWM, UN 3/20/1/11/1; NAZ, "Printing Report" (June 1915–June 1916), Historical Manuscripts, UCBWM, UN 3/20/1/11/8. For more on the American Board, see also the collection American Board of Commissioners for Foreign Missions (ABC), Houghton Library, Harvard University. Rennie traces the adoption of "Ndau" by the American Board missionaries (including the first published use in 1906) and argues that their usage of the term led to the "official" designation by Doke. Rennie, "Ideology and State Formation," 169. Ethnographers such as E. Dora Earthy and H. P. Junod soon adopted this expanded usage to describe the entire region from the Save River to the coast. The Portuguese were aware of the use of Ndau throughout the wider region. See AHM, "Revista de Manica e Sofala" (2a. Serie, no. 19, Setembro de 1905), 80. But they were not pleased with (Protestant) missionary instruction in Ndau and tried to prohibit it in their territory. AHM, Companhia de Moçambique, Secretaria Geral, Processos, "Missão Americana no Gogoi" (1921), Caixa 198.

36. Patrick Harries, "The Roots of Ethnicity: Discourse and the Politics of Language Construction in South-East Africa," *African Affairs* 346 (1988): 26.

37. Doke, *Unification of the Shona Dialects*, and *A Comparative Study in Shona Phonetics* (Johannesburg: University of the Witwatersrand Press, 1931).

38. Note that Shanga (or Machanga in Portuguese) on the coast is different from Sanga (or Quissanga, Chisanga) to the north. It is also not the same as Shangaan (or Changana in Portuguese), the name of a group of people in southern Mozambique south of the Save River.

39. Doke relied on Zulu-speaking informants for details about the "Ndau Group," and he did not gain a familiarity with the Mozambican region. Commenting on Doke's enduring classification of Shona into dialects, David Beach noted, "[I]t is curious how it seems to have stood the test of time in light of practical experience and further research." *The Shona and Their Neighbours* (Oxford: Blackwell, 1994), 29. The more recent work of C. H. Borland revisits the classification of eastern Shona into the two dialect clusters of Manyika and Ndau. See, for example, "Conflicting Methodologies of Shona Dialect Classification," *South African Journal of African Languages* 4, no. 1 (1983): 1–19; and "Internal Relationships in Southern Bantu," *South African Journal of African Languages* 6, no. 4 (1986): 139–41.

40. Harries, "Roots of Ethnicity," 39.

41. Ranger, *Invention of Tribalism*, 6; See also Beach, *Shona and Their Neighbours*, chap. 6.

42. Ranger, *Invention of Tribalism*, 6.

43. Terence Ranger demonstrates this in "Missionaries, Migrants, and the Manyika: The Invention of Ethnicity in Zimbabwe," in Leroy Vail, ed., *The Creation of Tribalism in Southern Africa* (Berkeley: University of California Press, 1989), 120.

44. Ranger, "Missionaries, Migrants, and the Manyika," 120, draws on David Beach's work in early Shona history.

45. Seven Laisse and Timothy Mataca, Machaze, Mozambique, 16 July 1998.

46. Doke, *Unification of the Shona Dialects*, 80.

47. The uncomplimentary term Shona is the name of the language spoken by 6,225,000 people in Zimbabwe in 1989 and 759,923 people in Mozambique, according to the 1980 census. According to Doke's report, there were about 150,000 Ndau speakers in the 1930s. One-third, or 50,000 people, were living on the Zimbabwean side of the border and the other two-thirds, about 100,000 people, were in Mozambique, according to the report. My own estimates, based on data from the 1930 and 1940 censuses in Mozambique, are slightly higher. For Mozambique alone, I estimate about 140,000 Ndau speakers in 1930 and 175,000 in 1940. In 1970 René Pélissier cited a figure of 750,000 for the number of Shona in Mozambique. Based on census data in each district, I estimate that slightly less than half would have been Ndau speakers. Doke, *Unification of the Shona Dialects*, appendix 3, 136; René Pélissier, *História de Moçambique: Formação e Oposição, 1854–1918* (Lisbon: Editorial Estampa, 1987–88), 1:39. A recent population count, based on an estimate from Andy M. Chebanne in 2000, puts the total number of Ndau speakers at 2,700,000 (with 1,900,000 in Mozambique and 800,000 in Zimbabwe). Chebanne's figures are cited in Raymond G. Gordon Jr., ed., *Ethnologue: Languages of the World*, 15th ed. (Dallas: SIL International, 2005), also available online at http://www.ethnologue.com/. See also Gregório Firmino, *A "Questão Linguística" na África Pós-Colonial: O Caso do Português e das Línguas Autóctones em Moçambique* (Maputo: Promédia, 2002).

48. As noted by Doke in his *Unification of the Shona Dialects* and by numerous elders, including Mubayi Mhlanga, Zamchiya, Zimbabwe, 13 July 1999; Jona Mwaoneni Makuyana, Zamchiya, Zimbabwe, 14 July 1999; and Mateus Simango, Zamchiya, Zimbabwe, 14 July 1999. (At times, many elders supplied similar information on a theme, but I list only a few names as examples.)

49. Sekai Sithole, Chikore, Zimbabwe, 29 June 1999; AHM, José Fontes Pessoa de Amorim, "Os 'Vatssangas' ou Mundaué" (Beira, 1956), Secção Especial, a. III, p. 6, no. 80.

50. Phillip Mutigwe, Chikore, Zimbabwe, 29 June 1999.

51. Marien Dziwandi, Nyanyadzi, Zimbabwe, 1 August 1999.

52. Shona is a tonal language. "Long ago" or "long back" is at least the end of the nineteenth century in this case. Phillip Mutigwe, Chikore, Zimbabwe, 29 June 1999; Siyanzi Raphius Gapara, Chikore, Zimbabwe, 1 July 1999; Robert Open Nkomo, Nyanyadzi, Zimbabwe, 1 August 1999.

53. Robert Open Nkomo, Nyanyadzi, Zimbabwe, 1 August 1999.

54. Phillip Mutigwe, Chikore, Zimbabwe, 29 June 1999.

55. Siyanzi Raphius Gapara, Chikore, Zimbabwe, 1 July 1999.

56. Ibid.

57. Phillip Mutigwe, Chikore, Zimbabwe, 29 June 1999.

58. Rennie, "Ideology and State Formation," 168–69.

59. Henri Philippe Junod, "A Contribution to the Study of Ndau Demography, Totemism, and History," *Bantu Studies* 8, no. 1 (March 1934): 18; Rennie, "Ideology and State Formation," 169.

60. João Julião da Silva, *Memoria sobre Sofalla* (1844), in João Julião da Silva, Zacarias Herculano da Silva, and Guilherme Ezequiel da Silva, *Memórias de Sofala* (Lisbon: Comissão Nacional para os Comemorações dos Descobrimentos Portugueses, 1998), 34, 49, 59, 67, 74–75. The editors of this collection of documents, José Fialho Feliciano and Victor Hugo Nicolau, note that the Mataos were "Vatombozis of Quissanga" who were Gaza Nguni subjects integrated into the military structure of these conquerors. Ibid., 34n10; Rennie, "Ideology and State Formation," 169.

61. St. Vincent W. Erskine, Route Map of the Gasa Country, in "Journey to Umzila's, South-East Africa, in 1871–1872," *Journal of the Royal Geographical Society* 45 (1875): 45–125, map facing p. 45.

62. Sarai Nyabanga Sithole, Zamchiya, Zimbabwe, 13 July 1999.

63. Ibid.

64. Jona Mwaoneni Makuyana, Zamchiya, Zimbabwe, 14 July 1999.

65. Ibid.; This was the conclusion of a 1905 Portuguese report. AHM, "Revista de Manica e Sofala" (2a. Serie, no. 18, Agosto de 1905), 65.

66. Ibid.

67. Ibid.

68. Mucherechete Dhlakama, Zamchiya, Zimbabwe, 13 July 1999. Mbuya Dhlakama was born in Maupfu across the border in Chikwekwete, Mozambique. For the Duma, see the work of Richard M. G. Mtetwa, "The 'Political' and Economic History of the Duma People of South-Eastern Rhodesia from the Early Eighteenth Century to 1945" (PhD diss., University of Rhodesia, 1976); On the Hlengwe, see James H. Bannerman, "Hlengweni: The History of the Hlengwe of the Lower Save and Lundi Rivers from the Late Eighteenth Century to the Mid-Twentieth Century," *Zimbabwean History* 12 (1981): 1–45.

69. Mucherechete Dhlakama, Zamchiya, Zimbabwe, 13 July 1999.

70. Desmond Dale, *Duramazwi: A Shona-English Dictionary* (Gweru, Zimbabwe: Mambo Press, 1981), 1.

71. M. Hannan, *Standard Shona Dictionary*, rev. ed. with addendum (Harare: College Press in conjunction with the Literature Bureau, 1984), xviii–xix.

72. Junod, "Contribution," 17.

73. John L. Comaroff, "Ethnicity, Nationalism, and the Politics of Difference in an Age of Revolution," in *The Politics of Difference: Ethnic Premises in a World of Power*, ed. Edwin N. Wilmsen and Patrick McAllister (Chicago: University of Chicago Press, 1996), 162–83.

74. John Wright, "Notes on the Politics of Being 'Zulu,' 1820–1920" (paper presented at the Conference on Ethnicity, Society, and Conflict in Natal, University of Natal, Pietermaritzburg, South Africa, 14–16 September 1992); Vail, *Creation of Tribalism.*

75. Colleen Kriger demonstrates how evidence of material culture can be used to examine changes in social, political, economic, and cultural relations over a wide region suffering from a paucity of other forms of historical evidence in *Pride of Men: Ironworking in 19th-Century West Central Africa* (Portsmouth, NH: Heinemann, 1999).

76. Riyarwi Mushoma, Chinaa, Chikore, Zimbabwe, 1 July 1999.

77. Alessandro Portelli, *The Death of Luigi Trastulli, and Other Stories: Form and Meaning in Oral History* (Albany: State University of New York Press, 1991), 2.

78. The Save River continues to serve as the western border of the Ndau-speaking region as it curves northward (from the mouth) in present-day Zimbabwe. Ndau speakers do not reside in the upper Pungwe area; they tend to live south of the Beira Corridor, a road that connects the port city of Beira with the city of Mutare in eastern Zimbabwe.

79. Although my knowledge of Ndau allowed me to communicate with people, some of the elders I encountered during fieldwork reacted as if I spoke strangely. To my relief, this was not due only to my American accent but was also a result of the Shona that I mixed in with Ndau—a product of language training with Zimbabweans in standard Shona. Elders would often exclaim, "Oh, she is speaking *Shona!*" when they realized that I was not using a "foreign" language such as Portuguese (in Mozambique) or English (in Zimbabwe). This distinction in language highlighted the perceived gap between Ndau and Shona among elders.

80. Elias Nyamunda also graciously assisted during several interviews in Vhimba, Zimbabwe. Transcripts of taped interviews from Zimbabwe are in English, while my Mozambican assistants transcribed interviews recorded in Mozambique into Portuguese.

81. I always sought permission to conduct and record each interview. After elders granted consent verbally, I would turn on the cassette recorder to begin taping. I received approval from the Research Council of Zimbabwe to conduct fieldwork and archival research in Zimbabwe as a research associate with the University of Zimbabwe, and a *Credencial* from the History Department at the Universidade Eduardo Mondlane facilitated fieldwork in central Mozambique.

82. Ian Hodder, "The Interpretation of Documents and Material Culture," in Norman K. Denzin and Yvonna S. Lincoln, eds., *Handbook of Qualitative Research* (London: Sage Publications, 1994); Ian Hodder, *Reading the Past* (Cambridge: Cambridge University Press, 1991); Ian Hodder, ed., *Symbolic and Structural Archaeology*

(Cambridge: Cambridge University Press, 1982). For an excellent example from southern Mozambique, see Heidi Gengenbach, "Where Women Make History: Pots, Stories, Tattoos, and Other Gendered Accounts of Community and Change in Magude District, Mozambique, c. 1800 to the Present" (PhD diss., University of Minnesota, 1999); and *Binding Memories: Women as Makers and Tellers of History in Magude, Mozambique* (New York: Columbia University Press, 2005), http://www.gutenberg-e.org.

83. As a sign of my appreciation for the time and generous sharing of knowledge from informants, elders who were interviewed received photographs of themselves. I usually presented them with an instant Polaroid photograph, and I also took a picture with my camera. A copy of this second picture was distributed to each person later. In addition to these photos, I offered each elder a small gift to thank them for the interview and express my gratitude. These tokens ranged from packets of seeds and bars of soap to razor blades and matches. At times I also reluctantly distributed cigarettes, particularly to chiefs, when other gifts seemed inappropriate or unavailable. My travels on foot precluded the transport of large or heavy gifts.

84. See Stephen Devereux and John Hoddinott, eds., *Fieldwork in Developing Countries* (Boulder: Lynne Rienner, 1993).

85. Jona Mwaoneni Makuyana, Zamchiya, Zimbabwe, 14 July 1999; field notes, Zamchiya, Zimbabwe, July 1999.

86. David McDermott Hughes, "Frontier Dynamics: Struggles for Land and Clients on the Zimbabwe-Mozambique Border" (PhD diss., University of California, Berkeley, 1999), 123.

87. One scene I witnessed in 1998 involved a group of young Zimbabweans having difficulty locating the right bus in Chimoio, Mozambique (the capital of Manica Province). The Mozambicans they encountered at the market were using the local language of Teve, spoken around Chimoio, rather than the Shona of these Zimbabweans. My assistant, Farai Raposa, who grew up in Chimoio and speaks Teve, helped these young men find their bus by bridging the gap between Teve and Shona. Implicit in this dilemma was the distinction that Mozambicans made between "Shona" (i.e., the language of "Zimbabwe") and Teve (the language of Chimoio), and Raposa was happy to offer this incident as an example of the language differences between Chimoio and the closest Zimbabwean city of Mutare near the border.

88. Hughes describes how people cross the border, "but emigration strips at least some people of rights and securities they regularly enjoy at home." "Frontier Dynamics," 119.

89. Jona Mwaoneni Makuyana, Zamchiya, Zimbabwe, 14 July 1999.

90. Ibid.

91. Idah Manyuni, Chikore, Zimbabwe, 28 June 1999.

92. This use has continued over time. See, for example, AHM, "Informações sobre Alguns Usos e Costumes Indigenas das Circumscripções: Manica," in "Relatorios e Informações," Annexo ao *Boletim Official* (1910), 107–8.

Chapter 2

Epigraph. Mordikai A. Hamutyinei and Albert B. Plangger, *Tsumo-Shumo: Shona Proverbial Lore and Wisdom* (Gweru, Zimbabwe: Mambo Press, 1987), 291.

1. Crawford Young, "Nationalism, Ethnicity, and Class in Africa: A Retrospective," *Cahiers d'Études Africaines* 103 (1986): 442. Young contrasts ethnicity as a focus for inquiry with nationalism, "a progressive and worthy topic."

2. Edwin Wilmsen and Patrick McAllister note that in South Africa before 1990, "[t]o discuss ethnicity was felt to legitimate its existence as a divisive force and thus to sanction the apartheid state." Edwin N. Wilmsen and Patrick McAllister, eds., *The Politics of Difference: Ethnic Premises in a World of Power* (Chicago: University of Chicago Press, 1996), vii.

3. Wilmsen and McAllister, *Politics of Difference*, vii–viii.

4. Kwame Anthony Appiah, *In My Father's House: Africa in the Philosophy of Culture* (Oxford: Oxford University Press, 1992), 175.

5. Wilmsen and McAllister, *Politics of Difference*, ix.

6. Comaroff and Comaroff, *Ethnography and the Historical Imagination*, 60. See also John Comaroff, "Ethnicity, Nationalism, and the Politics of Difference," 166.

7. Comaroff, "Ethnicity, Nationalism, and the Politics of Difference," 164. See also Young, "Nationalism, Ethnicity, and Class," 450.

8. Wilmsen and McAllister, *Politics of Difference*, viii.

9. Fredrik Barth, ed., *Ethnic Groups and Boundaries* (Boston: Little, Brown, 1969).

10. Thomas Spear and Richard Waller, eds., *Being Maasai: Ethnicity and Identity in East Africa* (Athens: Ohio University Press, 1993).

11. Ibid., 302.

12. Comaroff and Comaroff, *Ethnography and the Historical Imagination*, 54.

13. Vail, *Creation of Tribalism*.

14. The large number of mutually intelligible languages in southern Africa complicates the mix, for Africans developed communication networks through trade and faced few definable boundaries in terms of language. For a discussion of a sense of African unity in South Africa before officials worked to erect barriers around African identities, see the work of Brett Cohen, "'Something like a Blowing Wind': African Conspiracy and Coordination of Resistance to Colonial Rule in South Africa, 1876–1882" (PhD diss., Michigan State University, 2000).

15. J. Wright, "Politics of Being 'Zulu.'"

16. Fernand Braudel, *On History* (Chicago: University of Chicago Press, 1980), 4. Reprinted from the preface of Braudel, *The Mediterranean and the Mediterranean World in the Age of Philip II* (New York: Harper & Row, 1972); see also Braudel, *A History of Civilizations* (New York: A. Lane, 1994).

17. Two inspiring works from the region are Edward Alpers, *Ivory and Slaves in East Central Africa* (London: Heinemann, 1975); and Beach, *Shona and Their Neighbours*.

18. Ronald Atkinson, *The Roots of Ethnicity: The Origins of the Acholi of Uganda before 1800* (Philadelphia: University of Pennsylvania Press, 1994); and "The Evolution of Ethnicity among the Acholi of Uganda: The Precolonial Phase," *Ethnohistory* 36, no. 1 (1989): 19–43.

19. David Newbury, *Kings and Clans: Ijwi Island and the Lake Kivu Rift, 1780–1840* (Madison: University of Wisconsin Press, 1991).

20. Jan Vansina, *Paths in the Rainforests: Toward a Political Tradition in Equatorial Africa* (Madison: University of Wisconsin Press, 1990).

21. Ibid., 258.

22. Allen Isaacman and Barbara Isaacman, *Slavery and Beyond: The Making of Men and Chikunda Ethnic Identities in the Unstable World of South-Central Africa, 1750–1920* (Portsmouth, NH: Heinemann, 2004).

23. Elizabeth Eldredge, *A South African Kingdom: The Pursuit of Security in Nineteenth-Century Lesotho* (Cambridge: Cambridge University Press, 1993).

24. Ibid., 127.

25. Sandra Greene, *Gender, Ethnicity, and Social Change on the Upper Slave Coast: A History of the Anlo-Ewe* (Portsmouth, NH: Heinemann, 1996).

26. Greene is quoting Vail. Greene, *Gender, Ethnicity, and Social Change*, 14; and Vail, *Creation of Tribalism*, 15.

27. Ranger, *Invention of Tribalism*; and "Missionaries, Migrants, and the Manyika," 118–50.

28. See Masipula Sithole's critique, "Ethnicity and Democratization in Zimbabwe: From Confrontation to Accommodation," in *Ethnic Conflict and Democratization in Africa*, ed. Harvey Glickman (Atlanta: African Studies Association Press, 1995), 121–60. Greene also finds faults with this earlier approach by Ranger in *Gender, Ethnicity, and Social Change*.

29. Work remains to be done for the situation in neighboring central Mozambique. Herbert Chimhundu, "Early Missionaries and the Ethnolinguistic Factor during the 'Invention of Tribalism' in Zimbabwe," *Journal of African History* 33 (1992): 87.

30. John Keith Rennie, "Christianity, Colonialism, and the Origins of Nationalism among the Ndau of Southern Rhodesia, 1890–1935" (PhD diss., Northwestern University, 1973).

31. Rennie's short study on ideology and state formation in the Ndau region is an informative initial examination of the shaping of political and communal ideologies over several centuries. Rennie, "Ideology and State Formation."

32. "Letter from Diogo Alcáçova to the King" (1506), in *Documentos Sobre os Portugueses em Moçambique e na África Central, 1497–1840* (Lisbon: National Archives of Rhodesia, Centro de Estudos Históricos Ultramarinos, 1962–72; hereafter cited as *DPMAC*), 1:397; Elkiss, *Quest for an African Eldorado*, 16.

33. In the monsoon wind system, the prevailing direction of the wind reverses itself from season to season. In the Indian Ocean, travel from Mozambique to India was possible during the seasonal monsoon between April and September. Ships would reverse their course and sail to Mozambique from India in the months between November and February.

34. Sousa, *Asia Portuguesa*, in *RSEA*, 1:16.

35. Newitt, *History of Mozambique*, 4.

36. Ibid., 10–11.

37. Ibid., 10.

38. Fr. António da Conceição, "Tratado dos Rios de Cuama" (1696), in *O Chronista de Tissuary* 2, nos. 14–17 (1867): 15:63. Erosion has changed the shoreline of Sofala and destroyed the remains of the Portuguese fortress. The modern port is twenty miles to the north at Beira. Liesegang, "Archaeological Sites," 147–59; Elkiss, *Quest for an African Eldorado*, 72.

39. A mid-sixteenth-century Portuguese chronicler, Góis (Goes), wrote that four hundred households were at Sofala. Liesegang, "Archaeological Sites," 149.

40. Newitt, *History of Mozambique*, 79–80.

41. Sousa, *Asia Portuguesa*, in *RSEA*, 1:21.

42. Francisco Monclaro, "Account of the Journey Made by Fathers of the Company of Jesus with Francisco Barreto in the Conquest of Monomotapa in the Year 1569," in *RSEA*, 3:202–53.

43. Ibid., 3:226; João dos Santos, *Etiópia Oriental e Vária História de Cousas Notáveis do Oriente* (1609) (Lisbon: Comissão Nacional para as Comemorações dos Descobrimentos Portugueses, 1999).

44. Monclaro, "Journey by the Company of Jesus," in *RSEA*, 3:227.

45. Viewing the Mutapa state as an obstacle to their economic endeavors, the Portuguese drew up plans to conquer it in 1569 after the murder of the missionary Dom Gonçalo da Silveira at the Mutapa's court provided an excuse to invade. Francisco Barreto led the expedition up the Zambezi in 1571 to demand that the Mutapa accept Christian missionaries, eject the Moors, and promote friendly commerce. But the expedition was a tragic failure for the Portuguese and a sign that they would not completely dominate regional politics. "Determinação dos Letrados: Com q. Condiçoens se Podia Fazer Guerra aos Reys da Conquista de Portugal, Fala em Especial do Monomotapa" (1569), in *RSEA*, 3:150–56.

46. Scholars such as Erik Gilbert, Jonathan Reynolds, and David Northrup have argued that Europeans and Africans saw each other as equals during initial encounters on the continent. Gilbert and Reynolds point to the relatively peaceful contacts between Portuguese sailors and local populations in western and west-central Africa in the fifteenth century. Although these first impressions led to civil interactions, for the most part, the Portuguese takeover of Sofala was accompanied by an ongoing threat of violence to the local population living in southeast Africa. To the north, Portuguese control of Ilha de Moçambique and the use of force against several Swahili city-states came to define early interactions in the Indian Ocean. Swahili traders throughout the region would have informed locals of this violent behavior by the Portuguese. Northrup cites a quick Portuguese shift "from displays of power to acts of conquest" along the Swahili coast and contrasts this with encounters around Sofala that "moved at a slower and less violent pace." Nevertheless, a reputation of aggression (or the possibility of it) and firepower must have followed the Portuguese along the coast of Sofala and into the interior. Erik Gilbert and Jonathan T. Reynolds, *Africa in World History: From Prehistory to the Present* (Upper Saddle River, NJ: Pearson Educational, 2004), 156–57 and 201–6; David Northrup, *Africa's Discovery of Europe, 1450–1850* (New York: Oxford University Press, 2002), 39–41.

47. Dos Santos lived in Sofala from 1586 to 1590 and again from April 1594 to April 1595. In 1591 he left Sofala for Tete, where he stayed for eight months. He spent time in Sena and on Ilha de Moçambique, and from 1592 to 1594 he lived on the Quirimbas Islands. He returned to Portugal in 1600 and completed *Etiópia Oriental* in 1607. It was published in Évora, his birthplace, in 1609. Dos Santos later returned to Mozambique and lived in Sena. Manuel Lobato, Introduction to dos Santos, *Etiópia Oriental*, 7–9.

48. For dos Santos, "*Ethiopia Oriental*," or "Eastern Ethiopia," was the eastern coast of Africa from the southern tip to the Red Sea. Dos Santos, *Etiópia Oriental*, 73; and Lobato, Introduction to *Etiópia Oriental*, 24.

49. Lobato, Introduction to *Etiópia Oriental*, 21–22.

50. Dos Santos, *Etiópia Oriental*, 100.

51. Manuel Barreto, "Informação do Estado e Conquista dos Rios de Cuama" (1667), in *RSEA*, 3:436–508.

52. Ibid., 3:493. No currency is given for the revenue. The original Portuguese provided by Theal is "*sinco a dez mil de renda.*"

53. Ibid.

54. Ibid., 487.

55. See, for example, the lists of documents in Beach and de Noronha, "Shona and the Portuguese." David Beach graciously provided me with a copy of this unpublished collection, and I rely on it heavily here. See also Ana Cristina Ribeiro Marques Roque, "A Costa Oriental da Africa na Primeira Metade do Seculo XVI Segundo as Fontes Portuguesas da Epoca" (Tese de Mestrado, Universidade Nova de Lisboa, 1994); D. N. Beach, "Documents and African Society on the Zimbabwe Plateau before 1890," *Paideuma* 33 (1987): 129–45; and D. N. Beach, "Chronological list of documents from the beginning of Portuguese contact to the separation of Moçambique from Goa" (provisional copy provided by David Beach, February 1998).

56. For more on this decline in written evidence, see Beach, "African Society on the Zimbabwe Plateau," 129. There were also fewer Portuguese sources from other parts of Africa as Portuguese influence on the continent waned.

57. The collected, published documents hold much valuable information for the region and this study. Alongside these sources a handful of other narratives provide information about the Ndau region. They are found in less accessible nineteenth-century journals and several archives and libraries. I have consulted both the original Portuguese accounts and translated English versions of the documents, when available.

58. José Fialho Feliciano and Victor Hugo Nicolau, Introduction to *Memórias de Sofala* (1844), by João Julião da Silva, Zacarias Herculano da Silva, and Guilherme Ezequiel da Silva (Lisbon: Comissão Nacional para as Comemorações dos Descobrimentos Portugueses, 1998), 10; Newitt, *History of Mozambique*, 201.

59. These include studies such as Joaquim d'Almeida da Cunha, *Estudo acerca dos Usos e Costumes dos Banianes, Bathiás, Parses, Mouros, Gentios, e Indígenas* (Lourenço Marques, Mozambique: Imprensa Nacional, 1885).

60. Feliciano and Nicolau, "Introduction" to *Memórias de Sofala*, 16.

61. Ignácio Caetano Xavier, "Notícias dos Domínios Portuguezes na Costa de África Oriental" (1758), in António Alberto de Andrade, ed., *Relações de Moçambique Setecentista* (Lisbon: Agência Geral do Ultramar, 1955; hereafter cited as *RMS*), 143.

62. Ibid., 143–44.

63. António Alberto de Andrade, "Introdução aos Textos," in *RMS*, 22–23.

64. Xavier, "Notícias dos Domínios Portuguezes," in *RMS*, 186.

65. An alternate spelling of *reposta* is *resposta*. Both mean answer or reply. "Cafre," a Portuguese term that referred to Africans in general, meant infidel or unbeliever in its Arabic origins. Muslim traders first used "kaffir" in southeast Africa to refer to Africans who were not Muslim (i.e., not Swahili). The term remains in use today (particularly in some South African circles) as the derogatory "kaffir." One sixteenth-century published reference is in Goes (Góis), "Chronicle of King Dom Emanuel," in *RSEA*, 3:129. "The inhabitants of the country [the Mutapa kingdom] are black with woolly hair, and are commonly called Kaffirs by the settlers." S. I. G. Mudenge discusses the derivation of the term in *Political History of Munhumutapa*, xiv.

66. The historian Gerhard Liesegang, who saw the value of this report in the 1960s, wrote the introduction and notes to a published version in 1966. Carlos José dos Reis e Gama, *Reposta das Questoens sobre os Cafres*, introduction and notes by Gerhard Liesegang (Lisbon: Junta de Investigações do Ultramar, 1966).

67. One notable exception is the thorough *Etiópia Oriental* from the early seventeenth century by Fr. João dos Santos.

68. Liesegang, Introduction to Gama, *Reposta*, 7.

69. Ibid. According to Liesegang, Gama apparently produced a report in 1781 on the natural history of the region.

70. Ibid., 20. I refer to Gama as the author here until this case of alleged plagiarism is solved.

71. Ibid.

72. Ibid.

73. At AHM see, for example, J. F. Pereira Lisboa, "Questionario Acerca dos Indigenas do territorio de Manica e Sofala" (1906), and "Alguns Usos e Costumes Indígenas de Circumscripção de Sofala" (1907), both reports in Companhia de Moçambique, Secretaria Geral, Processos, Caixa 445; Luciano Lanne, "Notas Sobre Alguna Usos e Costumes Indígenas da Circumscripção de Mossurize" (1906), Companhia de Moçambique, Secretaria Geral, Processos, Caixa 445; "Respostas o Casamento" (1925), Companhia de Moçambique, Secretaria Geral, Processos, Caixa 445; "Relatorios e Informações," in Anexo ao *Boletim Official* (1910); Direccão dos Serviços dos Negócios Indígenas, "Monografia de Mossurize: Missão Etognóstica da Colónia de Moçambique" (n.d.); Direccão dos Serviços dos Negócios Indígenas, Tribunal Indígenas, "Condição de Usos e Costumes Gentilicos, Usos e Costumes Indígenas" (1909); Inspecção dos Serviços Administrativos e dos Negócios Indígenas (ISANI), "Inspecção as Circunscrições de Mossurize, Manica, Gorongoza e Chimoio" (1955). Later published works by António Rita-Ferreira followed in this vein and examined ethno-history and ethnic groupings in Mozambique.

74. Travel literature did not appear until the second half of the nineteenth century when Europeans, including several big-game hunters, wrote accounts of their "adventures" south of the Zambezi River.

75. George McCall Theal, "Abstract of Ethnographic Information Contained in Portuguese Records and Early Histories, Added to Papers on the Same Subject Published Some Years Ago by the Compiler of these Volumes," in *RSEA*, 7:392; Lobato, Introduction to *Etiópia Oriental*, 22.

76. Lobato, Introduction to *Etiópia Oriental*, 37; and dos Santos, *Etiópia Oriental*, 112.

77. Lobato, Introduction to *Etiópia Oriental*, 37.

78. Gama, *Reposta*, 20.

79. In the eighteenth century, for instance, there were *prazos* at Chiloane, Mambone, Chuparo, Ampara, Chironde, and Cheringoma, according to Malyn Newitt, *Portuguese Settlement on the Zambezi: Exploration, Land Tenure, and Colonial Rule in East Africa* (New York: Africana Publishing Company, 1973). See his map on p. 219.

80. Newitt, *History of Mozambique*, 30, 100.

81. Garlake, "Investigation of Manekweni, Mozambique," 25–47; and "Excavation of a *Zimbabwe*," 146–48; Barker, "Economic Models," 71–100.

82. Manyikweni was occupied up to the seventeenth century. Garlake, "Excavation of a *Zimbabwe*," 146.

83. Although apparently not yet building in stone, from at least the tenth century the Shona were "the most numerous and important people in the vast region of southeastern Africa between the Zambezi and Limpopo Rivers," according to Beach, *Shona and Their Neighbours*, 1, 99.

84. Barker, "Economic Models," 96; Sinclair, *Space, Time, and Social Formation*, 99.

85. At Manyikweni, for instance, analyses of faunal samples reveal that the community near the stone enclosure had a more lavish diet than the ordinary people farther away from the enclosure. Young cattle were slaughtered for an elite around the enclosure,

and other game were also eaten there. Of the bones recovered, antelope bones exceeded those of domestic livestock both within the enclosure and outside the stone walls. An intermediate level of society that ate sheep, goats, or game rather than cattle may have existed also. Others on the periphery ate mostly grain, wild foods, and meat acquired from hunting rather than consuming cattle, sheep, or goats. These ordinary subjects appear to have relied on agricultural products such as millet and sorghum for their subsistence while occasionally eating meat as a supplement. Garlake, "Excavation of a *Zimbabwe*," and "Investigation of Manekweni, Mozambique"; Barker, "Economic Models"; Sigvallius, "Faunal Remains from Manyikeni," in Sinclair, *Analyses from Excavations in Mozambique*, 27; Sinclair, *Space, Time, and Social Formation*, 96.

86. Connah, *African Civilizations*, 195.

87. Some initial work on examining these connections was carried out by Edward M. Andrews in 1905. AHM, Companhia de Moçambique, Secretaria Geral, Processos, "Pesquisas ao Norte de Madanda" (Beira, 10 de Julho de 1905), Caixa 198.

88. Wieschoff, *Zimbabwe-Monomotapa Culture;* Octávio Roza de Oliveira, *Amuralhados da Cultura Zimbáuè-Monomotapa de Manica e Sofala* (Lourenço Marques, Mozambique: Artes Gráficas, 1963); Octávio Roza de Oliveira, "Zimbáuès de Moçambique: Proto-História Africana," *Monumenta: Boletim da Commissão dos Monumentos Nacionais de Moçambique* 9 (1973): 31–64; and Bannerman, "Notes and Questions," 1, appendix 1.

89. Jan Vansina, "Historians, Are Archaeologists Your Siblings?" *History in Africa* 22 (1995): 370.

90. Ibid. See also Christopher R. DeCorse and Gerard L. Chouin, "Trouble with Siblings: Archaeological and Historical Interpretation of the West African Past," in *Sources and Methods in African History: Spoken, Written, Unearthed*, ed. Toyin Falola and Christian Jennings (Rochester, NY: University of Rochester Press, 2003), 7–15.

91. Vansina, "Historians, Are Archaeologists Your Siblings?" 398.

92. For details of various sites, see Wieschoff, *Zimbabwe-Monomotapa Culture;* Bannerman, "Notes and Questions"; and Oliveira, "Zimbáuès de Moçambique."

Chapter 3

Epigraph One. Fr. Felippe da Assumpção, "Brief Account of the Rivers of Cuama" (ca. 1698), in Beach and de Noronha, "Shona and the Portuguese," 1:270. (Quiteve is Teve.)
Epigraph Two. Dos Santos, *Ethiopia Oriental,* in *RSEA,* 7:208.

1. John Keith Rennie discusses this point in "Ideology and State Formation," 174.

2. Sofala, or *Bilad as-Sufala,* was viewed by Muslim merchants from the Arabian Peninsula as a region along the coast rather than one specific port. Elkiss, *Quest for an African Eldorado,* 3, 8.

3. The Ndau and their Shona-speaking neighbors probably exchanged goods with the Swahili first at Sofala and later along the Zambezi River to the north at the towns of Sena and Tete. Trading centers along rivers and on the plateau existed prior to any Portuguese presence in the area, but the Portuguese wanted to control the trading fairs with a *capitão mor* (administrative authority) and soldiers at each fair to increase their profits from the gold trade. The Portuguese attempted to conquer the Mutapa

state and take control of the inland goldfields, while the Swahili were relatively content to remain as middlemen.

4. See David Chanaiwa, "Politics and Long-Distance Trade in the Mwene Mutapa Empire during the Sixteenth Century," *International Journal of African Historical Studies* 5, no. 3 (1972): 424–35.

5. "Relação (Cópia) Feita pelo Padre Francisco de Monclaro, da Companhia de Jesus, da Expedição ao Monomotapa, Comandada por Francisco Barreto" (post-1573), in *DPMAC*, 8:390. See also "Memorias da Costa de Africa Oriental, e Algumas Reflexes Uteis para Estabelecer Melhor, e Fazer Mais Florente o Seu Commercio" (1762), in Luiz Fernando de Carvalho Dias, ed., *Fontes para História, Geografia, e Comércio de Moçambique, Séc. XVIII* (Lisbon: Junta das Missões Geográficas e de Investigações do Ultramar, 1954), 234 (also published in Andrade, *RMS*). Pedro Machado argues that Africans drove the trade in cloth in his study of Gujarati Vaniya merchants from South Asia. See Pedro Alberto da Silva Rupino Machado, "Gujarati Indian Merchant Networks in Mozambique, 1777–c. 1830" (PhD diss., School of Oriental and African Studies, University of London, 2005).

6. João de Barros, "Da Asia" (1522–1613), in *RSEA*, 6:266; Mudenge, *Political History of Munhumutapa*, 176–78; Mtetwa, " 'Political' and Economic History of the Duma," 272; and Beach, *Shona and Their Neighbours*, 73.

7. Beach, *Shona and Their Neighbours*, 73.

8. Ibid. Beach cites the one in five statistic for inhabitants who "lived within a reasonable distance" of gold sources.

9. Ibid.; Rennie, "Christianity, Colonialism, and Nationalism," 52; António Augusto Pereira Cabral, *Racas, Usos, e Costumes dos Indígenas de Província de Moçambique* (Lourenço Marques: Imprensa Nacional, 1925), 12. Cabral was Secretário dos Negócios Indígenas.

10. "Apontamentos de Gaspar Veloso" (1512), in *DPMAC*, 3:185, 187.

11. Machado, "Gujarati Indian Merchant Networks," 93.

12. NAZ, "Interview with Kapiro Chisvo" (born ca. 1868–78, interviewed by Dawson Munjeri, 15 December 1977), Oral History Interviews, AOH/31; Mtetwa, " 'Political' and Economic History of the Duma," 273.

13. "Papers Concerning Sofala and Mozambique" (ca. 1580–84?), in *RSEA*, 4:1–2.

14. Rennie, "Christianity, Colonialism, and Nationalism," 52.

15. The Buzi River was navigable for about the first one hundred miles, the Pungwe River for fifty to one hundred miles, and the Save River was passable to the present-day border with Zimbabwe, according to Rennie, "Christianity, Colonialism, and Nationalism," 52. Gerhard Liesegang notes that João Julião da Silva wrote in 1846 that boats could go up the first 150 km of the Save River to Maringa, and after that bark canoes were used. Liesegang, "Archaeological Sites on the Bay of Sofala," 152. In recent years the Save River has dried up in places, and this may have occurred in the past as well.

16. Rennie, "Christianity, Colonialism, and Nationalism," 37. For the history of Great Zimbabwe and Mutapa, see David Beach's comprehensive work on the Shona, including *Shona and Their Neighbours* and *Shona and Zimbabwe;* Mudenge, *Political History of Munhumutapa*; and Innocent Pikirayi, *The Archaeological Identity of the Mutapa State: Towards an Historical Archaeology of Northern Zimbabwe* (Uppsala, Sweden: Studies in African Archaeology 6, Department of Archaeology, Uppsala University, 1993).

17. Barreto, "Informação do Estado e Conquista dos Rios de Cuama" (1667), in *RSEA*, 3:479. A pasta was a measure of gold that weighed about 100 *meticals* (*meticais*), according to Mudenge, *Political History of Munhumutapa*, xviii.

18. Rennie, "Christianity, Colonialism, and Nationalism," 40–41, 52.

19. Ibid., 51.

20. This route was closer to many *prazos*. Pikirayi, *Archaeological Identity of Mutapa*, 109.

21. Barreto, "Informação do Estado e Conquista dos Rios de Cuama," in *RSEA*, 3:479.

22. Fr. Felippe da Assumpção, "Brief Account of the Rivers of Cuama" (ca. 1698), in "Shona and the Portuguese," 1:270. See also Barreto, "Informação do Estado e Conquista dos Rios de Cuama," in *RSEA*, 3:487, 489; and Luís António de Figueiredo, "Notícia do Continente de Moçambique e Abreviada Relação do seu Comércio" (1773), in Dias, *História, Geografia, e Comércio*, 262.

23. Conceição, "Tratado dos Rios de Cuama," 14:45.

24. Barreto, "Informação do Estado e Conquista dos Rios de Cuama," in *RSEA*, 3:487. Ambergris, a grayish, waxy substance from the intestines of sperm whales, was often found floating in tropical seas. It was used in some perfumes.

25. Ibid., 489; Bannerman notes that part of Teve near the serra Xiluva was a gold-bearing region with evidence of gold mining and washing in the eighteenth and nineteenth centuries. Bannerman, "Notes and Questions," 13. See also Ferão, "Account of the Portuguese Possessions within the Captaincy of Rios de Sena" (1810?), in *RSEA*, 7:378–79; Beach, *Shona and Zimbabwe*, 169.

26. João dos Santos noted the importance of cattle over gold for the people of Abutua, located in the interior on the southern part of the Zimbabwe Plateau. Dos Santos, *Etiópia Oriental*, 205.

27. Conceição, "Tratado dos Rios de Cuama," 15:63; Sousa, *Asia Portuguesa*, in *RSEA*, 1:15.

28. Beach, *Shona and Their Neighbours*, 111–12.

29. Ibid., 103.

30. Ibid., 114.

31. Ibid., chap. 4.

32. Alternate spellings include Teve (Quiteve, Uteve), Manica (Manyika), Barwe (Barue), and Danda (Madanda); and for smaller territories: Sanga (QuiSanga, Kisanga, Chisanga) and Machanga (Mashanga, Shanga).

33. Beach, *Shona and Zimbabwe*, 172.

34. Dos Santos, *Ethiopia Oriental*, in *RSEA*, 7:217; "Carta (Cópia) de Vasco Fernandes Homem para Luís da Silva" (1576), in *DPMAC*, 8:457–58.

35. Dos Santos, *Ethiopia Oriental*, in *RSEA*, 7:219–22; "Carta (Cópia) de Vasco Fernandes Homem para Luís da Silva," in *DPMAC*, 8:457–58.

36. Beach, *Shona and Zimbabwe*, 172–74.

37. Ibid., 174.

38. Conceição, "Tratado dos Rios de Cuama"; English translation from Beach and de Noronha, "Shona and the Portuguese," 1:200.

39. Ibid.

40. Rennie, "Ideology and State Formation," 164.

41. Ibid., 170.

42. Dos Santos, *Ethiopia Oriental*, in *RSEA*, 7:199; See also Rennie, "Ideology and State Formation," 167.

43. Dos Santos, *Ethiopia Oriental*, in *RSEA*, 7:272.

44. Ibid. *Empata* comes from the Shona verb *kubata*—to seize. Rennie, "Ideology and State Formation," 170.

45. Rennie, "Ideology and State Formation," 169–70.

46. Ibid., 169. For contrasting attitudes toward immigrants in recent times, see Hughes, "Frontier Dynamics."

47. Rennie, "Ideology and State Formation," 170.

48. Ibid., 170–71.

49. Ibid., 170.

50. Ibid., 171. In *Political History of Munhumutapa*, Mudenge discusses the Mutapa's insistence that all crawl as they approach the leader.

51. Rennie, "Ideology and State Formation," 171–72; dos Santos, *Ethiopia Oriental*, in *RSEA*, 7:199–200. Rainmaking is discussed further in chap. 6.

52. Rennie, "Ideology and State Formation," 172. See also Allen Isaacman, "Madzi-Manga, Mhondoro, and the Use of Oral Traditions: A Chapter in Barue Religious and Political History," *Journal of African History* 14, no. 3 (1973): 395–409.

53. Ibid., 171–73.

54. David Beach develops this paradigm convincingly in his extensive work on the Shona in Zimbabwe.

55. Beach, *Shona and Their Neighbours*, 110–12. The Shona worked out the upper gold reefs in the north and exhausted the southwestern goldfields.

56. The Duma subsequently established a confederacy to the west of the Save River. See Mtetwa, " 'Political' and Economic History of the Duma."

57. Manoel Rebello, "Proposal Submitted by the Residents of the Rios de Cuama to the Viceroy" (1698), in "Shona and the Portuguese," vol. 1.

58. Newitt, *History of Mozambique*, 201.

59. António Rita-Ferreira, *Povos de Moçambique: História e Cultura* (Porto: Afrontamento, 1975), 120–26.

60. Xavier, "Notícias dos Domínios Portuguezes," in *RMS*, 185; English translation from Beach and de Noronha, "Shona and the Portuguese," 2:58.

61. Xavier, "Notícias dos Domínios Portuguezes," in *RMS*, 186.

62. Mtetwa, " 'Political' and Economic History of the Duma," 271.

63. Ibid., 271–72.

64. Ibid., 271; "Relação (Cópia) Feito Pelo Padre Francisco de Monclaro da Companhia de Jesus, da Expedição ao Monomotapa, Comandada por Francisco Barreto," in *DPMAC*, 8:390.

65. The account appears often in the literature; see, for instance, the eighteenth-century report of Carlos José dos Reis e Gama, *Reposta*.

66. Ibid., 20.

67. Ibid. The invasion of the Gaza Nguni in the early nineteenth century changed these political realities for many of the Ndau, as they faced varying degrees of overrule by the Gaza Nguni (as discussed in chap. 7).

68. Rennie, "Ideology and State Formation," 169–70.

69. Ibid., 168. Chiluane was an important trading center for the Portuguese.

70. Beach, *Shona and Their Neighbours*, 104.

71. Newitt argues that Portuguese commercial infiltration led to a shift in the region's balance of power as African chiefs became involved in and dependent on commercial activities. *History of Mozambique*, 97.

72. Barreto, "Informação do Estado e Conquista dos Rios de Cuama," in *RSEA*, 3:487. There is also detailed evidence from the Portuguese about Manica.

73. Dos Santos, *Ethiopia Oriental*, in *RSEA*, 7:287.

74. "Apontamentos de Gaspar Veloso," in *DPMAC*, 3:183.

75. Liesegang, "Sofala, Beira e a sua Zona," 24–25; Beach, *Shona and Zimbabwe*, 168. The location of High Teve (*Alto Teve*), a ten-day journey from Sofala, was near the present-day city of Chimoio. Bannerman, "Notes and Questions," 13.

76. Andrew H. Mtetwa, "A History of Uteve under the Mwene Mutapa Rulers, 1480–1834: A Re-evaluation" (PhD diss., Northwestern University, 1984), v.

77. Ibid.

78. "Capitulos XX a XXV da Década IX da Ásia de Diogo do Couto" (post-1573), in *DPMAC*, 8:319; dos Santos, *Ethiopia Oriental*, in *RSEA*, 7:220. For a detailed description of the Portuguese in early Teve, see Mtetwa, "History of Uteve," chap. 4.

79. "Apontamentos de Gaspar Veloso," in *DPMAC*, 3:183.

80. Ferão, "Portuguese Possessions within Rios de Sena," in *RSEA*, 7:378–79; Beach, *Shona and Zimbabwe*, 169.

81. Gama's eighteenth-century report claims that the name of the king of Quiteve is not hereditary. *Reposta*, 20.

82. Dos Santos, *Ethiopia Oriental*, in *RSEA*, 7:201; Bhila, *Trade and Politics*, 75.

83. AHM, Artur José de Andrade Leitão, "Monografia Etnográfica sobre os Mateves" (1960?), Secção Especial, a. V, p. 7, no. 288.

84. Bannerman, "Notes and Questions," 16; dos Santos, *Ethiopia Oriental*, in *RSEA*, vol. 7.

85. "Traslado da Carta de D. António da Silveira para El-Rei" (post-1518), in *DPMAC*, 5:569.

86. Ibid., 567–69; "Carta de João Vaz de Almada, Capitão de Sofala, para El-Rei" (1516), in *DPMAC*, 4:291.

87. "Traslado da Carta de D. António da Silveira para El-Rei," in *DPMAC*, 5:569.

88. Rennie, "Christianity, Colonialism, and Nationalism," 67.

89. Ibid.; "Carta de João Vaz de Almada, Capitão de Sofala, para El-Rei," in *DPMAC*, 4:291.

90. Bhila, *Trade and Politics*, 2.

91. Rennie, "Ideology and State Formation," 168.

92. Rennie, "Christianity, Colonialism, and Nationalism," 66–67; Beach, *Shona and Zimbabwe*, 163, 169.

93. Rennie, "Ideology and State Formation," 168; My field experiences revealed that some locals in the highlands of Zimbabwe refer to *all* Ndau speakers in Mozambique as "Danda." See chap. 8 for further discussion of the blurred boundaries within the world of the Ndau. Freddy Sithole, Chikore, Zimbabwe, 29 June 1999; Allen Mundeta, Chikore, Zimbabwe, 29 June 1999.

94. Beach, *Shona and Zimbabwe*, 161.

95. This document was probably written by João Julião da Silva, according to Gerhard Liesegang. Noted in Rennie, "Christianity, Colonialism, and Nationalism," 116n29; Ferão, "Portuguese Possessions within Rios de Sena," in *RSEA*, 7:371–83; For a mid-twentieth-century description, see AHM, José Fontes Pessoa de Amorim, "Os 'Vatssangas' ou Mundaué" (Beira, 1956), Secção Especial, a. III, p. 6, no. 80.

96. J. K. Rennie, "From Zimbabwe to a Colonial Chieftaincy: Four Transformations of the Musikavanhu Territorial Cult in Rhodesia," in *Guardians of the Land*, ed.

J. M. Schoffeleers (Gweru, Zimbabwe: Mambo Press, 1978). Earlier fieldwork by Rennie in the Zimbabwe highlands and recent research from David McDermott Hughes on both sides of the border (in Vhimba and Gogoi) enhance a comparison of archival evidence and local histories from these Ndau areas.

97. Evidence for Sanga's Mutema dynasty does not go back farther than the late seventeenth century. Rennie, "From Zimbabwe to a Colonial Chieftancy," 258, 264; and "Christianity, Colonialism, and Nationalism"; Ferão, "Portuguese Possessions within Rios de Sena," in *RSEA*, 7:374, 377–78.

98. Rennie, "Ideology and State Formation," 168; Ferão, "Portuguese Possessions within Rios de Sena," in *RSEA*, 7:378.

99. Rennie, "Ideology and State Formation," 169.

100. Rennie, "From Zimbabwe to a Colonial Chieftancy," 266.

101. Ferão, "Portuguese Possessions within Rios de Sena," in *RSEA*, 7:378; Rennie, "Ideology and State Formation," 168.

102. Beach, *Shona and Zimbabwe*, 171.

103. Ibid. Beach speculates about this wealth.

104. Rennie, "Ideology and State Formation," 168–69.

105. Ibid.

106. Ibid.; NAZ, "Chindau-English and English-Chindau Vocabulary" (Rhodesian Branch of American Board Mission in South Africa, Binghamton, NY: 1915) GEN, AME; NAZ, "Brief Notes on the History of the Mission on its 60th Anniversary" (1953?), Historical Manuscripts, United Church Board for World Ministries, UN 3/8/5; NAZ, "Stations: Location and Special Work of Missionaries" (1916?), Historical Manuscripts, United Church Board for World Ministries, UN 3/20/1/11/1; NAZ, "Printing Report" (June 1915–June 1916), Historical Manuscripts, United Church Board for World Ministries, UN 3/20/1/11/8.

107. Also referred to as Shanga or Mashanga. AHM, João Maria da Piedade de Lencastre e Távora, "Os Vanhai (Sofala): Monografia Etnográfica" (1964), Secção Especial (não registrado); Rennie, "Ideology and State Formation," 169.

108. Liesegang in Gama, *Reposta*, 34n43.

109. Beach, *Shona and Their Neighbours*, 111.

110. Rennie, "Ideology and State Formation," 162–63.

111. Ibid., 164. Wilmsen and McAllister, *Politics of Difference*, viii.

112. For more on the *prazo* system, see Allen Isaacman, *Mozambique: The Africanization of a European Institution* (Madison: University of Wisconsin Press, 1972); Newitt, *Portuguese Settlement on the Zambezi*, and *History of Mozambique*, chap. 10. The holder was referred to as a *prazero*. The origins of the *prazos* stem from the sixteenth century.

113. Most married locally, and after the first generation *prazeros* tended to be of mixed descent. *Prazo* rulers relied on an army of slave soldiers known as the *Chikunda* and demanded tribute from local Africans under their control. For a study of these slave armies and their descendants, see Isaacman and Isaacman, *Slavery and Beyond*.

114. Newitt, *History of Mozambique*, 201.

115. Barreto, "Informação do Estado e Conquista dos Rios de Cuama," in *RSEA*, 3:487; Rennie, "Ideology and State Formation," 167. For detailed studies of the relationship between local inhabitants and *prazeros* such as Sisnando Dias Bayão and António Loba da Silva, see Isaacman, *Mozambique*, and Newitt, *Portuguese Settlement on the Zambezi*.

116. Newitt, *History of Mozambique*, 217–18.

117. Ibid.

118. Pikirayi, *Archaeological Identity of Mutapa*, 119.

119. Ibid., 155. See Liesegang, "Archaeological Sites on the Bay of Sofala."

120. Xavier, "Notícias dos Domínios Portuguezes," in *RMS*, 142.

121. Ibid., 72. This evidence is mainly from Portuguese documents.

122. See especially the work of Beach, *Shona and Their Neighbours*, and *Shona and Zimbabwe*; Mudenge, *Political History of Munhumutapa*; and Chanaiwa, "Politics and Long-Distance Trade."

123. Both Beach and Chanaiwa have noted this.

124. The leader of the Maravi people across the Zambezi River in the 1590s is referred to as Chunzo. "Extractos da Decada Composta por António Bocarro" (1569), in *RSEA*, 3:361.

125. "Carta de João Vaz de Almada, Capitão de Sofala, Para El-Rei," in *DPMAC*, 4:291; James H. Bannerman, "The Extent and Independence of the Mutapa, Torwa, Manyika, Barwe, and Teve States" (University of Zimbabwe Seminar Series, 20 July 1981).

Chapter 4

Epigraph One. Mubayi Mhlanga, Zamchiya, Zimbabwe, 13 July 1999.

Epigraph Two. Hamutyinei and Plangger, *Tsumo-Shumo*, 215.

1. This does not mean that women were always "passive actors and victims of patriarchal structures," as Carin Vijfhuizen points out in her study of a contemporary Ndau village in the 1990s, " 'The People You Live With': Gender Identities and Social Practices, Beliefs, and Power in the Livelihoods of Ndau Women and Men in a Village with an Irrigation Scheme in Zimbabwe" (PhD diss., Wageningen Agricultural University, Netherlands, 1998), 1. She discusses how "both women and men shape, change and reproduce rules, beliefs and normative value frames in practice and thereby shape those practices"; she argues that "both women and men, but especially women emerge as important negotiators, arbitrators and mediators in social relations" (14).

2. This assistance was reserved for times of dire need when the granaries of a homestead were empty. A Shona proverb cautions that the chief's place is for spending the day, but not the night. (*Dzimbabwe muswero, harina uraro.*) Hamutyinei and Plangger, *Tsumo-Shumo*, 306–7.

3. Indeed, colonial officials noted certain continuities from the time of dos Santos, although they tended to represent histories in the region as very static. See, for example, AHM, Armando Vaz Pereira Brites, "Monografia Etnográfica sobre a Sub-Raça 'Senas' " (Beira, post-1910?), Secção Especial, a. V, p. 7, no. 274, pp. 45–48.

4. Barth, *Ethnic Groups and Boundaries*.

5. Tonkin, McDonald, and Chapman, *History and Ethnicity*, 16.

6. When I asked for women's surnames during interviews, this created some confusion at times. Many women used the name of their own totem, while some followed Western custom and provided their husband's surname. The Nguni presence in the nineteenth century led to changes such as *moyo* (or *mwoyo*) becoming *nkomo* or *sithole*

and *muyambo* (or *mulambo/mlambo*) replacing *dziva*. Most of the Ndau elders I interviewed have names with Nguni origins.

7. As one informant in 1933 explained to H. P. Junod in "Contribution," 28; AHM, João Maria da Piedade de Lencastre e Távora, "Os Vanhai (Sofala): Monografia Etnográfica" (1964), Secção Especial (não registrado), 26.

8. Jona Mwaoneni Makuyana, Zamchiya, Zimbabwe, 14 July 1999.

9. Vijfhuizen, "People You Live With," 18.

10. Ibid.

11. Ibid.

12. John Kunjenjema, Chikore, Zimbabwe, 30 June 1999.

13. John Woka and Grace Chirawu, Chimanimani, Zimbabwe, 29 July 1999.

14. AHM, Luciano Lanne, "Notas sobre Alguns Usos e Costumes Indigenas da Circumscripção de Mossurize" (1906), Companhia de Moçambique, Secretaria Geral, Processos: Caixa 445, p. 14; John Keith Rennie, "Christianity, Colonialism, and Nationalism," 91.

15. Ibid., 90. Similarly, members of the pool totem must not drink water from certain areas such as the Save River.

16. John Kunjenjema, Chikore, Zimbabwe, 30 June 1999.

17. Phillip Mutigwe, Chikore, Zimbabwe, 29 June 1999.

18. Sarai Nyabanga Sithole, Zamchiya, Zimbabwe, 13 July 1999.

19. Junod, "Contribution," 28.

20. Quoted in Junod, "Contribution," 28.

21. Ibid.

22. Ibid., 29; A dead fetus (past six months in the womb) was to be buried separately from the mother, since the totem was of the father and not the mother. NAZ, "Bantu Domestic Life Part II" (no author—white mission doctor?, n.d.), Historical Manuscripts, United Church Board for World Ministries, UN 3/8/10.

23. Junod, "Contribution," 28.

24. Freddy Sithole, Chikore, Zimbabwe, 29 June 1999.

25. NAZ, "Letter, Erwin H. Richards to Kilbon, Secretary, American Zulu Mission, 24 October 1884, Mongwe, Inhambane," ABC (East Central Africa Mission, 1883–), MISC/AM 1.

26. Junod, "Contribution," 26–27.

27. Ibid., 27.

28. Fieldwork observations, 1998–99; Junod, "Contribution," 18.

29. H. P. Junod, "Notes on the Ethnological Situation in Portuguese East Africa on the South of the Zambezi," *Bantu Studies* 10 (1936): 295–96.

30. Dos Santos, *Ethiopia Oriental*, in *RSEA*, vol. 7.

31. Junod, "Notes on the Ethnological Situation," 295–96.

32. Dos Santos, *Ethiopia Oriental*, in *RSEA*, 7:200; Beach, *Shona and Their Neighbours*, 4, 28.

33. Beach, *Shona and Their Neighbours*, 4.

34. Shiriyedenga was the first Mutema, according to Rennie, "Christianity, Colonialism, and Nationalism," 90–91; Junod, "Contribution," 21–25.

35. Rennie, "Christianity, Colonialism, and Nationalism," 90–91; Junod, "Contribution," 21–25.

36. Junod, "Contribution," 21–25; Rennie, "Christianity, Colonialism, and Nationalism," 90.

37. Rennie, "Christianity, Colonialism, and Nationalism," 91.
38. Ibid.
39. Beach, *Shona and Zimbabwe*, 170–71.
40. Rennie, "Christianity, Colonialism, and Nationalism," 89.
41. Ibid., 66, 89.
42. Ibid., 89.
43. Vijfhuizen, "People You Live With," 18. See also Stephen C. Lubkemann, "Situating Wartime Migration in Central Mozambique: Gendered Social Struggle and the Transnationalization of Polygyny" (PhD diss., Brown University, 2000).
44. Rennie, "Christianity, Colonialism, and Nationalism," 76.
45. Vijfhuizen, "People You Live With," 27–28, 30. She refers to stages of bridewealth that include a first, *mabvunziro*, and second, *pfuma*, payment.
46. Ibid., 28.
47. Ibid., 27–28.
48. Ibid., 28–29. Vijfhuizen cites the general belief among the Ndau of Manesa that "something that is paid a high price for will be better taken care of than something obtained for nothing." However, this was not always the case. See, for example, AHM, "Informações sobre Alguns Usos e Costumes Indigenas das Circumscripções: Manica," in "Relatorios e Informações," Annexo ao *Boletim Official* (1910), 109–10.
49. Allen Mundeta, Chikore, Zimbabwe, 29 June 1999.
50. Field experiences 1998, 1999; and Vijfhuizen, "People You Live With," 27–28; for the early colonial period, see NAZ, "Civil Cases: NC Melsetter" (1906–22 and 1920–43), Civil Registers, S/666 and S/1068; NAZ, "NC Melsetter to CNC, Re: Native Divorces" (25 June 1906), Public Archives, Native Commissioner, Melsetter, NUE 1/1/1.
51. Monclaro, "Journey by the Company of Jesus," in *RSEA*, 3:230. In more recent times a new wife arrives with pots.
52. Ibid.
53. Gama, *Reposta*, 18.
54. Ibid., 18, 28. Similarly, an early twentieth-century account describes Ndau women as slaves of their husbands. AHM, Luciano Lanne, "Notas sobre Alguns Usos e Costumes Indigenas da Circumscripção de Mossurize" (1906), Companhia de Moçambique, Secretaria Geral, Processos: Caixa 445, p. 16.
55. Gama, *Reposta*, 18; AHM, "Informações sobre Alguns Usos e Costumes Indigenas das Circumscripções: Manica," in "Relatorios e Informações," Annexo ao *Boletim Official* (1910), 115–16.
56. Allen Mundeta, Chikore, Zimbabwe, 29 June 1999.
57. Freddy Sithole, Chikore, Zimbabwe, 29 June 1999.
58. Siyanzi Raphius Gapara, Chikore, Zimbabwe, 1 July 1999.
59. See, for instance, Hughes, "Frontier Dynamics," 94–95.
60. Allen Mundeta, Chikore, Zimbabwe, 29 June 1999.
61. Ibid.
62. Freddy Sithole, Chikore, Zimbabwe, 29 June 1999; Clientage arrangements, called *muganini* in the British record, continued into at least the 1920s. NAZ, "Munowenyu vs. Mazeranzera" (18 January 1922), Civil Cases, Chipinga, 1916–23, NUB 1/1/1.
63. Timóteo Mabessa Simango, Machanga, Sofala, Mozambique, 4 September 1998; AHM, "Revista de Manica e Sofala" (2a. Serie, no. 18, Agosto de 1905).

64. Allen Mundeta, Chikore, Zimbabwe, 29 June 1999; Michael Gelfand, *The Genuine Shona: Survival Values of an African Culture* (Gweru, Zimbabwe: Mambo Press, 1973), 167–70; AHM, "Informações sobre Alguns Usos e Costumes Indigenas das Circumscripções: Manica," in "Relatorios e Informações," Annexo ao *Boletim Official* (1910), 122; AHM, Luciano Lanne, "Notas sobre Alguns Usos e Costumes Indigenas da Circumscripção de Mossurize" (1906), Companhia de Moçambique, Secretaria Geral, Processos: Caixa 445, p. 15. Junod, "Notes on the Ethnological Situation," 305.

65. Timóteo Mabessa Simango, Machanga, Sofala, Mozambique, 4 September 1998.

66. Ibid.

67. Junod writes that neighbors of the Ndau to the north, the Zambezi Tonga, practiced *kufava*, similar to *uchinde*, as well. "Notes on the Ethnological Situation," 298.

68. Chinungu Mtetwa, Zamchiya, Zimbabwe, 13 July 1999.

69. Ibid.

70. Xavier, "Notícias dos Domínios Portuguezes," in *RMS*, 146; English translation from Beach and de Noronha, "Shona and the Portuguese," 2:31.

71. Gama, *Reposta*, 22.

72. Ibid.

73. Ibid., 28; AHM, "Informações sobre Alguns Usos e Costumes Indigenas das Circumscripções: Manica," in "Relatorios e Informações," Annexo ao *Boletim Official* (1910), 113–14.

74. Freddy Sithole, Chikore, Zimbabwe, 29 June 1999.

75. Ibid. Sithole also noted, "But now businessmen are the wealthy people."

76. Ellen Gapara and Siyanzi Raphius Gapara, Chikore, Zimbabwe, 1 July 1999.

77. Jona Mwaoneni Makuyana, Zamchiya, Zimbabwe, 14 July 1999.

78. Ibid. This could be the daughter of the soon-to-be-divorced man.

79. Idah Manyuni, Chikore, Zimbabwe, 28 June 1999. The verb "to sell" is used here, and later in the interview Manyuni states that the exchange of daughters was "not trading."

80. Sekai Sithole, Chikore, Zimbabwe, 29 June 1999.

81. NAZ, "Out Letters: NC Melsetter to CNC" (30 September 1897), Public Archives, Native Commissioner, Melsetter, NUE 2/1/2; Hughes, "Frontier Dynamics," 75.

82. Phillip Mutigwe, Chikore, Zimbabwe, 29 June 1999.

83. Hughes, "Frontier Dynamics," 75.

84. During many interviews elders recalled *mutengatore* arrangements, but it is not clear when (or if—and where) the practice ceased. In Vijfhuizen's study, "People You Live With," she does not mention the practice of *mutengatore*. The Portuguese were aware of the practice and wrote about it in the early twentieth century. One official insisted that the practice was waning. AHM, Cezar Augusto Cardotte, "Usos e Costumes dos Indigenas da Circumscripção de Manica" (1907), Companhia de Moçambique, Secretaria Geral, Processos, Caixa 445, p. 18; AHM, "Informações sobre Alguns Usos e Costumes Indigenas das Circumscripções: Manica," in "Relatorios e Informações," Annexo ao *Boletim Official* (1910), 112.

85. Mateus Simango, Zamchiya, Zimbabwe, 14 July 1999.

86. Idah Manyuni, Chikore, Zimbabwe, 28 June 1999; Freddy Sithole, Chikore, Zimbabwe, 29 June 1999; Siyanzi Raphius Gapara, Chikore, Zimbabwe, 1 July 1999.

87. Siyanzi Raphius Gapara, Chikore, Zimbabwe, 1 July 1999.

88. Chinungu Mtetwa, Zamchiya, Zimbabwe, 13 July 1999; Jona Mwaoneni Makuyana, Zamchiya, Zimbabwe, 14 July 1999.

89. Jona Mwaoneni Makuyana, Zamchiya, Zimbabwe, 14 July 1999.

90. Phillip Mutigwe, Chikore, Zimbabwe, 29 June 1999.

91. Ibid.; Sekai Sithole, Chikore, Zimbabwe, 29 June 1999.

92. Phillip Mutigwe, Chikore, Zimbabwe, 29 June 1999.

93. John Kunjenjema, Chikore, Zimbabwe, 30 June 1999.

94. Ibid.; Mubayi Mhlanga, Zamchiya, Zimbabwe, 13 July 1999.

95. Idah Manyuni, Chikore, Zimbabwe, 28 June 1999; Freddy Sithole, Chikore, Zimbabwe, 29 June 1999.

96. Idah Manyuni, Chikore, Zimbabwe, 28 June 1999; John Kunjenjema echoed this statement (Chikore, Zimbabwe, 30 June 1999).

97. Allen Mundeta, Chikore, Zimbabwe, 29 June 1999; Gelfand, *Genuine Shona*, 166.

98. Vijfhuizen, "People You Live With," 39.

99. Ibid., 250. Vijfhuizen notes that this term has also come to mean "daughter in law" among the Ndau of Manesa in the 1990s.

100. Allen Mundeta, Chikore, Zimbabwe, 29 June 1999; NAZ, "Deaths" (1904), Chipinga Register (1904–37), NUB 2/1/1; NAZ, "Interview with Amon Makufa Mlambo, born c. 1895" (interviewed by Dawson Munjeri, 13 December 1978 and 9 January 1979), Oral History Interviews, AOH/46; AHM, Luciano Lanne, "Notas sobre Alguns Usos e Costumes Indigenas da Circumscripção de Mossurize" (1906), Companhia de Moçambique, Secretaria Geral, Processos: Caixa 445, p. 27; AHM, Companhia de Moçambique, Secretaria Geral, Processos: J. F. Pereira Lisboa, "Alguns Usos e Costumes Indigenas da Circumscripção de Sofala" (1907), Caixa 445, p. 18; AHM, "Informações sobre Alguns Usos e Costumes Indigenas das Circumscripções: Manica," in "Relatorios e Informações," Annexo ao *Boletim Official* (1910), 107.

101. Allen Mundeta, Chikore, Zimbabwe, 29 June 1999.

102. Ibid.

103. Phoebe Mukokota, Chikore, Zimbabwe, 30 June 1999; AHM, "Revista de Manica e Sofala" (2a. Serie, no. 18, Agosto de 1905).

104. Ibid.

105. Ellen Gapara, Chikore, Zimbabwe, 1 July 1999.

106. "Marriage is like a path which all girls have to use." Hamutyinei and Plangger, *Tsumo-Shumo*, 215.

107. For an account of the role of gender in the shaping of ethnic identity in nineteenth-century Lesotho, see Eldredge, *South African Kingdom*.

108. *Hapana chisingawanisi*. Hamutyinei and Plangger, *Tsumo-Shumo*, 214.

109. Ndagumirwa Sigauke, Zamchiya, Zimbabwe, 13 July 1999.

110. Siyanzi Raphius Gapara, Chikore, Zimbabwe, 1 July 1999; Mubayi Mhlanga, Zamchiya, Zimbabwe, 13 July 1999; AHM, "Informações sobre Alguns Usos e Costumes Indigenas das Circumscripções: Manica," in "Relatorios e Informações," Annexo ao *Boletim Official* (1910), 123.

111. Siyanzi Raphius Gapara, Chikore, Zimbabwe, 1 July 1999.

112. Jona Mwaoneni Makuyana, Zamchiya, Zimbabwe, 14 July 1999.

113. Mubayi Mhlanga, Zamchiya, Zimbabwe, 13 July 1999.

114. Mateus Simango, Zamchiya, Zimbabwe, 14 July 1999.

115. Timóteo Mabessa Simango, Machanga, Sofala, Mozambique, 4 September 1998; this ceremony could also involve naming the child. AHM, "Informações sobre

Alguns Usos e Costumes Indigenas das Circumscripções: Manica," in "Relatorios e Informações," Annexo ao *Boletim Official* (1910), 115.

116. Mubayi Mhlanga, Zamchiya, Zimbabwe, 13 July 1999.

117. Ibid.

118. Chinungu Mtetwa (a midwife), Zamchiya, Zimbabwe, 13 July 1999; Sarai Nyabanga Sithole, Zamchiya, Zimbabwe, 13 July 1999.

119. Ibid.

120. AHM, "Informações sobre Alguns Usos e Costumes Indigenas das Circumscripções: Manica," in "Relatorios e Informações," Annexo ao *Boletim Official* (1910), 107; AHM, Cezar Augusto Cardotte, "Usos e Costumes dos Indigenas da Circumscripção de Manica" (1907), Companhia de Moçambique, Secretaria Geral, Processos, Caixa 445, p. 1.

121. Gama, *Reposta.*

122. Ibid.

123. NAZ, "Brief Notes on the History of the Mission on Its 60th Anniversary" (1953?), Historical Manuscripts, United Church Board for World Ministries, UN 3/8/5; the Portuguese continued to notice a dearth of twins in the Ndau region around Mossurize (on both sides of the border) in the early twentieth century. AHM, "Revista de Manica e Sofala" (2a. Serie, no. 20, Outubro de 1905), 94.

124. Jona Mwaoneni Makuyana, Zamchiya, Zimbabwe, 14 July 1999.

125. Gama, *Reposta,* 20.

126. Ibid.

127. Ibid., 16.

128. Ibid.

129. AHM, J. F. Pereira Lisboa, "Alguns Usos e Costumes Indigenas da Circumscripção de Sofala" (1907), Companhia de Moçambique, Secretaria Geral, Processos: Caixa 445, p. 44.

130. Gama, *Reposta,* 16.

131. *Dunhu kana Gomo raondomoka.* Siyanzi Raphius Gapara, Chikore, Zimbabwe, 1 July 1999.

132. Gama, *Reposta,* 17. The Portuguese term *Inhamaçango* is used for *nyamasango;* in the early twentieth century, mourning lasted for eight days. AHM, Companhia de Moçambique, Secretaria Geral, Processos: J. F. Pereira Lisboa, "Alguns Usos e Costumes Indigenas da Circumscripção de Sofala" (1907), Caixa 445, p. 43.

133. Chinungu Mtetwa, Zamchiya, Zimbabwe, 13 July 1999; AHM, "Informações sobre Alguns Usos e Costumes Indigenas das Circumscripções: Manica," in "Relatorios e Informações," Annexo ao *Boletim Official* (1910), 116; AHM, Luciano Lanne, "Notas sobre Alguns Usos e Costumes Indigenas da Circumscripção de Mossurize" (1906), Companhia de Moçambique, Secretaria Geral, Processos: Caixa 445, pp. 24–25.

134. Gama, *Reposta,* 17, and n. 32; cf. Sebastião Xavier Botelho, *Memoria Estatistica Sobre os Domínios Portuguezes na África Oriental* (Lisbon: Typ. de J. B. Morando, 1835), 150.

135. Sarai Nyabanga Sithole, Zamchiya, Zimbabwe, 13 July 1999; AHM, "Informações sobre Alguns Usos e Costumes Indigenas das Circumscripções: Manica," in "Relatorios e Informações," Annexo ao *Boletim Official* (1910), 116–18.

136. Siyanzi Raphius Gapara, Chikore, Zimbabwe, 1 July 1999.

137. Gama, *Reposta,* 18; AHM, "Informações sobre Alguns Usos e Costumes Indigenas das Circumscripções: Manica," in "Relatorios e Informações," Annexo ao *Boletim Official* (1910), 116–17.

138. Gama, *Reposta*, 19.
139. Ibid.
140. Dos Santos, *Ethiopia Oriental*, in *RSEA*, 7:289; see also dos Santos, *Etiópia Oriental*, 223.
141. Sarai Nyabanga Sithole, Zamchiya, Zimbabwe, 13 July 1999; AHM, "Informações sobre Alguns Usos e Costumes Indigenas das Circumscripções: Manica," in "Relatorios e Informações," Annexo ao *Boletim Official* (1910), 117–18.
142. Sarai Nyabanga Sithole, Zamchiya, Zimbabwe, 13 July 1999.
143. Jona Mwaoneni Makuyana, Zamchiya, Zimbabwe, 14 July 1999.
144. Ibid.
145. Sarai Nyabanga Sithole, Zamchiya, Zimbabwe, 13 July 1999; Mateus Simango, Zamchiya, Zimbabwe, 14 July 1999.
146. Sarai Nyabanga Sithole, Zamchiya, Zimbabwe, 13 July 1999.
147. Ibid.
148. Jona Mwaoneni Makuyana, Zamchiya, Zimbabwe, 14 July 1999.
149. Male heads of household were not buried inside the house. AHM, J. F. Pereira Lisboa, "Alguns Usos e Costumes Indigenas da Circumscripção de Sofala" (1907), Companhia de Moçambique, Secretaria Geral, Processos: Caixa 445, p. 43; Jona Mwaoneni Makuyana, Zamchiya, Zimbabwe, 14 July 1999.
150. Jona Mwaoneni Makuyana, Zamchiya, Zimbabwe, 14 July 1999.
151. Mubayi Mhlanga, Zamchiya, Zimbabwe, 13 July 1999; Jona Mwaoneni Makuyana, Zamchiya, Zimbabwe, 14 July 1999.
152. Mubayi Mhlanga, Zamchiya, Zimbabwe, 13 July 1999.
153. Ibid.
154. Malyn Newitt astutely argues this point in *History of Mozambique*, 46.
155. Siyanzi Raphius Gapara, Chikore, Zimbabwe, 1 July 1999.
156. Mubayi Mhlanga, Zamchiya, Zimbabwe, 13 July 1999; Chinungu Mtetwa, Zamchiya, Zimbabwe, 13 July 1999.
157. Mubayi Mhlanga, Zamchiya, Zimbabwe, 13 July 1999.
158. Dos Santos, *Etiópia Oriental.* Newitt makes this argument about ritual suicide in *History of Mozambique*, 46.
159. Chinungu Mtetwa, Zamchiya, Zimbabwe, 13 July 1999.
160. Ndagumirwa Sigauke, Zamchiya, Zimbabwe, 13 July 1999.
161. Chinungu Mtetwa, Zamchiya, Zimbabwe, 13 July 1999.
162. Mucherechete Dhlakama, Zamchiya, Zimbabwe, 13 July 1999.
163. Ibid.
164. Jona Mwaoneni Makuyana, Zamchiya, Zimbabwe, 14 July 1999.
165. Ibid.
166. Dos Santos, *Etiópia Oriental*, 91–92.
167. Ibid., 92.
168. Ibid.
169. Ibid., 89.
170. Sousa, *Asia Portuguesa*, in *RSEA*, 1:16.
171. Ibid.
172. Monclaro, "Journey by the Company of Jesus," in *RSEA*, 3:229.
173. Sousa, *Asia Portuguesa*, in *RSEA*, 1:15.
174. "Letter from the King [of Portugal] to the Viceroy of India" (1704), in *RSEA*, 5:13.

175. Joseph da Fonseca Coutinho, "Report on the Present Situation of the Conquistas of the Rivers of Soffalla" (1699), in "Shona and the Portuguese," vol. 1; "Letter from the King to the Viceroy of India" (1702), in *RSEA*, 5:7; see also a second letter from 1704 referring to the incident (see n. 174 above).
176. Coutinho, "Conquistas of the Rivers of Soffalla," in "The Shona and the Portuguese," vol. 1.
177. "King [of Portugal] to the Viceroy of India" (1704), in *RSEA*, 5:13.
178. "Copy of His Excellency's Communication" (1795), Dom Diogo de Souza to Carlos Joze dos Reys e Gama, from Moçambique, in "Shona and the Portuguese," vol. 2.
179. João Julião da Silva, "List of the Cloths and Effects that Lieutenant-Colonel João Julião da Silva Will Carry with Him for the Ceremonies and Expenses at Bandire" (1831), in "Shona and the Portuguese," vol. 2.
180. Ibid.
181. Phillip Mutigwe, Chikore, Zimbabwe, 29 June 1999.
182. Ibid.; John Kunjenjema, Chikore, Zimbabwe, 30 June 1999; Idah Manyuni, Chikore, Zimbabwe, 28 June 1999; NAZ, Peter Sithole, "Mission Work in Gazaland" (1973, based on interviews with students from 1893, 1907, etc.), Historical Manuscripts, United Church Board for World Ministries, UN 3/8/9.
183. John Kunjenjema, Chikore, Zimbabwe, 30 June 1999; Idah Manyuni, Chikore, Zimbabwe, 28 June 1999.
184. Siyanzi Raphius Gapara, Chikore, Zimbabwe, 1 July 1999.
185. Sarai Nyabanga Sithole, Zamchiya, Zimbabwe, 13 July 1999; Jona Mwaoneni Makuyana, Zamchiya, Zimbabwe, 14 July 1999. Makuyana says that the *mwadiwa* famine was the same as the *mutendeni* famine of 1912.
186. Sarai Nyabanga Sithole, Zamchiya, Zimbabwe, 13 July 1999.
187. Ibid.
188. Ibid.
189. Ibid.
190. NAZ, "Letters: H. J. Gibson to J. L. Barton" (19 October 1912), Historical Manuscripts, United Church Board for World Ministries, UN 3/2/1/6; the selling of children occurred again during a famine in 1915. NAZ, "Interview with Amon Makufa Mlambo, born c. 1895" (interviewed by Dawson Munjeri, 13 December 1978 and 9 January 1979), Oral History Interviews, AOH/46.
191. NAZ, "Letters, Misc., 1908–1912: G. Wilder to NC Meredith" (Chikore, 12 January 1909), Public Archives, Native Commissioner, Melsetter, NUE 1/3/2.
192. Simon Mundeta, Chikore, Zimbabwe, 28 June 1999; Siyanzi Raphius Gapara, Chikore, Zimbabwe, 1 July 1999; Jona Mwaoneni Makuyana, Zamchiya, Zimbabwe, 14 July 1999.
193. Mucherechete Dhlakama, Zamchiya, Zimbabwe, 13 July 1999.
194. Chinungu Mtetwa, Zamchiya, Zimbabwe, 13 July 1999.
195. Ibid.
196. Mubayi Mhlanga, Zamchiya, Zimbabwe, 13 July 1999.
197. Ibid.
198. John Kunjenjema, Chikore, Zimbabwe, 30 June 1999.
199. Sarai Nyabanga Sithole, Zamchiya, Zimbabwe, 13 July 1999; Jona Mwaoneni Makuyana, Zamchiya, Zimbabwe, 14 July 1999; AHM, João Maria da Piedade de Lencastre e Távora, "Os Vanhai (Sofala): Monografia Etnográfica" (1964), Secção Especial (não registrado), 21.

200. Ibid., 22.
201. Xavier, "Notícias dos Domínios Portuguezes," in *RMS*, 145. Xavier also provides details on fighting techniques.
202. Mateus Simango, Zamchiya, Zimbabwe, 14 July 1999.
203. Gama, *Reposta*, 22.
204. Ibid., 24.
205. Ibid., 22.
206. Ibid., 17.
207. Ibid., 22.
208. Ibid.

Chapter 5

Epigraph One. Chinungu Mtetwa, Zamchiya, Zimbabwe, 13 July 1999. A barbel is a species of catfish.
Epigraph Two. Hamutyinei and Plangger, *Tsumo-Shumo*, 424.

1. Many young Ndau women no longer practice some of the beauty techniques discussed here, such as *pika* and *nyora* (also called cicatrization), although they remain prevalent in the district of Machaze, Mozambique. Field notes, Manica: Machaze, 14–24 July 1998.
2. A similar point about shared connections was made at the exhibit "Body Art: Marks of Identity," American Museum of Natural History, New York, 20 November 1999–29 May 2000.
3. Gengenbach, "Where Women Make History," 369.
4. Ibid. See also Gengenbach, *Binding Memories.*
5. Donna Klumpp and Corinne Kratz, "Aesthetics, Expertise, and Ethnicity: Okiek and Maasai Perspectives on Personal Ornament," in *Being Maasai: Ethnicity and Identity in East Africa*, ed. Thomas Spear and Richard Waller (Athens: Ohio University Press, 1993), 195.
6. Dos Santos, *Etiópia Oriental*, 112; English translation from dos Santos, *Ethiopia Oriental*, in *RSEA*, 7:207. Dos Santos notes that women performed this task when they were not out working in their fields.
7. Sousa, *Asia Portuguesa* (1666–74), in *RSEA*, 1:15. Sousa was writing in the seventeenth century about the previous century.
8. Mudenge, *Political History of Munhumutapa*, 37 and 70n4.
9. In Teve, the areas were Macaia and Miràmbue. Gama, *Reposta*, 24–25.
10. Erskine, "Journey to Umzila's," 95.
11. Ibid.
12. Monclaro, "Relaçaõ da Viagem," in *RSEA*, 3:229.
13. Ibid. *Machira* is the Ndau word for pieces of cloth (sing., *jira*).
14. Ibid., 234; Barreto, "Informação do Estado e Conquista dos Rios de Cuama" (1667), in *RSEA*, 3:481.
15. Machado, "Gujarati Indian Merchant Networks," 97.
16. Dos Santos, *Etiópia Oriental*, 111; English translation from dos Santos, *Ethiopia Oriental*, in *RSEA*, 6:207.

17. This was a cotton cloth made in Cambay that was usually blue, red, or black, according to Mudenge, *Political History of Munhumutapa*, xi; Monclaro, "Relaçaõ da Viagem," in *RSEA*, 3:234–35.

18. Dos Santos, *Ethiopia Oriental*, in *RSEA*, 7:207.

19. Gama, *Reposta*, 26; Erskine, "Journey to Umzila's," 95.

20. Gama, *Reposta*, 26. An account from the early sixteenth century claimed that the Muslim residents of Sofala did not use dyes. "Description of the Situation, Customs, and Produce of Various Places of Africa" (ca. 1518), in *DPMAC*, 5:375.

21. Gama, *Reposta*, 23.

22. Ibid.

23. Jona Mwaoneni Makuyana, Zamchiya, Zimbabwe, 14 July 1999.

24. Bwanyi (Bwanye or Buene) is an island near Chiluane, south of Sofala. The Portuguese used it as their main base in the region during the nineteenth century. David Beach, *A Zimbabwean Past* (Gweru, Zimbabwe: Mambo Press, 1994), 247.

25. Xavier, "Notícias dos Domínios Portuguezes," in *RMS*, 146.

26. Erskine, "Journey to Umzila's," 97. A colonial official in the Eastern Highlands at Chimanimani noted at the end of the nineteenth century that most fiber was "principally of bark." NAZ, "Out Letters, NC Melsetter to CNC Salisbury" (20 October 1897), Public Archives, Native Commissioner, Melsetter, NUE 2/1/2.

27. Erskine, "Journey to Umzila's," 97.

28. Freddy Sithole, Chikore, Zimbabwe, 29 June 1999; Siyanzi Raphius Gapara, Chikore, Zimbabwe, 1 July 1999.

29. Siyanzi Raphius Gapara, Chikore, Zimbabwe, 1 July 1999.

30. Sarai Nyabanga Sithole, Zamchiya, Zimbabwe, 13 July 1999; Jona Mwaoneni Makuyana, Zamchiya, Zimbabwe, 14 July 1999.

31. Sousa, *Asia Portuguesa*, in *RSEA*, 1:15.

32. Xavier, "Notícias dos Domínios Portuguezes," in *RMS*, 146; English translation from Beach and de Noronha, "Shona and the Portuguese," 2:31.

33. Ndagumirwa Sigauke, Zamchiya, Zimbabwe, 13 July 1999.

34. "Situation, Customs, and Produce of Africa," in *DPMAC*, 5:375.

35. Idah Manyuni, Chikore, Zimbabwe, 28 June 1999.

36. Freddy Sithole, Chikore, Zimbabwe, 29 June 1999; Phillip Mutigwe, Chikore, Zimbabwe, 29 June 1999; Mateus Simango, Zamchiya, Zimbabwe, 14 July 1999.

37. Phillip Mutigwe, Chikore, Zimbabwe, 29 June 1999.

38. John Kunjenjema, Chikore, Zimbabwe, 30 June 1999.

39. Mubayi Mhlanga, Zamchiya, Zimbabwe, 13 July 1999.

40. Freddy Sithole, Chikore, Zimbabwe, 29 June 1999.

41. Ibid.

42. "Situation, Customs, and Produce of Africa," in *DPMAC*, 5:375; John Kunjenjema, Chikore, Zimbabwe, 30 June 1999.

43. Phillip Mutigwe, Chikore, Zimbabwe, 29 June 1999.

44. Ibid.

45. Celani Mutigwe, Chikore, Zimbabwe, 29 June 1999.

46. Monclaro, "Relaçaõ da Viagem," in *RSEA*, 3:229; Freddy Sithole, Chikore, Zimbabwe, 29 June 1999; Ndagumirwa Sigauke, Zamchiya, Zimbabwe, 13 July 1999; AHM, "Informações sobre Alguns Usos e Costumes Indigenas das Circumscripções: Manica," in "Relatorios e Informações," Annexo ao *Boletim Official* (1910), 107–8;

AHM, J. F. Pereira Lisboa, "Alguns Usos e Costumes Indigenas da Circumscripção de Sofala" (1907), Companhia de Moçambique, Secretaria Geral, Processos: Caixa 445, p. 4; NAZ, "Interview with Nhira Nzvere Chinhoyi" (born ca. 1870; interviewed by Dawson Munjeri, 4 May and 31 May 1978), Oral History Interviews, AOH/39; Beach, *Shona and Their Neighbours*, 158. See also Elizabeth Schmidt, *Peasants, Traders, and Wives: Shona Women in the History of Zimbabwe, 1870–1939* (Porstmouth, NH: Heinemann, 1992).

47. Monclaro, "Relaçaõ da Viagem," in *RSEA*, 3:229, 252.

48. Xavier, "Notícias dos Domínios Portuguezes," in *RMS*, 146; English translation from Beach and de Noronha, "Shona and the Portuguese," 2:31–32.

49. André Fernandes, "Letter from the Father André Fernandes to the Brother Luiz Froes at the College of Goa" (1560), in *RSEA*, 2:76.

50. Ibid.

51. Ibid.

52. John Kunjenjema, Chikore, Zimbabwe, 30 June 1999; Phoebe Mukokota, Chikore, Zimbabwe, 30 June 1999.

53. Sarai Nyabanga Sithole, Zamchiya, Zimbabwe, 13 July 1999.

54. Idah Manyuni, Chikore, Zimbabwe, 28 June 1999; Freddy Sithole, Chikore, Zimbabwe, 29 June 1999.

55. Gama, *Reposta*, 23.

56. Ibid., 23–24.

57. Ibid., 23.

58. Xavier, "Notícias dos Domínios Portuguezes," in *RMS*, 154–55.

59. Gama, *Reposta*, 23. Although the text reads "hands and feet," Gama is most likely referring to the common practice of wearing wire on the arms and legs.

60. Ibid.

61. Ibid., 23–24. Despite the presence of blacksmiths, Gama claimed that the Ndau did not know how to work gold or stone at the end of the eighteenth century.

62. Xavier, "Notícias dos Domínios Portuguezes," in *RMS*, 154, 174.

63. Monclaro, "Relaçaõ da Viagem," in *RSEA*, 3:234.

64. Ibid., 253.

65. Ibid.

66. Ibid., 235.

67. Dos Santos, *Etiópia Oriental*, 112. A *lupanga*, also known as a *panga*, is from the Shona word for knife: *banga* (sing.), *mapanga* (pl.).

68. Dos Santos, *Ethiopia Oriental*, in *RSEA*, 7:289. A *ndoro* is either a shell or a white, shell-like ornament that is usually worn on the chest. It is associated with chiefs and others who are said to have magical powers. Hannan, *Standard Shona Dictionary*, 443.

69. "Extracts from the *Decade* Written by Antonio Bocarro" (1631–49), in *RSEA*, 3:405.

70. E. Dora Earthy, *Valenge Women: The Social and Economic Life of Valenge Women of Portuguese East Africa, an Ethnographic Study* (London: Frank Cass, 1933), 212. Earthy lived among the Valenge north of the Limpopo River where Ndau spirits are believed to be prevalent. AHM, "Informações sobre Alguns Usos e Costumes Indigenas das Circumscripções: Manica," in "Relatorios e Informações," Annexo ao *Boletim Official* (1910), 107.

71. Valenge women to the south did not pierce their ears. Earthy, *Valenge Women*, 105.

72. John Kunjenjema, Chikore, Zimbabwe, 30 June 1999.
73. Philemon Khosa, Chikore, Zimbabwe, 28 June 1999.
74. Allen Mundeta, Chikore, Zimbabwe, 29 June 1999.
75. Amélia Mutume, Machanga, Sofala, Mozambique, 4 September 1998.
76. Sarai Nyabanga Sithole, Zamchiya, Zimbabwe, 13 July 1999.
77. Celani Mutigwe, Chikore, Zimbabwe, 29 June 1999.
78. Ndagumirwa Sigauke, Zamchiya, Zimbabwe, 13 July 1999; AHM, João Maria da Piedade de Lencastre e Távora, "Os Vanhai (Sofala): Monografia Etnográfica" (1964), Secção Especial (não registrado), 23.
79. Idah Manyuni, Chikore, Zimbabwe, 28 June 1999.
80. Sekai Sithole, Chikore, Zimbabwe, 29 June 1999.
81. Amélia Mutume, Machanga, Sofala, Mozambique, 4 September 1998.
82. Chinungu Mtetwa, Zamchiya, Zimbabwe, 13 July 1999.
83. Mucherechete Dhlakama, Zamchiya, Zimbabwe, 13 July 1999.
84. Phoebe Mukokota, Chikore, Zimbabwe, 30 June 1999; Allen Mundeta, Chikore, Zimbabwe, 29 June 1999.
85. Chinungu Mtetwa, Zamchiya, Zimbabwe, 13 July 1999.
86. The substance added to the wound may have been "medicine," since Desmond Dale defines *nyora* as a "tattoo mark, cicatrix, in which medicine has been added." Dale, *Shona-English Dictionary*, 163.
87. Erskine, "Journey to Umzila's," 95. See also Rennie, "Christianity, Colonialism, and Nationalism," 88.
88. St. Vincent W. Erskine, "Third and Fourth Journeys in Gaza, or Southern Mozambique, 1873 to 1874 and 1874 to 1875," *Journal of the Royal Geographical Society* 48 (1878): 30.
89. Yet we cannot be sure that Erskine did not see women with keloids as he headed north toward the Chimanimani mountains from the lower Save. He may have been looking only for scar tissue on women's faces, or perhaps he did not have the opportunity to view *nyora* and *pika* on other parts of the body such as the stomach or thighs. In addition, Erskine was forced to rely on his memory when he wrote his account of the journey, since all of his notebooks were lost in a flooded river. Erskine, "Journey to Umzila's," 45.
90. They did not mention any efforts by colonial officials or missionaries to suppress *pika* and *nyora*, although one Portuguese official, writing in 1948, claims that "civilized action" by missionaries ended these practices in the Concelho de Manica, which includes the Ndau areas of Dombe and Moribane (near present-day Sussendenga in Manica Province). AHM, José Cândido Magalhaes de Brito Rebelo, "Monografia Etnográfica sobre a População Indígena do Concelho de Manica" (1948), Secção Especial, a. III, p. 6, no. 38, p. 35.
91. Mubayi Mhlanga, Zamchiya, Zimbabwe, 13 July 1999.
92. Celani Mutigwe, Chikore, Zimbabwe, 29 June 1999.
93. Ibid.
94. Ndagumirwa Sigauke, Zamchiya, Zimbabwe, 13 July 1999.
95. Sarai Nyabanga Sithole, Zamchiya, Zimbabwe, 13 July 1999.
96. Jona Mwaoneni Makuyana, Zamchiya, Zimbabwe, 14 July 1999.
97. Celani Mutigwe, Chikore, Zimbabwe, 29 June 1999.
98. Chinungu Mtetwa, Zamchiya, Zimbabwe, 13 July 1999.
99. Jona Mwaoneni Makuyana, Zamchiya, Zimbabwe, 14 July 1999.

100. Amélia Mutume, Machanga, Sofala, Mozambique, 4 September 1998.
101. Erskine, "Journey to Umzila's," 95; Erskine, "Third and Fourth Journeys in Gaza," 30.
102. Junod, "Notes on the Ethnological Situation," 296.
103. Earthy, *Valenge Women*, 105.
104. "Situation, Customs, and Produce of Africa," in *DPMAC*, 5:375.
105. Mubayi Mhlanga, Zamchiya, Zimbabwe, 13 July 1999.
106. Ibid.
107. Ibid.
108. Erskine, "Third and Fourth Journeys in Gaza," 30.
109. Sarai Nyabanga Sithole, Zamchiya, Zimbabwe, 13 July 1999.
110. She described the look as "dirty" and claimed that at least one European named Neilson made the Ndau cut their hair before speaking to him. NAZ, "Interview with Susara Catrina Johanna Webster, nee Odendaal (b. 7 May 1894)" (25 April 1973), Oral History Archives, Oral/WE 3.
111. Francisco Monclaro, "Narrative (Copy) by Father Francisco de Monclaro, of the Society of Jesus, of the Expedition to Monomotapa, Led by Francisco Barreto," in *DPMAC*, 8:325–429, 381. cf. another version of Monclaro, "Relaçaõ da Viagem," in *RSEA*, 3:229.
112. Dos Santos, *Ethiopia Oriental*, in *RSEA*, 7:207.
113. Ibid.
114. Dos Santos, *Ethiopia Oriental*, in *RSEA*, 7:289.
115. Phillip Mutigwe, Chikore, Zimbabwe, 29 June 1999.
116. Ndagumirwa Sigauke, Zamchiya, Zimbabwe, 13 July 1999.
117. Farther south, the walls of Valenge houses bore many designs earlier in the twentieth century. Earthy, *Valenge Women*, 238, Plate XVII.
118. Beach, *Shona and Their Neighbours*, 48.
119. Sarai Nyabanga Sithole, Zamchiya, Zimbabwe, 13 July 1999.
120. Ibid.
121. Chinungu Mtetwa, Zamchiya, Zimbabwe, 13 July 1999.
122. John Kunjenjema, Chikore, Zimbabwe, 30 June 1999.
123. Catherine Dhlakama, Chikore, Zimbabwe, 30 June 1999; AHM, "Informações sobre Alguns Usos e Costumes Indigenas das Circumscripções: Manica," in "Relatorios e Informações," Annexo ao *Boletim Official* (1910), 108.
124. This was also the case earlier in the twentieth century. AHM, João Maria da Piedade de Lencastre e Távora, "Os Vanhai (Sofala): Monografia Etnográfica" (1964), Secção Especial (não registrado), 20.
125. NAZ, "J. N. Eksteen to CNC" (27 September 1897), Public Archives, Native Commissioner, Ndanga, N 9/2/1. Observed in N'danga District, on the west side of the Save River.
126. Ndagumirwa Sigauke, Zamchiya, Zimbabwe, 13 July 1999.
127. Gama, *Reposta*, 24.
128. Chinungu Mtetwa, Zamchiya, Zimbabwe, 13 July 1999.
129. Sarai Nyabanga Sithole, Zamchiya, Zimbabwe, 13 July 1999.
130. Sekai Sithole, Chikore, Zimbabwe, 29 June 1999.
131. John Kunjenjema, Chikore, Zimbabwe, 30 June 1999; Catherine Dhlakama, Chikore, Zimbabwe, 30 June 1999; Mubayi Mhlanga, Zamchiya, Zimbabwe, 13 July

1999; AHM, "Informações sobre Alguns Usos e Costumes Indigenas das Circumscripções: Manica," in "Relatorios e Informações," Annexo ao *Boletim Official* (1910), 108.

132. Jona Mwaoneni Makuyana, Zamchiya, Zimbabwe, 14 July 1999.
133. Mucherechete Dhlakama, Zamchiya, Zimbabwe, 13 July 1999.
134. Ibid.; Sarai Nyabanga Sithole, Zamchiya, Zimbabwe, 13 July 1999.
135. Phoebe Mukokota, Chikore, Zimbabwe, 30 June 1999; Jona Mwaoneni Makuyana, Zamchiya, Zimbabwe, 14 July 1999.
136. Mubayi Mhlanga, Zamchiya, Zimbabwe, 13 July 1999; Mateus Simango, Zamchiya, Zimbabwe, 14 July 1999.
137. Siyanzi Raphius Gapara, Chikore, Zimbabwe, 1 July 1999.
138. Celani Mutigwe, Chikore, Zimbabwe, 29 June 1999; Ndagumirwa Sigauke, Zamchiya, Zimbabwe, 13 July 1999.
139. Celani Mutigwe, Chikore, Zimbabwe, 29 June 1999.
140. Mucherechete Dhlakama, Zamchiya, Zimbabwe, 13 July 1999.
141. Ellen Gapara, Chikore, Zimbabwe, 1 July 1999.
142. Chinungu Mtetwa, Zamchiya, Zimbabwe, 13 July 1999.
143. Sarai Nyabanga Sithole, Zamchiya, Zimbabwe, 13 July 1999.
144. Catherine Dhlakama, Chikore, Zimbabwe, 30 June 1999.
145. Ellen Gapara, Chikore, Zimbabwe, 1 July 1999.
146. Jona Mwaoneni Makuyana, Zamchiya, Zimbabwe, 14 July 1999.
147. Fernandes, "Father André Fernandes to Brother Luiz Froes," in *RSEA*, 2:76.
148. Fynn [Henry Francis], "Delagoa Bay (1823)," in *RSEA*, 2:481.
149. Allen Mundeta, Chikore, Zimbabwe, 29 June 1999; see, for instance, the discussion of tattoos in nineteenth-century southern Mozambique in Gengenbach, "Where Women Make History," chap. 5. Early twentieth-century descriptions appear in AHM, "Relatorios e Informações," Annexo ao *Boletim Official* (1910); and Cabral, *Racas, Usos e Costumes*, 27–28. (Cabral was Secretário dos Negócios Indígenas.)
150. Klumpp and Kratz, "Aesthetics, Expertise, and Ethnicity," 195.

Chapter 6

Epigraph One. Sarai Nyabanga Sithole, Zamchiya, Zimbabwe, 13 July 1999. Sithole was describing Mbonyeya's rainmaking power from the Musikavanhu chieftaincy.
Epigraph Two. Hamutyinei and Plangger, *Tsumo-Shumo*, 304.
Epigraph Three. Ibid., 320.

1. Ibid., 412. *Panonwiwa doro, panonzikwa nemhere.* Another proverb warns, "(Snuff) tobacco creates no grudge like beer" (*Fodya haina shura sedoro*), implying the rudeness of refusing to offer beer to visitors. Ibid., 434.
2. Siyanzi Raphius Gapara, Chikore, Zimbabwe, 1 July 1999; Sekai Sithole, Chikore, Zimbabwe, 29 June 1999; field notes, Zimbabwe, Zamchiya, July 1999.
3. Hughes, "Frontier Dynamics," 142.
4. Vijfhuizen, "People You Live With," 265.
5. The *dare* is not only the court, but also the village meeting place for men and the body that has judicial or executive authority. Hannan, *Standard Shona Dictionary*, 111.
6. Hamutyinei and Plangger, *Tsumo-Shumo*, 304.

7. Idah Manyuni, Chikore, Zimbabwe, 28 June 1999; Sarai Nyabanga Sithole, Zamchiya, Zimbabwe, 13 July 1999.

8. They are still performed today. Philemon Khosa, Chikore, Zimbabwe, 29 July 1999; Mucherechete Dhlakama, Zamchiya, Zimbabwe, 13 July 1999; NAZ, "Out Letters, NC Melsetter to CNC Salisbury" (2 April, 30 June, 31 August, and 20 October 1897), Public Archives, Native Commissioner, Melsetter, NUE 2/1/2; NAZ, "NC Melsetter to Longden" (11 February 1897), Civil Commissioner and Magistrate (1895–98), DM 2/9/1.

9. Mucherechete Dhlakama, Zamchiya, Zimbabwe, 13 July 1999.

10. Ibid.

11. Ibid.; Allen Mundeta, Chikore, Zimbabwe, 29 June 1999; Mubayi Mhlanga, Zamchiya, Zimbabwe, 13 July 1999; Philemon Khosa, Chikore, Zimbabwe, 29 July 1999.

12. Allen Mundeta, Chikore, Zimbabwe, 29 June 1999.

13. Mubayi Mhlanga, Zamchiya, Zimbabwe, 13 July 1999.

14. John Kunjenjema, Chikore, Zimbabwe, 30 June 1999.

15. Ibid.

16. Mateus Simango, Zamchiya, Zimbabwe, 14 July 1999; AHM, João Maria da Piedade de Lencastre e Távora, "Os Vanhai (Sofala): Monografia Etnográfica" (1964), Secção Especial (não registrado), 28.

17. Dos Santos, *Etiópia Oriental*; English translation from dos Santos, *Ethiopia Oriental*, in *RSEA*, 7:199.

18. Ibid.

19. Ibid. During fieldwork, I also participated in these "coming and goings" as I sought interviews with certain chiefs. In the nineteenth century, American missionaries complained of being "forced to wait for weeks" before Ngungunyana would talk with them. NAZ, "Local History," 6–7 (1934? background and history of Rhodesia to 1897, compiled for schoolchildren), Historical Manuscripts, United Church Board for World Ministries, UN 3/8/1.

20. Sarai Nyabanga Sithole, Zamchiya, Zimbabwe, 13 July 1999.

21. Ibid. Mbonyeya displayed rainmaking powers around 1895 until his death in 1947, according to Rennie, "From Zimbabwe to a Colonial Chieftaincy," 257, 278.

22. Sarai Nyabanga Sithole, Zamchiya, Zimbabwe, 13 July 1999.

23. Ibid.

24. Mubayi Mhlanga, Zamchiya, Zimbabwe, 13 July 1999.

25. Ibid.

26. Beach, *Shona and Zimbabwe*; Rennie, "From Zimbabwe to a Colonial Chieftaincy," 257–85; Gloria Waite, "Public Health in Precolonial East-Central Africa" in Steven Feierman and John M. Janzen, eds., *The Social Basis of Health and Healing in Africa* (Berkeley: University of California Press, 1992), 221.

27. Waite notes that this substance was probably *mteyo*. Waite, "Public Health in Precolonial East-Central Africa," 221.

28. Ibid.; Rennie, "From Zimbabwe to a Colonial Chieftaincy," 260, 264.

29. Waite, "Public Health in Precolonial East-Central Africa," 222; Rennie, "From Zimbabwe to a Colonial Chieftaincy," 260.

30. Bhila, *Trade and Politics*; Waite, "Public Health in Precolonial East-Central Africa," 222.

31. Waite, "Public Health in Precolonial East-Central Africa," 222.

32. Rennie, "Christianity, Colonialism, and Nationalism," 68–69, and "From Zimbabwe to a Colonial Chieftaincy," 261, 263; Hughes, "Frontier Dynamics," 38.

33. Coastal delegations brought presents for rain into the 1920s, according to Rennie, "From Zimbabwe to a Colonial Chieftaincy," 257, 262.

34. Erskine noted this in the 1870s in "Journey to Umzila's," 121. The Gaza Nguni presence also led to many changes, including a disregard for territorial shrines (as discussed ahead in chap. 7). Rennie, "Ideology and State Formation," 184.

35. Rennie, "From Zimbabwe to a Colonial Chieftaincy," 270.

36. Ibid., 272–80.

37. Erskine, "Third and Fourth Journeys in Gaza," 34.

38. Ibid.

39. Idah Manyuni, Chikore, Zimbabwe, 28 June 1999; Siyanzi Raphius Gapara, Chikore, Zimbabwe, 1 July 1999.

40. John Kunjenjema, Chikore, Zimbabwe, 30 June 1999.

41. Freddy Sithole, Chikore, Zimbabwe, 29 June 2000; Siyanzi Raphius Gapara, Chikore, Zimbabwe, 1 July 1999; Sekai Sithole, Chikore, Zimbabwe, 29 June 1999.

42. Siyanzi Raphius Gapara, Chikore, Zimbabwe, 1 July 1999.

43. Sekai Sithole, Chikore, Zimbabwe, 29 June 1999.

44. Phillip Mutigwe, Chikore, Zimbabwe, 29 June 2000; Jona Mwaoneni Makuyana, Zamchiya, Zimbabwe, 14 July 1999. Sekuru Makuyana argues that "when *muchongoyo* is performed, even white people would nod their heads in appreciation following the sequence of the dance."

45. Sekai Sithole, Chikore, Zimbabwe, 29 June 1999. She commented that ceremonies such as this one have been replaced by "modern" ceremonies.

46. Freddy Sithole, Chikore, Zimbabwe, 29 June 2000.

47. Ellen Gapara, Chikore, Zimbabwe, 1 July 1999.

48. Ibid.

49. Freddy Sithole, Chikore, Zimbabwe, 29 June 2000.

50. Dos Santos also noted that inhabitants of the Sofala hinterland recognized "a great God, whom they call Moungo." This Portuguese priest argued, however, that "they have a confused knowledge . . . but they do not pray or command themselves to him." *Ethiopia Oriental*, in *RSEA*, 7:199.

51. Xavier, "Notícias dos Domínios Portuguezes," in *RMS*, 147; English translation from Beach and de Noronha, "Shona and the Portuguese," 2:32.

52. Gama, *Reposta*, 15–16.

53. Dos Santos, *Ethiopia Oriental*, in *RSEA*, 7:197.

54. Gama, *Reposta*, 15.

55. Ibid., 17.

56. Sousa, *Asia Portuguesa*, in *RSEA*, 1:24–25.

57. Ibid. Although Sousa's description is not entirely accurate, it is understandable that his confusion arises from his own Catholic perspective.

58. Dos Santos, *Ethiopia Oriental*, in *RSEA*, 7:200.

59. Vijfhuizen, "People You Live With," 36.

60. Gama, *Reposta*, 17.

61. AHM, Luciano Lanne, "Notas sobre Alguns Usos e Costumes Indigenas da Circumscripção de Mossurize" (1906), Companhia de Moçambique, Secretaria Geral, Processos: Caixa 445, p. 19.

62. Gama, *Reposta*, 17–18.

63. Ibid., 19; Xavier, "Notícias dos Domínios Portuguezes," in *RMS*, 147.

64. Jona Mwaoneni Makuyana, Zamchiya, Zimbabwe, 14 July 1999.

65. These figures applied household medicines and profited as "deceivers" (the word used is *enganadoras*), from the perspective of Gama, *Reposta*, 16.

66. AHM, "Informações sobre Alguns Usos e Costumes Indigenas das Circumscripções: Manica," in "Relatorios e Informações," Annexo ao *Boletim Official* (1910), 113; later, money was a form of payment as well, but this occurred rarely. Allen Mundeta, Chikore, Zimbabwe, 29 June 1999.

67. Dos Santos, *Ethiopia Oriental*, in *RSEA*, 7:204.

68. Ibid.

69. Ibid.

70. Gama, *Reposta*, 19. Gama reviled the Ndau for using *moavi*. See also AHM, "Informações sobre Alguns Usos e Costumes Indigenas das Circumscripções: Manica," in "Relatorios e Informações," Annexo ao *Boletim Official* (1910), 120; and AHM, J. F. Pereira Lisboa, "Alguns Usos e Costumes Indigenas da Circumscripção de Sofala" (1907), Companhia de Moçambique, Secretaria Geral, Processos: Caixa 445, pp. 45, 77. Both sources note that *moavi* (*mauve*) is no longer used.

71. Dos Santos, *Ethiopia Oriental*, in *RSEA*, 8:204–5; a similar practice is also mentioned in AHM, "Informações sobre Alguns Usos e Costumes Indigenas das Circumscripções: Manica" in "Relatorios e Informações," Annexo ao *Boletim Official* (1910), 120. Another practice involving boiling water is noted in AHM, José Cândido Magalhaes de Brito Rebelo, "Monografia Etnográfica sobre a População Indígena do Concelho de Manica" (1948), Secção Especial, a. III, p. 6, no. 38, p. 17. And for one using crocodiles in the Save River, see AHM, João Maria da Piedade de Lencastre e Távora, "Os Vanhai (Sofala): Monografia Etnográfica" (1964), Secção Especial (não registrado), 28.

72. Dos Santos, *Ethiopia Oriental*, in *RSEA*, 8:204–5.

73. AHM, Luciano Lanne, "Notas sobre Alguns Usos e Costumes Indigenas da Circumscripção de Mossurize" (1906), Companhia de Moçambique, Secretaria Geral, Processos: Caixa 445, pp. 40–41. See also AHM, Cezar Augusto Cardotte, "Usos e Costumes dos Indigenas da Circumscripção de Manica" (1907), Companhia de Moçambique, Secretaria Geral, Processos, Caixa 445, p. 1; AHM, (no author), "Alguns Usos e Costumes Indigenas da Sub-Circumscripção de Chiloane" (1907), Companhia de Moçambique, Secretaria Geral, Processos, Caixa 445.

74. *Jenga mhosva / ndiye muiti wezvakaipa.* Hamutyinei and Plangger, *Tsumo-Shumo*, 200; AHM, Luciano Lanne, "Notas sobre Alguns Usos e Costumes Indigenas da Circumscripção de Mossurize" (1906), Companhia de Moçambique, Secretaria Geral, Processos: Caixa 445, p. 40; AHM, J. F. Pereira Lisboa, "Alguns Usos e Costumes Indigenas da Circumscripção de Sofala" (1907), Companhia de Moçambique, Secretaria Geral, Processos: Caixa 445, p. 78.

75. Dos Santos noted that the king's drunken state during the ceremony was "a very usual thing." *Ethiopia Oriental*, in *RSEA*, 8:196.

76. Ibid., 8:197.

77. Ibid.

78. Ibid.

79. In this case, the term Zulu was used to refer to the Gaza Nguni. Further details are provided in chap. 7. Allen Mundeta, Chikore, Zimbabwe, 29 June 1999. Mundeta also notes that the Manyika and Zezuru have "other spirit mediums that tell them what to do, but not in this area."

80. Simon Mundeta and Allen Mundeta, Chikore, Zimbabwe, 29 June 1999.

81. Catherine Dhlakama, Chikore, Zimbabwe, 30 June 1999.

82. Steven Feierman, "Colonizers, Scholars, and the Creation of Invisible Histories," in *Beyond the Cultural Turn: New Directions in the Study of Society and Culture*, ed. Victoria E. Bonnell and Lynn Hunt (Berkeley: University of California Press, 1999), 210n12, 187.

83. Vijfhuizen, "People You Live With," 265.

84. John Kunjenjema, Chikore, Zimbabwe, 30 June 1999.

85. Dos Santos, *Ethiopia Oriental*, in *RSEA*, 7:208; Jona Mwaoneni Makuyana, Zamchiya, Zimbabwe, 14 July 1999.

86. Dos Santos, *Ethiopia Oriental*, in *RSEA*, 7:208; AHM, "Revista de Manica e Sofala" (2a. Serie, no. 20, Outubro de 1905), 94–95; Sarai Nyabanga Sithole, Zamchiya, Zimbabwe, 13 July 1999; AHM, J. F. Pereira Lisboa, "Questionario acerca dos Indigenas do Territorio de Manica e Sofala" (1906), Companhia de Moçambique, Secretaria Geral, Processos: Caixa 445, p. 3.

87. Sarai Nyabanga Sithole, Zamchiya, Zimbabwe, 13 July 1999.

88. Sousa, *Asia Portuguesa*, in *RSEA*, 1:24–25.

89. David Hughes discusses colonial interventions and the suppression of these methods in "Frontier Dynamics," 143; AHM, J. F. Pereira Lisboa, "Questionario acerca dos Indigenas do Territorio de Manica e Sofala" (1906), Companhia de Moçambique, Secretaria Geral, Processos: Caixa 445, p. 4.

90. VaTarangwa, Chikore, Zimbabwe, 28 June 1999; AHM, J. F. Pereira Lisboa, "Questionario acerca dos Indigenas do Territorio de Manica e Sofala" (1906), Companhia de Moçambique, Secretaria Geral, Processos: Caixa 445, p. 3.

91. Gama, *Reposta*, 20.

92. These valued items were also used to secure marriage arrangements (as discussed in chap. 4). Phillip Mutigwe, Chikore, Zimbabwe, 29 June 2000; Siyanzi Raphius Gapara and Ellen Gapara, Chikore, Zimbabwe, 1 July 1999; Mucherechete Dhlakama, Zamchiya, Zimbabwe, 13 July 1999; Idah Manyuni, Chikore, Zimbabwe, 28 June 1999; VaTarangwa, Chikore, Zimbabwe, 28 June 1999; AHM, Luciano Lanne, "Notas sobre Alguns Usos e Costumes Indigenas da Circumscripção de Mossurize" (1906), Companhia de Moçambique, Secretaria Geral, Processos: Caixa 445, p. 13; AHM, Cezar Augusto Cardotte, "Usos e Costumes dos Indigenas da Circumscripção de Manica" (1907), Companhia de Moçambique, Secretaria Geral, Processos, Caixa 445, p. 27.

93. VaTarangwa, Chikore, Zimbabwe, 28 June 1999; AHM, Cezar Augusto Cardotte, "Usos e Costumes dos Indigenas da Circumscripção de Manica" (1907), Companhia de Moçambique, Secretaria Geral, Processos, Caixa 445, p. 7.

94. Mubayi Mhlanga, Zamchiya, Zimbabwe, 13 July 1999.

95. A proverb reflects this desperate act: *Mhosvakadzi muripo mwene*. A woman's fine is her very self. Hamutyinei and Plangger, *Tsumo-Shumo*, 314.

96. Allen Mundeta, Chikore, Zimbabwe, 29 June 1999.

97. Ibid.

98. Catherine Dhlakama, Chikore, Zimbabwe, 30 June 1999.

99. Chinungu Mtetwa, Zamchiya, Zimbabwe, 13 July 1999; dos Santos, *Ethiopia Oriental*, in *RSEA*, 7:201.

100. Dos Santos, *Ethiopia Oriental*, in *RSEA*, 7:201–2. "Inhama," or *nyama*, also means "meat."

101. Dos Santos, *Ethiopia Oriental*, in *RSEA*, 7:202.

102. Ibid. Dos Santos describes two instruments called *ambira*. One resembles the finger piano (called *mbira* today) made out of flat rods of iron on wood and played inside a gourd. The other was a type of xylophone. Henrik Ellert argues that dos Santos was describing the *matepe mbira*, also known as *sansa* or *sansi* in Mozambique. Ellert, *Material Culture of Zimbabwe* (Harare: Longman, 1984), 62.

103. Dos Santos, *Ethiopia Oriental*, in *RSEA*, 7:203.

104. Gama mentions the leaders of Quisssanga, Madanda, and Butonga in *Reposta*, 21.

105. Ibid.

106. Ibid.

107. Ibid.

108. Ibid.

109. Monclaro, "Relaçaõ da Viagem," in *RSEA*, 3:227.

110. Ibid.; dos Santos, *Etiópia Oriental*, 89–90.

111. Monclaro, "Relaçaõ da Viagem," in *RSEA*, 3:227.

112. Chinungu Mtetwa, Zamchiya, Zimbabwe, 13 July 1999.

113. Monclaro, "Relaçaõ da Viagem," in *RSEA*, 3:227.

114. AHM, João Maria da Piedade de Lencastre e Távora, "Os Vanhai (Sofala): Monografia Etnográfica" (1964), Secção Especial (não registrado), 18; Gama, *Reposta*, 21.

115. John Kunjenjema, Chikore, Zimbabwe, 30 June 1999.

116. Vijfhuizen, "People You Live With," 26.

Chapter 7

Epigraph One. Jona Mwaoneni Makuyana, Zamchiya, Zimbabwe, 14 July 1999.
Epigraph Two. John Kunjenjema, Chikore, Zimbabwe, 30 June 1999.

1. Michael Taussig, *Shamanism, Colonialism, and the Wild Man: A Study in Terror and Healing* (Chicago: University of Chicago Press, 1987), 4.

2. Ibid., 5.

3. Chinua Achebe, quoted in Appiah, *In My Father's House*, 177.

4. Appiah, *In My Father's House*, 177.

5. Ibid.

6. Ibid., 178.

7. Ibid.

8. Pierre Nora, "Between Memory and History: Les Lieux de Memoire," *Representations* 26 (spring 1989): 7–24.

9. See, for example, Portelli, *Death of Luigi Trastulli*.

10. Jona Mwaoneni Makuyana described Ngungunyana as "a problem" during an interview in Zamchiya, Zimbabwe, 14 July 1999.

11. For more on the causes and consequences of the dramatic changes that took place during this time, often referred to as the *Mfecane*, see works such as Carolyn Hamilton, ed., *The Mfecane Aftermath* (Johannesburg: Witwatersrand University Press, 1996); Elizabeth Eldredge, "Sources of Conflict in Southern Africa, ca. 1800–1830: The 'Mfecane' Reconsidered," *Journal of African History* 33, no. 1 (1992): 1–35, and "Migration, Conflict, and Leadership in Early Nineteenth-Century South Africa: The Case of Matiwane," in *Paths toward the Past: African Historical Essays in Honor of Jan Vansina*, ed. Robert W. Harms et al. (Atlanta: African Studies Association Press, 1994),

39–75; Carolyn Hamilton, "The Character and Objects of Chaka: A Reconsideration of the Making of Shaka as 'Mfecane' Motor," *Journal of African History* 33 (1992): 37–63; J. D. Omer-Cooper, "Has the Mfecane a Future? A Response to the Cobbing Critique," *Journal of Southern African Studies* 19, no. 2 (June 1993): 273–94, and *The Zulu Aftermath* (London: Longmans, 1966); Jeff Peires, "Paradigm Deleted: The Materialist Interpretation of the Mfecane," *Journal of Southern African Studies* 19, no. 2 (June 1993): 295–313; John Wright, "Political Mythology and the Making of Natal's Mfecane," *Canadian Journal of African Studies* 23, no. 2 (1989): 272–91; and Julian Cobbing, "The Mfecane as Alibi: Thoughts on Dithakong and Mbolompo," *Journal of African History* 29 (1988): 487–519.

12. These included Zwangendaba, Maseko, and Nxaba. Maseko left the Ndau area and crossed the Zambezi River around 1839. Zwangendaba, the leader of one group that crossed the Zambezi River near Zumbo in 1835, eventually settled in Tanzania, twelve hundred miles from his birthplace, where his followers came to be known as the Ngoni. Gerhard Liesegang, "Nguni Migrations between Delagoa Bay and the Zambezi, 1821–1839," *African Historical Studies* 3, no. 2 (1970): 317–37; Omer-Cooper, *Zulu Aftermath*.

13. According to David Beach, Nxaba entered the Save Valley in 1827 and conquered Mutema's territory of Sanga. *Shona and Zimbabwe*, 177; see also Liesegang, "Nguni Migrations," 325, 337.

14. Both Nxaba and Soshangane are credited with an attack on Sofala in 1836, but Liesegang argues that the Gaza Nguni under Soshangane were not involved in this raid. Gerhard Liesegang, "Aspects of Gaza Nguni History, 1821–1897," *Rhodesian History* 6 (1975): 3n9, and "Nguni Migrations," 317, 325–27; AHM, "Relatorio sobre as Ilhas do Archipelago de Bazaruto e Pescarias de Perolas" (Francisco Pena, Bazaruto, 31 de Dezembro de 1909), in "Relatorios e Informações," Annexo ao *Boletim Official* (1910), 404–5.

15. This was the area between the coastal town of Inhambane and the Save River to the north.

16. Beach, *Shona and Their Neighbours*, 27.

17. Omer-Cooper, *Zulu Aftermath*, 58. Liesegang notes that the kingdom was named after Soshangane's grandfather. "Nguni Migrations," 328.

18. Mzila struggled with his brother Mawewe in a succession war from 1858 to 1862.

19. For details on Ngungunyana's rise to power as a "usurper" who was "not the legitimate heir," see Douglas Wheeler, "Gungunyane the Negotiator: A Study in African Diplomacy," *Journal of African History* 9, no. 4 (1968): 585–602.

20. In 1888 American missionaries attempting to visit Ngungunyana at his capital (about thirty miles from Mount Selinda) noted that he "was in complete control of the country." Their account alludes to life "under the cruel hand of Gungunyana" as one good reason for white rule and missionary influence. NAZ, "Local History," 6–7 (1934? background and history of Rhodesia to 1897, compiled for schoolchildren), Historical Manuscripts, United Church Board for World Ministries, UN 3/8/1; AHM, "Relação Nominal dos Regulos que Antigamente Eram Subordinados," Fundo do Século XIX, Governo do Distrito de Sofala, Caixa 3, Sala 8.

21. Those who came to be called "Ndau" would say *Ndau-we, Ndau-we* (We salute you! We salute you!) to exclaim deference (as discussed in chap. 1). Sekai Sithole, Chikore, Zimbabwe, 29 June 1999; AHM, José Fontes Pessoa de Amorim, "Os 'Vatssangas' ou Mundaué" (Beira, 1956), Secção Especial, a. III, p. 6, no. 80.

22. Gerhard Liesegang, for instance, argues that the word came into use after the conquests of Nqaba to designate local assimilated men who wore Nguni dress and used Nguni armaments. Liesegang, "Sofala, Beira e a sua Zona," 32. But J. Keith Rennie argues that an earlier reference is apparently from a Portuguese document that mentions "Mujao" traders who crossed the Save River in 1739 to trade their gold for cloth at Inhambane. This reference to "Mujao" is similar to "Ndjao," the Inhambane version of "Ndau." Rennie, "Ideology and State Formation," 168–69.

23. Or *madzviti*. Martinho Manhacha Jackson Simango, Machanga, Sofala, Mozambique, 5 September 1998. Mulenje Macama William Simango, Buzi, Sofala, Mozambique, 23 September 1998. The term *xibitzi*, or *chibitzi*, is probably derived from *dzviti*, meaning "invader" (or "warrior" in common usage), i.e., the Nguni. *Dzviti* is also an abusive term for a Ndebele person, according to Dale in *Shona English Dictionary*, 54. Beach points out that the Shona called all Nguni speakers *madzviti*, thus creating some confusion. *Shona and Their Neighbours*, 139. See also Rennie, "Christianity, Colonialism, and Nationalism," 145.

24. Achebe quoted in Appiah, *In My Father's House*, 177.

25. Rennie, "Christianity, Colonialism, and Nationalism."

26. Elders used the Ndau term *mabziti* here. Mulenje Macama William Simango, Buzi, Sofala, Mozambique, 23 September 1998. See also Rennie, "Christianity, Colonialism, and Nationalism," 145.

27. Luís Mangate Bill Mapossa (Group Interview with Chefe Agostinho Manduze Jorge Chiteve Simango, Régulo ChiTeve), Machanga, Sofala, Mozambique, 12 September 1998.

28. Wheeler's study of Ngungunyana notes that the leader's mother was a Ndau. He also speculates that Ngungunyana's military leader, Maguiguana, may have been Ndau as well, or else he may have come from the neighboring Chope or Valenge to the south. "Gungunyane the Negotiator," 589.

29. Rennie, "Christianity, Colonialism, and Nationalism," 147; and Walter Rodney, "The Year 1895 in Southern Mozambique: African Resistance to the Imposition of European Colonial Rule," *Journal of the Historical Society of Nigeria* 5 (1971): 517.

30. This figure, cited in Monica Wilson and Leonard Thompson, *A History of South Africa to 1870* (Boulder: Westview Press, 1983), 100, comes from Alfred T. Bryant, *Olden Times in Zululand and Natal, Concerning Earlier Political History of the Eastern-Nguni Clans* (London: Longmans, Green and Co., 1929).

31. Liesegang, "Sofala, Beira e a sua Zona," 32; AHM, José Fontes Pessoa de Amorim, "Os 'Vatssangas' ou Mundaué" (Beira, 1956), Secção Especial, a. III, p. 6, no. 80; the use of *nhamussoro* continues today in southern Mozambique. See Gengenbach, "Where Women Make History."

32. Idah Manyuni, Chikore, Zimbabwe, 28 June 1999. Manyuni explained, "We are now a mixed pot; it is no longer Ndaus only." One Portuguese official referred to "modifications" in Ndau culture due to the Nguni presence. AHM, José Fontes Pessoa de Amorim, "Os 'Vatssangas' ou Mundaué" (Beira, 1956), Secção Especial, a. III, p. 6, no. 80.

33. Taussig, *Shamanism, Colonialism, and the Wild Man*, 5.

34. Ibid.

35. John Kunjenjema, Chikore, Zimbabwe, 30 June 1999. Similarly, one local history makes the argument that Ngungunyana "put cruel people in important positions." NAZ, Albert Hlatywayo, "The African History in the Nineteenth Century" (n.d.), Papers of Charles Stephen Davies (1906–71), DA 8/2/2.

36. José Paulo Maduca Simango, Machanga, Sofala, Mozambique, 4 September 1998.

37. Freddy Sithole, Chikore, Zimbabwe, 29 June 1999. Historically the Nguni ancestors of the Shangaan, the Zulu, and the Ndebele did share a common language and culture, so these connections are not inaccurate.

38. For instance, *Moyo* became *Sithole* or *Nkomo*.

39. Allen Mundeta, Chikore, Zimbabwe, 29 June 1999.

40. This statement comes from J. Keith Rennie's 1970 interview with M. Hlatcwayo, quoted in "Christianity, Colonialism, and Nationalism," 145.

41. Phillip Mutigwe, Chikore, Zimbabwe, 29 June 1999.

42. See Hughes, "Frontier Dynamics," 40.

43. Ibid., 40–41. Mountain strongholds, such as that of Mtassa, were an obstacle to successful Nguni raids in the 1880s in Manicaland, according to Wheeler, "Gungunyane the Negotiator," 585–86.

44. NAZ, "Interview with Herbert Dzvairo" (b. 1905; interviewed by Dawson Munjeri, 30 January 1979), Oral History Interviews, AOH/47; a similar statement was made by Sekuru Mlambo: "You see, we are the Ndau and at the same time we are the Shangaan." NAZ, "Interview with Amon Makufa Mlambo, born c. 1895" (interviewed by Dawson Munjeri, 13 December 1978 and 9 January 1979), Oral History Interviews, AOH/46.

45. Rennie has noted this in his informative work on ideologies. See "Ideology and State Formation," 184.

46. Rennie, "From Zimbabwe to a Colonial Chieftaincy," 258.

47. Rennie, "Ideology and State Formation," 184.

48. Ibid., 182.

49. Timóteo Mabessa Simango, Machanga, Sofala, Mozambique, 4 September 1998.

50. Fernando Vitorino Tuzine, Machanga, Sofala, Mozambique, 4 September 1998; Rennie, "Christianity, Colonialism, and Nationalism," 137.

51. For more on the "ambulatory enslavement" derived from the Nguni system of *kukhonza*, see See Patrick Harries, "Slavery, Social Incorporation, and Surplus Extraction: The Nature of Free and Unfree Labour in South-East Africa," *Journal of African History* 22 (1981): 309–30. He describes relationships "of extreme servility and exploitation" that he defines as slavery (311).

52. For detailed examples of *kukhonza* in Gogoi and Vhimba, see Hughes, "Frontier Dynamics." This offer of obedience is also noted in Rennie, "Christianity, Colonialism, and Nationalism," 147.

53. Fernando Vitorino Tuzine, Machanga, Sofala, Mozambique, 4 September 1998; Rennie, "Ideology and State Formation," 183.

54. Rennie, "Christianity, Colonialism, and Nationalism," 146.

55. Ibid.

56. Vail, *Creation of Tribalism*, 15.

57. Albeit rarely. Junod, "Contribution," 22; Rennie, "Christianity, Colonialism, and Nationalism," 77; AHM, "Revista de Manica e Sofala" (1a. Serie, no. 3, Maio de 1904), 33–34.

58. Rodney, "1895 in Southern Mozambique," 516.

59. Ibid. Parallels may exist with Shaka and his mother, Nande, in South Africa. An alternate spelling of *Empiumbecasane* is *Impiucazamo*.

60. Ibid., 517.

61. Rennie, "Ideology and State Formation," 184. Rennie notes that members of the royal family were "dispersed in towns around the state."

62. Both Sandra Greene and Elizabeth Eldredge make this point. Greene, *Gender, Ethnicity, and Social Change*; Eldredge, *South African Kingdom.*

63. Diana Jeater, *Marriage, Perversion, and Power: The Construction of Moral Discourse in Southern Rhodesia, 1894–1930* (Oxford: Clarendon Press, 1993), 19.

64. NAZ, "Letter, NC Melsetter to CNC, Salisbury" (9 March 1896), Public Archives, Native Commissioner, Melsetter, NUE 2/1/1; Rennie, "From Zimbabwe to a Colonial Chieftaincy," 183–84.

65. Phillip Mutigwe, Chikore, Zimbabwe, 29 June 1999; NAZ, "Letter, NC Melsetter to CNC, Salisbury" (9 March 1896); and "Out Letters, L. C. Meredith to CNC" (2 April 1896), Public Archives, Native Commissioner, Melsetter, NUE 2/1/1.

66. Rennie, "Ideology and State Formation," 186.

67. Ibid.

68. Hughes, "Frontier Dynamics," 40.

69. Rennie, "Ideology and State Formation," 184.

70. João Guerra Muchanga, Machanga, Sofala, Mozambique, 4 September 1998; Luís Santana Machave, Machanga, Sofala, Mozambique, 4 September 1998; Mateus Simango, Zamchiya, Zimbabwe, 14 July 1999.

71. Ndau women did, however, share a "body language" visible to others through jewelry and decorative markings such as tattoos and scarification.

72. Idah Manyuni, Chikore, Zimbabwe, 28 June 1999; Phillip Mutigwe, Chikore, Zimbabwe, 29 June 1999.

73. Idah Manyuni, Chikore, Zimbabwe, 28 June 1999.

74. Or *mabziti*. Phillip Mutigwe, Chikore, Zimbabwe, 29 June 1999; Idah Manyuni, Chikore, Zimbabwe, 28 June 1999.

75. Idah Manyuni, Chikore, Zimbabwe, 28 June 1999; Phillip Mutigwe, Chikore, Zimbabwe, 29 June 1999.

76. The sense here is of identity rather than ownership. Mhlanga went on to state, "Those without pierced ears were said to be from across the Save; we call those people vaDuma. But now such distinctions are no more. Long back on the way to Mutare if you were stranded you could not put up for the night where people could see you because they would kill you." Mubayi Mhlanga, Zamchiya, Zimbabwe, 13 July 1999; similar sentiments about ear piercing and identity were expressed by others such as Siyanzi Raphius Gapara, Chikore, Zimbabwe, 1 July 1999; and Mateus Simango, Zamchiya, Zimbabwe, 14 July 1999.

77. Phillip Mutigwe, Chikore, Zimbabwe, 29 June 1999.

78. Ibid.

79. Freddy Sithole, Chikore, Zimbabwe, 29 June 1999.

80. VaTarangwa, Chikore, 28 June 1999.

81. Catherine Dhlakama, Chikore, Zimbabwe, 30 June 1999; Chinungu Mtetwa, Zamchiya, Zimbabwe, 13 July 1999.

82. Catherine Dhlakama, Chikore, Zimbabwe, 30 June 1999.

83. Sekai Sithole, Chikore, Zimbabwe, 29 June 1999.

84. Allen Mundeta, Chikore, Zimbabwe, 29 June 1999.

85. Phillip Mutigwe, Chikore, Zimbabwe, 29 June 1999.

86. Chinungu Mtetwa, Zamchiya, Zimbabwe, 13 July 1999.

87. Siyanzi Raphius Gapara, Chikore, Zimbabwe, 1 July 1999.

88. Ellen Gapara, Chikore, Zimbabwe, 1 July 1999.

89. Mateus Simango, Zamchiya, Zimbabwe, 14 July 1999.

90. Chinungu Mtetwa, Zamchiya, Zimbabwe, 13 July 1999; see also Phoebe Mukokota, Chikore, Zimbabwe, 30 June 1999.

91. Freddy Sithole, Chikore, Zimbabwe, 29 June 1999.

92. Ranger, "Missionaries, Migrants and the Manyika"; see also the other chapters in Vail's groundbreaking volume, *The Creation of Tribalism in Southern Africa.*

93. This warrants further study. See Carolyn Nordstrom, *A Different Kind of War Story* (Philadelphia: University of Pennsylvania Press, 1997).

94. Rennie also refers to the "ample testimony" about the king's ability "to order mutilation, killing and expropriation of property as punishments for offences." "Ideology and State Formation," 184.

95. Most began to bury their bones to avoid punishment. Timóteo Mabessa Simango, Machanga, Sofala, Mozambique, 4 September 1998.

96. Isaias Veremo Dhlakama, Chibabava, Sofala, Mozambique, 15 September 1998. Described in Gama, *Reposta.*

97. Pedro Bapiro Gafuro, Machanga, Sofala, Mozambique, 4 September 1998; João Guerra Muchanga, Machanga, Sofala, Mozambique, 4 September 1998; Filimon Dongonda Simango, Dongonda, Chibabava, Sofala, Mozambique, 15 September 1998. An American missionary report from 1884, commenting on Mzila's treatment of his allies, noted a "number of deserted kraals to be met with everywhere. It is no exaggeration, I think, to say that over a strip of country 75 miles wide extending north and south a much greater distance, not more than one kraal in every three remained inhabited." This was also a time of famine, so communities may have fled in search of food rather than to escape the wrath of Mzila's warriors. NAZ, "Letter, Erwin H. Richards to Kilbon, Secretary, American Zulu Mission, 24 October 1884, Mongwe, Inhambane," ABC (East Central Africa Mission, 1883–), MISC/AM 1.

98. Cases of sexual assault as "punishment" by the Gaza Nguni were also noted in interviews. Jona Mwaoneni Makuyana, Zamchiya, Zimbabwe, 14 July 1999.

99. John Kunjenjema, Chikore, Zimbabwe, 30 June 1999.

100. Ibid. Ngungunyana would order the death of a person "by sinking a sharp wooden peg into their head through their back into the ground," according to Jona Mwaoneni Makuyana, Zamchiya, Zimbabwe, 14 July 1999.

101. John Kunjenjema, Chikore, Zimbabwe, 30 June 1999; Jona Mwaoneni Makuyana, Zamchiya, Zimbabwe, 14 July 1999; AHM, Luciano Lanne, "Notas sobre Alguns Usos e Costumes Indigenas da Circumscripção de Mossurize" (1906), Companhia de Moçambique, Secretaria Geral, Processos: Caixa 445, p. 26.

102. Siyanzi Raphius Gapara, Chikore, Zimbabwe, 1 July 1999.

103. Phillip Mutigwe, Chikore, Zimbabwe, 29 June 1999.

104. Wilson Mhlanga, "The Story of Ngwaqazi: The History of the Amatshangana," *NADA* 25 (1948): 72; NAZ, "Letter, NC Melsetter to Secretary, Native Department" (12 October 1895), Public Archives, Native Commissioner, Melsetter, NUE 2/1/1; NAZ, "Richards to Kilbon, 24 October 1884," ABC (East Central Africa Mission, 1883–), MISC/AM 1. Richards claimed that Ngungunyana, in 1884, informed him of the time it took to reach Bilene.

105. Rennie, "Ideology and State Formation," 187. Wheeler notes that estimates ranged from 40,000 to 100,000 people. "Gungunyane the Negotiator," 589. A Portuguese account from May 1889 records Ngungunyana's arrival at Mossurize with

about 10,000 men en route to Mandhlakazi (Manjacaz) in the south. AHM, José Casaleiro da Alegria Rodrigues(?) (Mussurize, 13 de Maio de 1889), Fundo do Século XIX, Governo do Distrito de Sofala, 8–17/M2(2).

106. NAZ, "Local History of the Vandau People before the 20th Century" (Dumisani Mhlanga, n.d.), Papers of Charles Stephen Davies (1906–71), DA 8/2/1-2. This "history" refers to Mzila as "the Vandau chief."

107. AHM, Armando Vaz Pereira Brites, "Monografia Etnográfica sobre a Sub-Raça 'Senas' " (Beira, post-1910?), Secção Especial, a. V, p. 7, no. 274, p. 41; Rennie, "Ideology and State Formation," 187. This presence, most likely quite substantial, is understudied.

108. Phillip Mutigwe, Chikore, Zimbabwe, 29 June 1999.

109. Ibid.

110. Ibid.

111. Ibid.; Chief Mpungu was said to be "a son of Mzila and therefore a half-brother of Ngungunyana." NAZ, "Local History," 6 (1934? background and history of Rhodesia to 1897, compiled for schoolchildren), Historical Manuscripts, United Church Board for World Ministries, UN 3/8/1.

112. NAZ, Peter Sithole, "Mission Work in Gazaland" (1973, based on interviews with students from 1893, 1907, etc.), Historical Manuscripts, United Church Board for World Ministries, UN 3/8/9.

113. NAZ, "Interview with Amon Makufa Mlambo, born c. 1895" (interviewed by Dawson Munjeri, 13 December 1978 and 9 January 1979), Oral History Interviews, AOH/46.

114. Ibid.

115. Wilmsen and McAllister, *Politics of Difference*.

116. Ibid., viii. For a similar argument about Shangaan identity in South Africa, see Isak Niehaus, "Ethnicity and the Boundaries of Belonging: Reconfiguring Shangaan Identity in the South African Lowveld," *African Affairs* 101 (2002): 557–83.

117. Wilmsen and McAllister, *Politics of Difference*, viii.

Chapter 8

Epigraph One. Ellen Gapara, Chikore, Zimbabwe, 1 July 1999.
Epigraph Two. Idah Manyuni, Chikore, Zimbabwe, 28 June 1999.

1. As Idah Manyuni mentioned through metaphor. Chikore, Zimbabwe, 28 June 1999.

2. Jona Mwaoneni Makuyana, Zamchiya, Zimbabwe, 14 July 1999.

3. Ibid. Makuyana continued, "Mahohoma [a district administrator in the colonial government] is the one who destroyed Shangani; he said that we are Ndaus. This is because people used to say 'Ndau' as a greeting and also when referring to places. So he called us VaNdau, 'AmaNdau.' "

4. Mateus Simango, Zamchiya, Zimbabwe, 14 July 1999. Simango also cites Mahohoma as "the one who divided us into Ndau and Shangani."

5. John Kunjenjema, Chikore, Zimbabwe, 30 June 1999.

6. Ibid.

7. Freddy Sithole, Chikore, Zimbabwe, 29 June 1999. This is the Ndau term for Gaza Nguni warriors. VaSithole was about eighty years old when he made this comment.

8. Idah Manyuni, Chikore, Zimbabwe, 28 June 1999.

9. Bertha Munedzi, Mhakwe, Zimbabwe, 30 July 1999.

10. Mbuya Dhliwayo, Mhakwe, Zimbabwe, 30 July 1999.

11. Celani Mutigwe, Chikore, Zimbabwe, 29 June 1999.

12. Phoebe Mukokota, Chikore, Zimbabwe, 30 June 1999.

13. Philemon Khosa, Chikore, Zimbabwe, 29 July 1999.

14. Ellen Gapara, Chikore, Zimbabwe, 1 July 1999.

15. As is the case in Rogo, Nigeria, according to Abdul Raufu Mustapha, "Identity Boundaries, Ethnicity, and National Integration in Nigeria," in *Ethnic Conflicts in Africa*, ed. Okwudiba Nnoli (Dakar, Senegal: CODESRIA, 1998), 30.

16. Hughes, "Frontier Dynamics," 56.

17. Ibid., 59.

18. Ibid.

19. Variety would not be a characteristic of recent arrivals. D. E. Needham, E. K. Mashingaidze, and N. Bhebe, *From Iron Age to Independence: A History of Central Africa* (Harare: Longman, 1984), 39.

20. John Kunjenjema, Chikore, Zimbabwe, 30 June 1999.

21. Ibid.

22. Celani Mutigwe, Chikore, Zimbabwe, 29 June 1999.

23. Phillip Mutigwe, Chikore, Zimbabwe, 29 June 1999.

24. Idah Manyuni, Chikore, Zimbabwe, 28 June 1999.

25. Ibid.

26. Freddy Sithole, Chikore, Zimbabwe, 29 June 1999. Ndau is a tonal language. To the west, in the Save River Valley, the tone is different as well.

27. Ibid. VaSithole is referring to the tone and accent of the language speaker.

28. Allen Mundeta, Chikore, Zimbabwe, 29 June 1999.

29. Ibid.

30. Ibid. Another insult is a claim that the Danda are dirty and do not bathe due to a lack of water in their region. AHM, José Fontes Pessoa de Amorim, "Os 'Vatssangas' ou Mundaué" (Beira, 1956), Secção Especial, a. III, p. 6, no. 80.

31. NAZ, "Interview with Jonah Tarwiwa Chitombo, born c. 1898–1904" (interviewed by Dawson Munjeri, 5 and 11 September 1979), Oral History Interviews, AOH/61.

32. Jeanne Marie Penvenne discusses the "centrifugal forces which challenge the bounded political entity called Mozambique" in Penvenne, "Mozambique: A Tapestry of Conflict," in David Birmingham and Phyllis M. Martin, eds., *History of Central Africa: The Contemporary Years since 1960* (New York: Longman, 1998), 233.

33. VaTarangwa, Chikore, Zimbabwe, 28 June 1999.

34. Ibid.

35. Mubayi Mhlanga, Zamchiya, Zimbabwe, 13 July 1999. Hlengwe is spoken to the south of the Save River. The northern limit of the Ndau area is around Rusitu, since people speak Manyika (another dialect of Shona) beyond Chimanimani, according to elders such as Jona Mwaoneni Makuyana, Zamchiya, Zimbabwe, 14 July 1999.

36. Mateus Simango, Zamchiya, Zimbabwe, 14 July 1999. To the south, explained Allen Mundeta, the Hlengwe area and the Chiredzi area are no longer considered to be part of the Ndau region. Mundeta, Chikore, Zimbabwe, 29 June 1999.

37. Eric Wolf, *Europe and the People without History* (Berkeley: University of California Press, 1997).

38. This is reflected in the Mozambican rejection of school texts written in Zimbabwean standard Shona at the primary level.

39. The initial support for Afonso Dhlakama, Renamo's president since 1980, "derived almost entirely from the N'dau speakers of central Mozambique," according to Alex Vines in *Renamo: Terrorism in Mozambique* (Bloomington: Indiana University Press, 1991), 16. Renamo became a political party after the war ended in 1992, and both Dhlakama and Renamo continue to receive support from the Ndau region in national elections.

40. Ibid., 63–64.

41. Ndabaningi Sithole founded ZANU (Ndonga) in 1963 as a faction of ZANU (PF), the ruling party since independence in 1980. Masipula Sithole, "Ethnicity and Democratization in Zimbabwe: From Confrontation to Accommodation," in *Ethnic Conflict and Democratization in Africa*, ed. Harvey Glickman (Atlanta: African Studies Association Press, 1995), 148–51.

42. Ibid., 151.

43. Sithole argues that demands for inclusion (rather than secession) are "one healthy aspect of ethnicitiy in Zimbabwe." "Ethnicity and Democratization in Zimbabwe," 149.

44. United Nations, "Culture: UNESCO Wants World Heritage to Include Tradition" (UN Wire, 21 November 2000; posted on the H-Net discussion list on Research in African Primary Sources, http://www.h-net.org/~afrsrch/).

45. UNESCO, "World Culture Report 2000: Cultural Diversity, Conflict, and Pluralism," http://www.unesco.org/culture/worldreport/; also published as *Cultural Diversity, Conflict, and Pluralism* by Arizpe S. Lourdes and Ann-Belinda Preis (Paris: UNESCO, 2000).

46. Michel Cahen has detailed Renamo's transition from an armed organization to a political party between 1992 and 1994 in *Os Outros: Um Historiador em Moçambique, 1994* (Basel: P. Schlettwein, 2004). He argues that the war did not assume an ethnic character, but was a postcolonial implosion (xvi–xvii). See also Cahen, *Mozambique: La Révolution Implosée: Études sur 12 Ans d'Indépendance, 1975–1987* (Paris: L'Harmattan, 1987).

47. Dhlakama, for instance, suggested that his party might establish a new headquarters in the city of Beira, the capital of the province of Sofala and home to many Ndau speakers. Many areas in this central province were Renamo strongholds during the war. "Could Zimbabwe Intervene Again?" *Financial Gazette*, 10 February 2000.

48. In 1994 Dhlakama also failed to campaign in the southern part of Mozambique, exacerbating regional divides, and Cahen argues that this was a grave error in his campaign strategy. Renamo did attempt to marshal support from the margins, including marginalized ethnicities such as the Ndau. *Os Outros*, xx.

49. Mustapha, "Identity Boundaries, Ethnicity, and National Integration," 30.

50. Ibid.

51. Ibid., 27.

52. Ibid.

53. Ibid.

54. Ibid., 47.

55. Michel Cahen, "Nationalism and Ethnicities: Lessons from Mozambique," in *Ethnicity Kills? The Politics of War, Peace, and Ethnicity in Subsaharan Africa*, eds. Einar Braathen, Morten Boas, and Gjermund Saether (New York: St. Martin's Press, 2000), 168. See also Cahen, *Os Outros*.

56. Ibid.

57. Ibid.

58. Sithole, "Ethnicity and Democratization in Zimbabwe," 151–52.

59. Ibid., 153.

60. Ibid.

61. Ibid.

62. Comaroff, "Ethnicity, Nationalism, and the Politics of Difference," 163.

63. Commenting on the "*invention* of tribalism" thesis, Masipula Sithole remarked, "But we all know that all inventions are real." "Ethnicity and Democratization in Zimbabwe," 123. See also, for example, J. Wright, "Politics of Being 'Zulu.' "

64. Cahen, *Os Outros*, xvi. See also AHM, José Alberto Gomes de Melo Branquinho, "Prospecção das Forças Tradicionais: Manica e Sofala" (1966), Secção Especial, a. III, p. 6, no. 19.

65. Appiah, *In My Father's House*, 178.

66. Ibid., 179.

67. Ibid.

68. Ibid. Appiah writes, " 'Race' in Europe and 'tribe' in Africa are central to the way in which the objective interests of the worst-off are distorted."

69. *Kare haagari ari kare.* Hamutyinei and Plangger, *Tsumo-Shumo*, 291.

GLOSSARY OF NDAU AND PORTUGUESE WORDS

bira. Religious ceremony of thanksgiving for care by ancestors
curva. Annual gift to a ruler; tribute
dare. Court of a chief
feira. Regional market or trading fair
fumo. Local ruler or chief
gudza (**pl.** *magudza*). Coverings of woven strips or strings from baobab, musasa, and fig trees
Joni. Johannesburg, South Africa
madzviti. Warriors
makoto. Rainmaking ceremonies
mudzimu (**pl.** *vadzimu*). Spirit elder of a family; soul of a dead relative
mutupo (**pl.** *mitupo*). Totem of a clan
n'anga. Traditional Ndau healer
nhamussoro. Healer
nyamasango. Ruler of the woodland; midlevel ruler
nyora. Scarification
pika. Tattoos
prazo. Portuguese crown estate in southeast Africa
prazero. Portuguese or Afro-Portuguese holder of a crown estate
régulo. Local ruler or chief
sadza. Maize meal staple of Ndau diet
sertanejo. Afro-Portuguese backwoodsman of the interior
zimbabwe. Stone structure inhabited by rulers and elites

BIBLIOGRAPHY

Archives

Mozambique

Arquivo do Património Cultural (ARPAC), Maputo and Beira
Arquivo Histórico de Moçambique (AHM), Maputo
Companhia de Moçambique
Direccão dos Serviços dos Negócios Indígenas
Fundo do Século XIX, Governo do Distrito de Sofala
Inspecção dos Serviços Administrativos e dos Negócios Indígenas (ISANI)
Secção Especial

Zimbabwe

National Archives of Zimbabwe (NAZ), Harare
Civil Registers (S)
Historical Manuscripts, United Church Board for World Ministries [UCBWM] (UN Series)
Oral History Interviews (AOH)
Public Archives, Native Commissioner, Melsetter (N, NUE)

Portugal

Biblioteca da Ajuda, Lisboa
Biblioteca Nacional de Lisboa
Biblioteca da Sociedade de Geografia de Lisboa
Arquivo Histórico Ultramarino, Lisboa
Avulsos de Moçambique
Diversos de Moçambique

United States

Houghton Library, Harvard University, Cambridge
American Board of Commissioners for Foreign Missions (ABC)

Published Primary Documents and Government Sources

Andrade, António Alberto de, ed. *Relações de Moçambique Setecentista* [*RMS*]. Lisbon: Agência Geral do Ultramar, 1955.

Barreto, Manuel. "Informação do Estado e Conquista dos Rios de Cuama Vulgar e Verdadeiramente Chamados Rios de Ouro." 1667. *Boletim da Sociedade de Geografia de Lisboa* 4, no. 1 (1883): 33–59.

Beach, D. N., and H. de Noronha, eds. "The Shona and the Portuguese, 1575–1890." 2 vols. Mimeo. Harare, 1980.

Boletim do Governo do Estado da India (1865).

Boletim Official (1910).

Boletim da Sociedade de Estudos da Colónia de Moçambique.

Botelho, Sebastião Xavier. *Memoria Estatistica Sobre os Domínios Portuguezes na África Oriental.* Lisbon: Typ. de J. B. Morando, 1835.

Cabral, António Augusto Pereira. *Racas, Usos e Costumes dos Indígenas de Província de Moçambique.* Lourenço Marques, Mozambique: Imprensa Nacional, 1925.

Conceição, Fr. António de. "Tratado dos Rios de Cuama." 1696. *O Chronista de Tissuary* 2, nos. 14–17 (1867): 39–45, 63–69, 84–92, 105–11.

Cunha, Joaquim d'Almeida da. *Estudo acerca dos Usos e Costumes dos Banianes, Bathiás, Parses, Mouros, Gentios e Indígenas.* Lourenço Marques, Mozambique: Imprensa Nacional, 1885.

Dias, Luíz Fernando de Carvalho, ed. *Fontes para História, Geografia, e Comércio de Moçambique, Séc. XVIII.* Lisbon: Junta das Missões Geográficas e de Investigações do Ultramar, 1954.

Documentos Sobre os Portugueses em Moçambique e na África Central, 1497–1840 [DPMAC]. 9 vols. Lisbon: National Archives of Rhodesia, Centro de Estudos Históricos Ultramarinos, 1962–72.

dos Santos, João. *Etiópia Oriental e Vária História de Cousas Notáveis do Oriente.* 1609. Lisbon: Comissão Nacional para as Comemorações dos Descobrimentos Portugueses, 1999.

Erskine, St. Vincent W. "Journey of Exploration to the Mouth of the River Limpopo." 1868. *Journal of the Royal Geographical Society* 39 (1869): 233–76.

———. "Journey to Umzila's, South-East Africa, in 1871–1872." *Journal of the Royal Geographical Society* 45 (1875): 45–125.

———. "Third and Fourth Journeys in Gaza, or Southern Mozambique, 1873 to 1874 and 1874 to 1875." *Journal of the Royal Geographical Society* 48 (1878): 25–56.

Gama, Carlos José dos Reis e. *Reposta das Questoens sobre os Cafres.* 1796. Introduction and notes by Gerhard Liesegang. Lisbon: Junta de Investigações do Ultramar, 1966.

Lanne, Luciano. *Reposta ao Questionário Etnográfico acerca da População Indígena da Provincia de Moçambique, Circunscrição de Mossurize.* Mossurize: Companhia de Moçambique, 1916.

Lopes, Gustavo de Bivar Pinto. *Respostas ao Questionário Etnográfico.* Beira: Imprensa da Companhia de Moçambique, 1928.

Moçambique—Documentário Trimestral.

Monclaro, Francisco. "Relaçaõ da Viagem que Fizeram os Padres da Companhia de Jesus com Francisco Barreto na Conquista de Monomotapa no Anno de 1569, Feita Pelo Padre Monclaro, da Mesma Companhia." *Boletim da Sociedade de Geografia de Lisboa.* 4a série, nos. 10–11 (1885): 492–508, 542–62.

Monumenta: Boletim da Comissão dos Monumentos Nacionais de Moçambique.

Moraes, Henrique Bravo de. "Informação Sobres os Rios de Cuama e Sofala." 1700–1703. In *Uma Informação Inédita Sobre Moçambique Setecentista.* Introduction and notes by Leopoldo da Rocha. Lisbon: Casa Portuguesa, 1975.

Revista de Manica e Sofala (1904–11).

Silva, João Julião da, Zacarias Herculano da Silva, and Guilherme Ezequiel da Silva. *Memórias de Sofala*. 1844. Introduction and notes by José Fialho Feliciano and Victor Hugo Nicolau. Lisbon: Comissão Nacional para as Comemorações dos Descobrimentos Portugueses, 1998.

Theal, George McCall, ed. *Records of South-Eastern Africa* [*RSEA*]. 1898–1903. A facsimile of the first edition printed by W. Clowes, London, for the government of the Cape Colony. 9 vols. Cape Town: C. Struik, 1964.

Secondary Sources

Alexander, Jocelyn. "The Local State in Post-War Mozambique: Political Practice and Ideas about Authority." *Africa* 67, no. 1 (1997): 1–26.

———. "Terra e Autoridade Política no Pós-Guerra em Moçambique: O Caso da Província de Manica." *Arquivo* 16 (October 1994): 3–94.

Alexander, Jocelyn, JoAnn McGregor, and Terence Ranger. *Violence and Memory: One Hundred Years in the "Dark Forests" of Matabeleland*. Portsmouth, NH: Heinemann, 2000.

Alpers, Edward. *Ivory and Slaves in East Central Africa*. London: Heinemann, 1975.

Anderson, Benedict. *Imagined Communities: Reflections on the Origin and Spread of Nationalism*. New York: Verso, 1991.

Antunes, Luis Frederico Dias. "A Actividade da Companhia de Comércio: Baneanes de Diu em Moçambique, 1686–1777." Tese de Mestrado, Universidade Nova de Lisboa, 1992.

Appiah, Kwame Anthony. "The Case for Contamination." *New York Times Magazine*, 1 January 2006, 30–37, 52.

———. *Cosmopolitanism: Ethics in a World of Strangers*. New York: W. W. Norton, 2006.

———. *In My Father's House: Africa in the Philosophy of Culture*. New York: Oxford University Press, 1992.

Atkinson, Ronald. "The Evolution of Ethnicity among the Acholi of Uganda: The Precolonial Phase." *Ethnohistory* 36, no. 1 (1989): 19–43.

———. *The Roots of Ethnicity: The Origins of the Acholi of Uganda before 1800*. Philadelphia: University of Pennsylvania Press, 1994.

Axelson, Eric. *Portuguese in South-East Africa, 1488–1600*. Johannesburg: C. Struik, 1973.

———. *Portuguese in South-East Africa, 1600–1700*. Johannesburg: Witwatersrand University Press, 1969.

Bannerman, James H. "Bvumba—Estado Pré-Colonial Shona em Manica, na Fronteira Entre Moçambique e o Zimbabwe." *Arquivo* 13 (April 1993): 81–98.

———. "The Extent and Independence of the Mutapa, Torwa, Manyika, Barwe, and Teve States." University of Zimbabwe Seminar Series, 20 July 1981.

———. "Hlengweni: The History of the Hlengwe of the Lower Save and Lundi Rivers from the Late Eighteenth Century to the Mid-Twentieth Century." *Zimbabwean History* 12 (1981): 1–45.

———. "Land Tenure in Central Mozambique: Past and Present." Paper prepared for MARRP, Chimoio, Mozambique, 1993.

———. "Notes and Questions Regarding the Archaeology, Language, and Ethno-History of Central Moçambique between the Zambezi and Save Rivers." Paper presented at the Tenth Pan African Archaeological Congress, Harare, Zimbabwe, June 1995.

———. "Towards a History of the Hlengwe People of the South of Rhodesia." *NADA* 9, no. 5 (1978): 483–96.

Baptista, Joaquim Renato. *Africa Oriental: Caminho de Ferro da Beira a Manica.* Lisbon: Imprensa Nacional, 1892.

Barker, Graeme. "Economic Models for the Manekweni *Zimbabwe*, Mozambique." *Azania* 13 (1978): 71–100.

Barth, Fredrik., ed. *Ethnic Groups and Boundaries.* Boston: Little, Brown, 1969.

Baxter, P. T. W., Jan Hultin, and Alessandro Triulzi. *Being and Becoming Oromo.* Lawrenceville, NJ: Red Sea Press, 1996.

Beach, D. N. "Documents and African Society on the Zimbabwe Plateau before 1890." *Paideuma* 33 (1987): 129–45.

———. "Fontes Para a História de Manica e Sofala no Arquivo Nacional do Zimbabwe." *Arquivo* 6 (October 1989): 347–67.

———. "Mutapa: An Alternative Approach to the Study of Titles in Shona History." *Rhodesian History* 6 (1975): 97–99.

———. "The Mutapa Dynasty: A Comparison of Documentary and Traditional Evidence." *History in Africa* 3 (1976): 1–17.

———. *The Shona and Their Neighbours.* Oxford: Blackwell, 1994.

———. *The Shona and Zimbabwe, 900–1850: An Outline of Shona History.* Gweru, Zimbabwe: Mambo Press, 1980.

———. "The Zimbabwe Plateau and Its Peoples." In *History of Central Africa*, vol. 1. Edited by David Birmingham and Phyllis M. Martin, 245–77. New York: Longman, 1983.

———. *A Zimbabwean Past.* Gweru, Zimbabwe: Mambo Press, 1994.

Bhila, H. H. K. *Trade and Politics in a Shona Kingdom.* Harlow, Essex, UK: Longman, 1982.

———. "Trade and the Survival of an African Polity: The External Relations of Manyika from the Sixteenth to the Early Nineteenth Century." *Rhodesian History* 8 (1976): 1–11.

Birmingham, David, and Phyllis M. Martin, eds. *History of Central Africa.* 2 vols. New York: Longman, 1983.

———. *History of Central Africa: The Contemporary Years since 1960.* New York: Longman, 1998.

Bonnell, Victoria E., and Lynn Hunt, eds. *Beyond the Cultural Turn: New Directions in the Study of Society and Culture.* Berkeley: University of California Press, 1999.

Borland, C. H. "Conflicting Methodologies of Shona Dialect Classification." *South African Journal of African Languages* 4, no. 1 (1983): 1–19.

———. "Internal Relationships in Southern Bantu." *South African Journal of African Languages* 6, no. 4 (1986): 139–41.

Bourdillon, M. F. C. *The Shona Peoples: An Ethnography of the Contemporary Shona, with Special Reference to Their Religion.* Gweru, Zimbabwe: Mambo Press, 1976.

Braathen, Einar, Morten Boas, and Gjermund Saether, eds. *Ethnicity Kills? The Politics of War, Peace, and Ethnicity in Subsaharan Africa.* New York: St. Martin's Press, 2000.

Braudel, Fernand. *A History of Civilizations.* New York: A. Lane, 1994.

———. *The Mediterranean and the Mediterranean World in the Age of Philip II.* New York: Harper and Row, 1972.

Braudel, Fernand. *On History*. Chicago: University of Chicago Press, 1980.

Bravman, Bill. *Making Ethnic Ways: Communities and Their Transformations in Taita, Kenya, 1800–1950*. Portsmouth, NH: Heinemann, 1998.

Bryant, Alfred T. *Olden Times in Zululand and Natal, Concerning Earlier Political History of the Eastern-Nguni Clans*. London: Longmans, Green and Co., 1929.

Cahen, Michel. *Mozambique: La Révolution Implosée: Études sur 12 Ans d'Indépendance, 1975–1987*. Paris: L'Harmattan, 1987.

————. "Nationalism and Ethnicities: Lessons from Mozambique." In *Ethnicity Kills? The Politics of War, Peace, and Ethnicity in Subsaharan Africa*. Edited by Einar Braathen et al., 163–87. New York: St. Martin's Press, 2000.

————. *Os Outros: Um Historiador em Moçambique, 1994*. Basel: P. Schlettwein, 2004.

Chanaiwa, David. "Politics and Long-Distance Trade in the Mwene Mutapa Empire during the Sixteenth Century." *International Journal of African Historical Studies* 5, no. 3 (1972): 424–35.

Chimhundu, Herbert. "Early Missionaries and the Ethnolinguistic Factor during the 'Invention of Tribalism' in Zimbabwe." *Journal of African History* 33 (1992): 87–109.

Chingono, Mark. "Mulheres, Guerra e Transformaçao na Província de Manica: Uma Herança Ambígua." *Arquivo* 16 (October 1994): 95–134.

Cobbing, Julian. "The Mfecane as Alibi: Thoughts on Dithakong and Mbolompo." *Journal of African History* 29 (1988): 487–519.

Coelho, Trinidade. *Dezoito Annos em Africa: Notas e Documentos para a Biografia do Conselheiro José d'Almeida*. Lisbon: Typ. de A. de Mendonça, 1898.

Cohen, Brett. " 'Something like a Blowing Wind': African Conspiracy and Coordination of Resistance to Colonial Rule in South Africa, 1876–1882." PhD diss., Michigan State University, 2000.

Cohen, David William. "The Undefining of Oral Tradition." *Ethnohistory* 36, no. 1 (Winter 1989): 9–18.

Comaroff, John L. "Ethnicity, Nationalism, and the Politics of Difference in an Age of Revolution." In *The Politics of Difference: Ethnic Premises in a World of Power*. Edited by Edwin N. Wilmsen and Patrick McAllister, 162–83. Chicago: University of Chicago Press, 1996.

Comaroff, John L., and Jean Comaroff. *Ethnography and the Historical Imagination*. Boulder: Westview Press, 1992.

————. *Of Revelation and Revolution*. Vol. 1, *Christianity, Colonialism, and Consciousness in South Africa*. Chicago: University of Chicago Press, 1991.

Connah, Graham. *African Civilizations: An Archaeological Perspective*. Cambridge: Cambridge University Press, 2001.

Cooper, Frederick. *Colonialism in Question: Theory, Knowledge, History*. With one chapter coauthored by Rogers Brubaker. Berkeley: University of California Press, 2005.

Dale, Desmond. *Duramazwi: A Shona-English Dictionary*. Gweru, Zimbabwe: Mambo Press, 1981.

Davison, Jean. *Gender, Lineage, and Ethnicity in Southern Africa*. Boulder: Westview Press, 1997.

DeCorse, Christopher R., and Gerard L. Chouin. "Trouble with Siblings: Archaeological and Historical Interpretation of the West African Past." In *Sources and Methods in African History: Spoken, Written, Unearthed*. Edited by Toyin Falola and Christian Jennings, 7–15. Rochester, NY: University of Rochester Press, 2003.

Denzin, Norman K., and Yvonna S. Lincoln, eds. *Handbook of Qualitative Research*. London: Sage Publications, 1994.

Devereux, Stephen, and John Hoddinott, eds. *Fieldwork in Developing Countries*. Boulder: Lynne Rienner, 1993.

Dhliwayo, Kholisile David. "External Traders in the Hinterland of Sofala, 1810–1889." Master's thesis, School of Oriental and African Studies, University of London, 1977.

Doke, Clement M. *Bantu: Modern Grammatical, Phonetical, and Lexicographic Studies since 1860*. London: Published for International African Institute by Dawsons of Pall Mall, 1967.

———. *A Comparative Study in Shona Phonetics*. Johannesburg: University of the Witwatersrand Press, 1931.

———. *Report on the Unification of the Shona Dialects*. Hertford, UK: Printed for the Government of Southern Rhodesia by S. Austin and Sons, 1931.

Dube, R. "Family History: A Case Study from Southern Zimbabwe." History Department BA Honours thesis, University of Zimbabwe, 1989.

Earthy, E. Dora. *Valenge Women: The Social and Economic Life of Valenge Women of Portuguese East Africa, an Ethnographic Study*. London: Frank Cass, 1933.

Ehret, Christopher. "Language Change and the Material Correlates of Language and Ethnic Shift." *Antiquity* 62 (1988): 564–74.

Ehret, Christopher, and Margaret Kinsman. "Shona Dialect Classification and Its Implications for Iron Age History in Southern Africa." *International Journal of African Historical Studies* 14, no. 3 (1981): 401–43.

Ehret, Christopher, and Merrick Posnansky. *The Archaeological and Linguistic Reconstruction of African History*. Berkeley: University of California Press, 1982.

Eldredge, Elizabeth. "Migration, Conflict, and Leadership in Early Nineteenth-Century South Africa: The Case of Matiwane." In *Paths toward the Past: African Historical Essays in Honor of Jan Vansina*. Edited by Robert W. Harms, Joseph C. Miller, David S. Newbury and Michele D. Wagner, 39–75. Atlanta: African Studies Association Press, 1994.

———. "Sources of Conflict in Southern Africa, ca. 1800–1830: The 'Mfecane' Reconsidered," *Journal of African History* 31, no. 1 (1992): 1–35.

———. *A South African Kingdom: The Pursuit of Security in Nineteenth-Century Lesotho*. Cambridge: Cambridge University Press, 1993.

———. "Women in Production: The Economic Role of Women in Nineteenth-Century Lesotho." *Signs: Journal of Women in Culture and Development* 16, no. 4 (1991): 707–31.

Elkiss, T. H. *The Quest for an African Eldorado: Sofala, Southern Zambezia, and the Portuguese, 1500–1865*. Waltham, MA: Crossroads Press, 1981.

Ellert, Henrik. *The Material Culture of Zimbabwe*. Harare: Longman, 1984.

Emerson, Robert M., Rachel I. Fretz, and Linda L. Shaw. *Writing Ethnographic Fieldnotes*. Chicago: University of Chicago Press, 1995.

Feierman, Steven, and John M. Janzen, eds. *The Social Basis of Health and Healing in Africa*. Berkeley: University of California Press, 1992.

Feliciano, José Fialho, and Victor Hugo Nicolau. Introduction and Notes to *Memórias de Sofala* (1844), by João Julião da Silva, Zacarias Herculano da Silva, and Guilherme Ezequiel da Silva. Lisbon: Comissão Nacional para as Comemorações dos Descobrimentos Portugueses, 1998.

Firmino, Gregório. *A "Questão Linguística" na África Pós-Colonial: O Caso do Português e das Línguas Autóctones em Moçambique.* Maputo: Promédia, 2002.

Garlake, Peter. "Excavation of a *Zimbabwe* in Mozambique." *Antiquity* 50, no. 198 (June 1976): 146–48.

———. "An Investigation of Manekweni, Mozambique." *Azania* 11 (1976): 25–47.

Geffray, Christian. *A Causa das Armas: Antropologia da Guerra Contemporânea em Moçambique.* Porto: Edições Afrontamento, 1991.

Gelfand, Michael. *The Genuine Shona: Survival Values of an African Culture.* Gweru, Zimbabwe: Mambo Press, 1973.

Gengenbach, Heidi. *Binding Memories: Women as Makers and Tellers of History in Magude, Mozambique.* Chichester, New York: Columbia University Press, 2005, http://www.gutenberg-e.org.

———. "Naming the Past in a 'Scattered' Land: Memory and the Power of Women's Naming Practices in Southern Mozambique." *International Journal of African Historical Studies* 33 (2000): 523–42.

———. "Where Women Make History: Pots, Stories, Tattoos, and Other Gendered Accounts of Community and Change in Magude District, Mozambique, c. 1800 to the Present." PhD diss., University of Minnesota, 1999.

Gilbert, Erik, and Jonathan T. Reynolds. *Africa in World History: From Prehistory to the Present.* Upper Saddle River, NJ: Pearson Educational, 2004.

Gordon Jr., Raymond G., ed. *Ethnologue: Languages of the World.* 15th ed. Dallas: SIL International, 2005; also available at http://www.ethnologue.com.

Gray, Richard, and David Birmingham, eds. *Pre-Colonial African Trade: Essays on Trade in Central and Eastern Africa before 1900.* New York: Oxford University Press, 1970.

Greene, Sandra. *Gender, Ethnicity, and Social Change on the Upper Slave Coast: A History of the Anlo-Ewe.* Portsmouth, NH: Heinemann, 1996.

Guy, Jeff. "Analysing Pre-Capitalist Societies in Southern Africa." *Journal of Southern African Studies* 14, no. 1 (October 1987): 18–37.

Hall, Margaret, and Tom Young. *Confronting Leviathan: Mozambique since Independence.* Athens: Ohio University Press, 1997.

Hall, Martin. *The Changing Past: Farmers, Kings, and Traders in Southern Africa, 200–1860.* Cape Town: David Philip, 1987.

Hamilton, Carolyn. " 'The Character and Objects of Chaka': A Reconsideration of the Making of Shaka as 'Mfecane' Motor." *Journal of African History* 33 (1992): 37–63.

———. "Ideology and Oral Traditions: Listening to the Voices from Below." *History in Africa* 14 (1987): 67–86.

———, ed. *The Mfecane Aftermath.* Johannesburg: Witwatersrand University Press, 1996.

———. *Terrific Majesty: The Powers of Shaka Zulu and the Limits of Historical Invention.* Cambridge: Harvard University Press, 1998.

Hamilton, Carolyn, and John Wright. "The Making of the amaLala: Ethnicity, Ideology, and Relations of Subordination in a Precolonial Context." *South African Historical Journal* 22 (November 1990): 3–23.

Hamutyinei, Mordikai A., and Albert B. Plangger, *Tsumo-Shumo: Shona Proverbial Lore and Wisdom.* Gweru, Zimbabwe: Mambo Press, 1987.

Hannan, M. *Standard Shona Dictionary.* Rev. ed. with addendum. Harare: College Press in conjunction with the Literature Bureau, 1984.

Harries, Patrick. "The Anthropologist as Historian and Liberal: H. A. Junod and the Thonga." *Journal of Southern African Studies* 8, no. 1 (1981): 37–50.

Harries, Patrick. "The Roots of Ethnicity: Discourse and the Politics of Language Construction in South-East Africa." *African Affairs* 346 (1988): 25–52.

———. "Slavery, Social Incorporation, and Surplus Extraction: The Nature of Free and Unfree Labour in South-East Africa." *Journal of African History* 22 (1981): 309–30.

———. *Work, Culture, and Identity: Migrant Laborers in Mozambique and South Africa, c. 1860–1910.* Portsmouth, NH: Heinemann, 1994.

Henriksen, Thomas H. *Mozambique: A History.* London: Rex Collings, 1978.

Hobsbawm, Eric, and Terence Ranger, eds. *The Invention of Tradition.* Cambridge: Cambridge University Press, 1983.

Hodder, Ian. "The Interpretation of Documents and Material Culture." In *Handbook of Qualitative Research.* Edited by Norman K. Denzin and Yvonna S. Lincoln, 393–402. London: Sage Publications, 1994.

———. *Reading the Past.* Cambridge: Cambridge University Press, 1991.

———, ed. *Symbolic and Structural Archaeology.* Cambridge: Cambridge University Press, 1982.

Holleman, J. F. "Accommodating the Spirit amongst Some North-Eastern Shona Tribes." *Rhodes-Livingstone Paper Number 22.* New York, 1953.

Horowitz, Donald. *Ethnic Groups in Conflict.* Berkeley: University of California Press, 1985.

Hughes, David McDermott. "Disputed Territory and Dependent People: Rethinking Land Tenure on the Zimbabwe-Mozambique Border." Paper Presented to the International Association for the Study of Common Property Meetings. Berkeley, 5–8 June 1996.

———. "Frontier Dynamics: Struggles for Land and Clients on the Zimbabwe-Mozambique Border." PhD diss., University of California, Berkeley, 1999.

———. "Mozambican Refugees and the Politics of Vulnerability." Paper presented to the American Anthropological Association annual meetings, Washington DC, 19–23 November 1997.

———. "When Parks Encroach upon People: Expanding National Parks in the Rusitu Valley, Zimbabwe." *Cultural Survival Quarterly* 20, no. 1 (1996): 36–40.

Isaacman, Allen. "Madzi-Manga, Mhondoro, and the Use of Oral Traditions: A Chapter in Barue Religious and Political History." *Journal of African History* 14, no. 3 (1973): 395–409.

———. *Mozambique: The Africanization of a European Institution.* Madison: University of Wisconsin Press, 1972.

———. "The Origin, Formation, and Early History of the Chikunda of South Central Africa." *Journal of African History* 13, no. 3 (1972): 443–61.

Isaacman, Allen, and Barbara Isaacman. *Mozambique: From Colonialism to Revolution.* Boulder: Westview Press, 1983.

———. *Slavery and Beyond: The Making of Men and Chikunda Ethnic Identities in the Unstable World of South-Central Africa, 1750–1920.* Portsmouth, NH: Heinemann, 2004.

———. *The Tradition of Resistance: The Zambezi Valley, 1850–1921.* London: Heinemann Educational, 1976.

Jackson, Robert H., and Gregory Maddox. "The Creation of Identity: Colonial Society in Bolivia and Tanzania." *Comparative Studies in Society and History* 35, no. 2 (1993): 263–84.

Jeater, Diana. *Marriage, Perversion, and Power: The Construction of Moral Discourse in Southern Rhodesia, 1894–1930.* Oxford: Clarendon Press, 1993.

José, Alexandrino, and Paula Maria G. Meneses, eds. *Moçambique: 16 Anos de Historiografia: Focos, Problemas, Metodologias, Desadios para a Década de 90.* Maputo: Colecção Painel Moçambicano, 1991.

Junod, Henri Philippe. "A Contribution to the Study of Ndau Demography, Totemism, and History." *Bantu Studies* 8, no. 1 (March 1934): 17–37.

———. "Notes on the Ethnological Situation in Portuguese East Africa on the South of the Zambezi." *Bantu Studies* 10 (1936): 293–313.

———. *Os Indigenas de Moçambique no Século XVI e Começo do XVII.* Lourenço Marques, Mozambique: Imprensa Nacional, 1939.

Klumpp, Donna, and Corinne Kratz. "Aesthetics, Expertise, and Ethnicity: Okiek and Maasai Perspectives on Personal Ornament." In *Being Maasai: Ethnicity and Identity in East Africa.* Edited by Thomas Spear and Richard Waller, 195–221. Athens: Ohio University Press, 1993.

Kriger, Colleen. "Iron Working in Nineteenth-Century Central Africa." PhD diss., York University, 1992.

———. *Pride of Men: Ironworking in 19th-Century West Central Africa.* Portsmouth, NH: Heinemann, 1999.

Lan, David. *Guns and Rain: Guerrillas and Spirit Mediums in Zimbabwe.* London: James Currey, 1985.

Larson, Pier. *History and Memory in the Age of Enslavement: Becoming Merina in Highland Madagascar, 1770–1822.* Portsmouth, NH: Heinemann, 2000.

Liesegang, Gerhard. "Archaeological Sites on the Bay of Sofala." *Azania* 7 (1972): 147–59.

———. "Aspects of Gaza Nguni History, 1821–1897." *Rhodesian History* 6 (1975): 1–14.

———. Introduction and notes to *Reposta das Questoens sobre os Cafres* (1796), by Carlos José dos Reis e Gama. Lisbon: Junta de Investigações do Ultramar, 1966.

———. "Nguni Migrations between Delagoa Bay and the Zambezi, 1821–1839." *African Historical Studies* 3, no. 2 (1970): 317–37.

———. "Sofala, Beira e a sua Zona." *Arquivo* 6 (October 1989): 21–64.

———. "Territorialidades Sociais e Identidades com Referencia a Moçambique." Paper presented to the Open Course, Para Uma Sociologia dos Processos Identitarios em Moçambique, Universidade Eduardo Mondlane, Maputo, 27 March 1998.

Lobato, Manuel. Introduction to *Etiópia Oriental e Vária História de Cousas Notáveis do Oriente* (1609), by João dos Santos. Lisbon: Comissão Nacional para as Comemorações dos Descobrimentos Portugueses, 1999.

Lowe, Chris. "Talking about 'Tribe': Moving from Stereotypes to Analysis." *Africa Action Background Paper.* November 1997, available at http://www.africaaction.org/bp/ethall.htm.

Lubkemann, Stephen C. "Situating Wartime Migration in Central Mozambique: Gendered Social Struggle and the Transnationalization of Polygyny." PhD diss., Brown University, 2000.

MacGonagle, Elizabeth. "Mightier than the Sword: The Portuguese Pen in Ndau History." *History in Africa* 28 (2001): 169–86.

———. "A Mixed Pot: History and Identity in the Ndau Region of Mozambique and Zimbabwe, 1500–1900." PhD diss., Michigan State University, 2002.

Machado, Pedro Alberto da Silva Rupino. "Gujarati Indian Merchant Networks in Mozambique, 1777–c. 1830." PhD diss., School of Oriental and African Studies, University of London, 2005.

Mamdani, Mahmood. *Citizen and Subject: Contemporary Africa and the Legacy of Late Colonialism*. Princeton: Princeton University Press, 1996.

——. *When Victims Become Killers: Colonialism, Nativism, and the Genocide in Rwanda*. Princeton: Princeton University Press, 2001.

Mhlanga, Wilson. "The Story of Ngwaqazi: The History of the Amatshangana." *NADA* 25 (1948): 70–73.

Miller, Daniel, and Christopher Tilley. *Ideology, Power, and Prehistory*. Cambridge: Cambridge University Press, 1984.

Mkanganwi, K. G. "The Relationships of Coastal Ndau to the Shona Dialects of the Interior." *African Studies* 21 (1972): 11–37.

Moore, Henrietta L. *Space, Text, and Gender: An Anthropological Study of the Marakwet of Kenya*. Cambridge: Cambridge University Press, 1986.

Moore, Sally Falk. *Anthropology and Africa: Changing Perspectives on a Changing Scene*. Charlottesville: University Press of Virginia, 1994.

Morais, João M. F. "Fontes Historiograficas e Arqueologia em Moçambique." *Leba* (Lisbon) 7 (1992): 301–17.

Moura, Armando Reis. "Sobre os Vandaus (Sofala-Moçambique)." In *Moçambique— Aspectos da Cultura Material*. Separata de C. E. A. Coimbra, Portugal: Instituto de Antropologia, Universidade de Coimbra, 1986.

Mtetwa, Andrew H. "A History of Uteve under the Mwene Mutapa Rulers, 1480–1834: A Re-evaluation." PhD diss., Northwestern University, 1984.

Mtetwa, Richard M. G. "The 'Political' and Economic History of the Duma People of South-Eastern Rhodesia from the Early Eighteenth Century to 1945." PhD diss., University of Rhodesia, 1976.

Mudenge, S. I. G. *A Political History of Munhumutapa, c. 1400–1902*. Harare: Zimbabwe Publishing House, 1988.

——. "Role of Trade in the Rozvi Empire: A Re-appraisal." *Journal of African History* 15 (1974): 373–91.

Needham, D. E., E. K. Mashingaidze, and N. Bhebe. *From Iron Age to Independence: A History of Central Africa*. Harare: Longman, 1984.

Neil-Tomlinson, Barry. "The Mozambique Chartered Company, 1892–1910." PhD diss., School of Oriental and African Studies, University of London, 1980.

Newbury, David. *Kings and Clans: Ijwi Island and the Lake Kivu Rift, 1780–1840*. Madison: University of Wisconsin Press, 1991.

Newitt, Malyn. *A History of Mozambique*. Bloomington: Indiana University Press, 1995.

——. *Portuguese Settlement on the Zambezi: Exploration, Land Tenure, and Colonial Rule in East Africa*. New York: Africana Publishing Company, 1973.

Niehaus, Isak. "Ethnicity and the Boundaries of Belonging: Reconfiguring Shangaan Identity in the South African Lowveld." *African Affairs* 101 (2002): 557–83.

Nnoli, Okwudiba, ed. *Ethnic Conflicts in Africa*. Dakar, Senegal: CODESRIA, 1998.

Nora, Pierre. "Between Memory and History: Les Lieux de Memoire." *Representations* 26 (Spring 1989): 7–24.

Nordstrom, Carolyn. *A Different Kind of War Story.* Philadelphia: University of Pennsylvania Press, 1997.

Northrup, David. *Africa's Discovery of Europe, 1450–1850.* New York: Oxford University Press, 2002.

Oliveira, Octávio Roza de. *Amuralhados da Cultura Zimbáuè-Monomotapa de Manica e Sofala.* Lourenço Marques: Artes Gráficas, 1963.

———. "Zimbáuès de Moçambique: Proto-História Africana." *Monumenta: Boletim da Commissão dos Monumentos Nacionais de Moçambique* 9 (1973): 31–64.

Omer-Cooper, J. D. "Has the Mfecane a Future? A Response to the Cobbing Critique." *Journal of Southern African Studies* 19, no. 2 (June 1993): 273–94.

———. *The Zulu Aftermath.* London: Longmans, 1966.

Peires, Jeff. "Paradigm Deleted: The Materialist Interpretation of the Mfecane." *Journal of Southern African Studies* 19, no. 2 (June 1993): 295–313.

Pélissier, René. "Exploitation du Facteur Ethnique au Mozambique pendant la Conquàte Coloniale." In *Les Ethnies Ont une Histoire.* Edited by Jean-Pierre Chrétien and Gérard Prunier, 247–57. Paris: Karthala, 1989.

———. *História de Moçambique: Formação e Oposição, 1854–1918.* 2 vols. Lisbon: Editorial Estampa, 1987–88.

———. *Naissance du Mozambique: Résistance et Révoltes Anticoloniales, 1854–1918.* 2 vols. Orgeval, France: Pélissier, 1984.

Phimister, I. R. "Pre-Colonial Gold Mining in Southern Zambezia: A Reassessment." *African Social Research* 21 (June 1976): 1–30.

Pikirayi, Innocent. *The Archaeological Identity of the Mutapa State: Towards an Historical Archaeology of Northern Zimbabwe.* Uppsala, Sweden: Studies in African Archaeology 6, Department of Archaeology, Uppsala University, 1993.

———. "The Traditions of Nyanga." University of Zimbabwe History Department, unpublished MA paper, 1986.

Portelli, Alessandro. *The Death of Luigi Trastulli, and Other Stories: Form and Meaning in Oral History.* Albany: State University of New York Press, 1991.

Pwiti, G. "Trade and Economies in Southern Africa: The Archaeological Evidence." *Zambezia* 18, no. 2 (1991): 119–29.

Randles, W. G. L. *L'empire du Monomotapa du XVe au XIXe siècle.* Paris: Mouton, 1975.

———. *The Empire of Monomotapa: From the Fifteenth to the Nineteenth Century.* Translated by R. S. Roberts. Gweru, Zimbabwe: Mambo Press, 1979.

Ranger, Terence. *The Invention of Tribalism in Zimbabwe.* Gweru, Zimbabwe: Mambo Press, 1985.

———. "Missionaries, Migrants and the Manyika: The Invention of Ethnicity in Zimbabwe." In *The Creation of Tribalism in Southern Africa.* Edited by Leroy Vail, 118–50. Berkeley: University of California Press, 1989.

Rennie, John Keith. "Christianity, Colonialism, and the Origins of Nationalism among the Ndau of Southern Rhodesia, 1890–1935." PhD diss., Northwestern University, 1973.

———. "From Zimbabwe to a Colonial Chieftaincy: Four Transformations of the Musikavanhu Territorial Cult in Rhodesia." In *Guardians of the Land.* Edited by J. M. Schoffeleers, 257–85. Gweru, Zimbabwe: Mambo Press, 1978.

———. "Ideology and State Formation: Political and Communal Ideologies among the South-Eastern Shona, 1500–1890." In *State Formation in Eastern Africa.* Edited by Ahmed Idho Salim, 162–94. Nairobi: Heinemann Educational, 1984.

Rita-Ferreira, António. *Agrupamento e Caracterização Étnica dos Indígenas de Moçambique.* Lisbon: Junta de Investigações do Ultramar, 1958.

————. *Bibliografia Etnológica de Moçambique.* Lisbon: Junta de Investigações do Ultramar, 1961.

————. "The Ethno-History and the Ethnic Grouping of the Peoples of Moçambique." *South African Journal of African Affairs* 3, no. 1 (1973): 56–76.

————. *Fixação Portuguesa e História Pré-Colonial de Moçambique.* Lisbon: Instituto de Investigação Científica Tropical/Junta de Investigações Científicas do Ultramar, 1982.

————. *Povos de Moçambique: História e Cultura.* Porto: Afrontamento, 1975.

Rodney, Walter. "The Year 1895 in Southern Mozambique: African Resistance to the Imposition of European Colonial Rule." *Journal of the Historical Society of Nigeria* 5 (1971): 509–36.

Roque, Ana Cristina Ribeiro Marques. "A Costa Oriental da Africa na Primeira Metade do Seculo XVI Segundo as Fontes Portuguesas da Epoca." Tese de Mestrado, Universidade Nova de Lisboa, 1994.

Schmidt, Elizabeth. *Peasants, Traders, and Wives: Shona Women in the History of Zimbabwe, 1870–1939.* Portsmouth, NH: Heinemann, 1992.

Serra, Carlos, ed. *Racismo, Etnicidade e Poder: Um Estudo em Cinco Cidades de Moçambique.* Maputo: Universidade Eduardo Mondlane, 2000.

Sinclair, Paul J. J. "Archaeology in Eastern Africa: An Overview of Current Chronological Issues." *Journal of African History* 32 (1991): 179–219.

————. "Chibuene—an Early Trading Site in Southern Mozambique." *Paideuma* 28 (1982): 149–64.

————. *Space, Time, and Social Formation: A Territorial Approach to the Archaeology and Anthropology of Zimbabwe and Mozambique, c. 0–1700 A.D.* Uppsala: Department of Archaeology, Uppsala University, 1987.

Sinclair, Paul J. J., ed. *Analyses of Slag, Iron, Ceramics, and Animal Bones from Excavations in Mozambique.* Maputo: Universidade Eduardo Mondlane, 1988.

Sithole, Masipula. "Ethnicity and Democratization in Zimbabwe: From Confrontation to Accommodation." In *Ethnic Conflict and Democratization in Africa.* Edited by Harvey Glickman, 121–60. Atlanta: African Studies Association Press, 1995.

Smith, Alan K. "The Indian Ocean Zone." In *History of Central Africa*, vol. 1. Edited by David Birmingham and Phyllis M. Martin, 205–44. New York: Longman, 1983.

————. "The Peoples of Southern Mozambique: An Historical Survey." *Journal of African History* 15, no. 4 (1973): 565–80.

Smith, Anthony D. *The Ethnic Revival.* New York: Cambridge University Press, 1981.

Sopa, António. "A Identidade em Historia." Paper presented to the Open Course, Para Uma Sociologia dos Processos Identitarios em Moçambique, Universidade Eduardo Mondlane, Maputo, 20 March 1998.

Souto, Amelia Neves de. *Guia Bibliográfico.* Maputo: Centro de Estudos Africanos, Universidade Eduardo Mondlane, 1996.

Spear, Thomas, and Richard Waller, eds. *Being Maasai: Ethnicity and Identity in East Africa.* Athens: Ohio University Press, 1993.

Stack, John, ed. *The Primordial Challenge: Ethnicity in the Contemporary World.* Westport, CT: Greenwood Press, 1986.

Taussig, Michael. *Shamanism, Colonialism, and the Wild Man: A Study in Terror and Healing.* Chicago: University of Chicago Press, 1987.

Thompson, Leonard, ed. *African Societies in Southern Africa.* New York: Praeger, 1969.

Tilley, Christopher, ed. *Reading Material Culture.* Oxford: Blackwell, 1990.

Tonkin, Elizabeth, Maryon McDonald, and Malcolm Chapman, eds. *History and Ethnicity.* New York: Routledge, 1989.

UNESCO. "World Culture Report 2000: Cultural Diversity, Conflict, and Pluralism." http://www.unesco.org/culture/worldreport/. Also published as *Cultural Diversity, Conflict, and Pluralism* by Arizpe S. Lourdes and Ann-Belinda Preis. Paris: UNESCO, 2000.

United Nations. "Culture: UNESCO Wants World Heritage to Include Tradition." UN Wire, 21 November 2000. Posted on the H-Net discussion list on Research in African Primary Sources, http://www.h-net.org/~afrsrch/.

Vail, Leroy, ed. *The Creation of Tribalism in Southern Africa.* Berkeley: University of California Press, 1989.

Vansina, Jan. "Historians, Are Archeologists Your Siblings?" *History in Africa* 22 (1995): 369–408.

———. *Living with Africa.* Madison: University of Wisconsin Press, 1994.

———. *Paths in the Rainforests: Toward a Political Tradition in Equatorial Africa.* Madison: University of Wisconsin Press, 1990.

Vijfhuizen, Carin. " 'The People You Live With': Gender Identities and Social Practices, Beliefs, and Power in the Livelihoods of Ndau Women and Men in a Village with an Irrigation Scheme in Zimbabwe." PhD diss., Wageningen Agricultural University, Netherlands, 1998.

Vines, Alex. *Renamo: Terrorism in Mozambique.* Bloomington: Indiana University Press, 1991.

Webster, David. "*Abafazi Bathonga Bafihlakala*: Ethnicity and Gender in a KwaZulu Border Community." In *Tradition and Transition in Southern Africa: Festschrift for Philip and Iona Meyer.* Edited by Andrew D. Spiegel and Patrick A. McAllister, 243–71. New Brunswick, NJ: Transaction Publishers, 1991.

Werbner, Richard. *Tears of the Dead: The Social Biography of an African Family.* Washington, DC: Smithsonian Institution Press, 1991.

Werbner, Richard, and Terence Ranger, eds. *Postcolonial Identities in Africa.* Atlantic Highlands, NJ: Zed Books, 1996.

Wheeler, Douglas. "Gungunyane the Negotiator: A Study in African Diplomacy." *Journal of African History* 9, no. 4 (1968): 585–602.

Wieschoff, H. A. *The Zimbabwe-Monomotapa Culture in Southeast Africa.* Menasha, WI: George Banta, 1941.

Wilmsen, Edwin N., and Patrick McAllister, eds. *The Politics of Difference: Ethnic Premises in a World of Power.* Chicago: University of Chicago Press, 1996.

Wilson, Ken. "Cults of Violence and Counter-Violence in Mozambique." *Journal of Southern African Studies* 18, no. 3 (1992): 527–83.

Wilson, Monica, and Leonard Thompson. *A History of South Africa to 1870.* Boulder: Westview Press, 1983.

Wolf, Eric. *Europe and the People without History.* Berkeley: University of California Press, 1997.

Wright, Donald. *The World and a Very Small Place in Africa: A History of Globalization in Niumi, The Gambia.* Armonk, NY: M. E. Sharpe, 2004.

Wright, John. "Notes on the Politics of Being 'Zulu,' 1820–1920." Paper presented at the Conference on Ethnicity, Society, and Conflict in Natal, University of Natal, Pietermaritzburg, South Africa, 14–16 September 1992.

Wright, John. "Political Mythology and the Making of Natal's Mfecane." *Canadian Journal of African Studies* 23, no. 2 (1989): 272–91.

Young, Crawford. "Nationalism, Ethnicity, and Class in Africa: A Retrospective." *Cahiers d'Études Africaines* 103 (1986): 421–95.

Field Interviews, 1998–99

Manica Province, Mozambique

Agostinho, Amelia. Dombe, Sede, Distrito de Sussundenga, 7 July 1998.

Alvar, Balamiera. Rotanda, Bairro Sede, Distrito de Sussundenga, 2 July 1998.

Ana, (Mbuya), Selinda, (Mbuya), and Lucia (Mbuya). Chitobe, Sede, Distrito de Machaze, 19 July 1998.

Basopo, Eliza. Espungabera, Sede, Distrito de Mossurize, 27 July 1998.

Cecilia, (Mbuya), and Goshwe Sitole. Espungabera, Sede, Distrito de Mossurize, 27 July 1998.

Chingera, (Mbuya). Guezane, Distrito de Machaze, 17 July 1998.

Chiquerwa, Wilson. Dacata, Distrito de Mossurize, 28 July 1998.

Chisanati, Timo Ngesi. Dombe Sede, Distrito de Sussundenga, 9 July 1998.

Dubuya, Manuel. Dacata, Distrito de Mossurize, 28 July 1998.

Gama, Emilia. Bairro Sede, Rotanda, Distrito de Sussundenga, 4 July 1998.

Gangenjani, Semu. Sussundenga, Sede, Distrito de Sussundenga, 4 August 1998.

Group Interview with Nyanga Mbiri Mupunga, Mangiza Munzanga, James Dundo, Albino Joni, Fazenda Soni, Makinase Mupinde, et al. Mupunga, Distrito de Sussundenga, 10 July 1998.

Group Interview with Regulo Mateus Faduku et al., Chipambuleque, Distrito de Machaze, 15 July 1998.

Gundana, Joshua. Dombe, Sede, Distrito de Sussundenga, 7 July 1998.

Gwanga, (Mbuya). Guezane, Distrito de Machaze, 17 July 1998.

Inhasi, (Mbuya). Chimunkono, Distrito de Sussundenga, 8 July 1998.

João, Rosinda, and Musota Fifteen. Sussundenga, Sede, Distrito de Sussundenga, 4 August 1998.

Kamba, Viola. Sussundenga, Sede, Distrito de Sussundenga, 4 August 1998.

Kaniera, Robert. Musambudzi, Rotanda, Distrito de Sussundenga, 3 July 1998.

Kumbi, Josia Matavera. Tuca-Tuca, Distrito de Machaze, 20 July 1998.

Laisse, Seven, and Timothy Mataca (guia). Guezane, Distrito de Machaze, 16 July 1998.

Lovemore, Wanda. Rotanda, Bairro Sede, Distrito de Sussundenga, 2 July 1998.

Machawa, Mateus. Chitobe, sede, Distrito de Machaze, 19 July 1998.

Mafuia, Luis Nhica. Chiurairue, Distrito de Mossurize, 29 July 1998.

Mafuria, Timothy Moso Sitole. Chiurairue, Distrito de Mossurize, 29 July 1998.

Magude, Nelson Paulo Paweta. Rotanda, Bairro Sede, Distrito de Sussundenga, 2 July 1998.

Magumisse, Jossia and July Sofakai (guia). Dombe, Sede, Distrito de Sussundenga, 7 July 1998.

Mahamu, Murivana. Dacata, Distrito de Mossurize, 28 July 1998.

Makadui, Chako. Guezane, Distrito de Machaze, 17 July 1998.

Maki, Mutasi. Sussundenga, Sede, Distrito de Sussundenga, 4 August 1998.

Makosi, Pedro. Tuca-Tuca, Distrito de Machaze, 20 July 1998.

Marokana, Mixon. Chiurairue, Distrito de Mossurize, 29 July 1998.

Mashanja, (Mbuya), and Phillipe Sunguro. Rotanda, Bairro Sede, Distrito de Sussundenga, 2 July 1998.

Mashawo, Mazete Mixon. Dacata, Distrito de Mossurize, 28 July 1998.

Mashiri, Peter. Rotanda, Bairro Sede, Distrito de Sussundenga, 2 July 1998.

Matakera, Jose. Rotanda, Bairro Sede, Distrito de Sussundenga, 2 July 1998.

Mbadzo, Manuel Antonio. Rotanda, Bairro Sede, Distrito de Sussundenga, 2 July 1998.

Mbajaninga, Champs. Guezane, Distrito de Machaze, 16 July 1998.

Mberi, Kenneth. Rotanda, Bairro Sede, Distrito de Sussundenga, 2 July 1998.

Mlombo, Zuze Chingomana. Dacata, Distrito de Mossurize, 28 July 1998.

Moyana, Tafula. Guezane, Distrito de Machaze, 17 July 1998.

Muchalenyi, Timu Nbweseni. Dacata, Distrito de Mossurize, 28 July 1998.

Muchanga, Albert Laisse. Chiurairue, Distrito de Mossurize, 29 July 1998.

Muchanga, Henriques Musindo. Chiurairue, Distrito de Mossurize, 29 July 1998.

Muchanga, Kemsi Mambachange Mapungwana. Espungabera, Sede, Distrito de Mossurize, 27 July 1998.

Muchanga, Lucia. Chiurairue, Distrito de Mossurize, 29 July 1998.

Muchanga, Sofasoque Pande. Espungabera, Sede, Distrito de Mossurize, 27 July 1998.

Mudengo, Francisco Roki. Chitobe, Sede, Distrito de Machaze, 19 July 1998.

Mukwawaya, Benjamini Mikiseni. Chimunkono, Distrito de Sussundenga, 8 July 1998.

Musinwa, Feniasi Mikiseni. Musambudzi, Rotanda, Distrito de Sussundenga, 3 July 1998.

Musororo, Vaina, and Binda Domu Mosunza. Rotanda, Bairro Sede, Distrito de Sussundenga, 2 July 1998.

Mutanda, Mangiza. Chimunkono, Distrito de Sussundenga, 8 July 1998.

Mutimumkulo, Solomon and Ana Mutimumkulo. Tuca-Tuca, Distrito de Machaze, 20 July 1998.

Mutisi, Paulino. Chitobe, Sede, Distrito de Machaze, 19 July 1998.

Muvanekwa, Brandy Matonga. Dacata, Distrito de Mossurize, 28 July 1998.

Nemhasi, (Mbuya). Espungabera, Sede, Distrito de Mossurize, 27 July 1998.

Ngini, Isaac. Chiurairue, Distrito de Mossurize, 29 July 1998.

Rice, Chimoio, and Reina Mucheka. Musambudzi, Rotanda, Distrito de Sussundenga, 3 July 1998.

Sangatana, Round. Musambudzi, Rotanda, Distrito de Sussundenga, 4 July 1998.

Save Group Interview, Grupo 1: James Matseva, Sargeni Nyamunda, Samuel Chisingi and Around Tivane, Chidoco (Save), Distrito de Machaze, 23 July 1998.

Save Group Interview, Grupo 2: Selinda Nyambi Perisela, Tasi Bokuta, Tawasi Shaluk, Naisai Chishongue and Nyamani Chisatu Basoka, Chidoco (Save), Distrito de Machaze, 23 July 1998.

Save Group Interview, Grupo 3: Ngozi Mateja, Chiruvani Sitolo Zuka and Manhasi Sitoye, Chidoco (Save), Distrito de Machaze, 23 July 1998.

Save Group Interview, Grupo 4: Tawasi Sibanda, Zamuse Nyamunda, Nyokasi Mutani, Munyani Nyamunda and Anasi Sibanda, Chidoco (Save), Distrito de Machaze, 23 July 1998.

Save Group Interview, Grupo 5: Makokali Chitandu, Paulina Changu, (?) Chilovane Tsonga, Moyasi Changu, Josi Miyambo, Moyasi Ngwenya, Yokasi Tivane and Mujai Tiwana, Chidoco (Save), Distrito de Machaze, 23 July 1998.

Save Group Interview, Grupo 6: Mushawa Nyanzi, Totowani Machava, Mangeni Matesva, Musami Nyambani and Maria Azitangu, Chidoco (Save), Distrito de Machaze, 23 July 1998.

Save Group Interview, Grupo 7: Nyasala Sibandi, Chikavana Mataweya, Manhasi Maliga, Pukwane Machisi Simango, Tawasi Simango and Salimina Tchislangu, Chidoco (Save), Distrito de Machaze, 23 July 1998.

Save Group Interview, Grupo 8: Ndaina Sete, Moyasi Abasizi, Cecilia Secheni, Sara Sitoi and Tavasi Chipinini, Chidoco (Save), Distrito de Machaze, 23 July 1998.

Save Group Interview, Grupo 9: Julieta Coana, Chibemva Sitole, Makokani Shauke and Julivani Ngwenya, Chidoco (Save), Distrito de Machaze, 23 July 1998.

Simpson, Tazwira, and Zefenius Simpson. Musambudzi, Rotanda, Distrito de Sussundenga, 3 July 1998.

Sito, Filipe. Guezane, Distrito de Machaze, 17 July 1998.

Siyanda, Mario Joao, Feliz Mikiroso, Amelia Joao and Luisa Mukwiyo. Dombe Sede, Distrito de Sussundenga, 9 July 1998.

Sunguri, Zacariah. Musambudzi, Rotanda, Distrito de Sussundenga, 3 July 1998.

Valemo, Sebastiao. Chitobe Sede, Distrito de Machaze, 22 July 1998.

Vurandi, Lazaro. Chimunkono, Distrito de Sussundenga, 8 July 1998.

Watchi, Ndasi. Sussundenga, Sede, Distrito de Sussundenga, 4 August 1998.

Sofala Province, Mozambique

Anônimo. Buzi, Distrito de Buzi, 24 September 1998.

Bonessa, Pedro Fernando. Machanga Sede, Distrito de Machanga, 11 September 1998.

Dhlakama, Isaias Veremo (2a. vez). Chibabava Sede, Distrito de Chibabava, 15 September 1998.

Gofuro, Pedro Bapiro. Zona de Zivava, Distrito de Machanga, 4 September 1998.

Group Interview with Chefe Agostinho Manduze Jorge Chiteve Simango (Régulo ChiTeve) e Luis Mangate Bili Mapossa, Régulo ChiTeve, Distrito de Machanga, 12 September 1998.

Machava, Luis Santana. Machanga Sede, Distrito de Machanga, 4 September 1998; 8 September 1998.

Machava, Marachana Twende. Dongonda, Distrito de Chibabava, 15 September 1998.

Magona, Julia Kua João. Machanga Sede, Distrito de Machanga, 7 September 1998.

Mapare, Manuel (regulo de Guara-Guara) and others. Guara-Guara, Distrito de Buzi, 23 September 1998.

Maposa, Notissa Mabalana. Dongonda, Distrito de Chibabava, 15 September 1998.

Mapossa, Mateus Mbangenene (Chefe tradicional de Moligue). Moligue, Distrito de Chibabava, 18 September 1998.

Matavata, Carlos Alberto with Mamundu Ismael e Arbino João Zebunanye. Buzi Sede, Distrito de Buzi, 21 September 1998.

Mavijo, Mwari, and Psipa Chauque. Machanga Sede, Distrito de Machanga. 8 September 1998.

Minyamba, Maibasi. Chibabava Sede, Distrito de Chibabava, 14 September 1998.

Moyana, Manuel. Dongonda, Distrito de Chibabava, 15 September 1998.

Muchanga, Augusto Magodo Sangulo. Muvi, Distrito de Machanga, 6 September 1998; Machanga Sede, 7 September 1998.

Muchanga, Chimwiasi. Chibabava Sede, Distrito de Chibabava, 14 September 1998.
Mugadue, Macotore José Mafusse (Regulo de Muzungue). Muxungue, Distrito de Chibabava, 16 September 1998.
Mugadui, Matasi. Dongonda, Distrito de Chibabava, 15 September 1998.
Mussalaulo, José. Muvi, Distrito de Machanga, 6 September 1998.
Mutume, Amélia. Machanga Sede, Distrito de Machanga, 4 September 1998.
Ndazondwa, John. Mupini, Distrito de Machanga, 8 September 1998.
Ngilazi, David. Chibabava Sede, Distrito de Chibabava, 15 September 1998.
Nguenha, Dajonganhi Ussene. Muvi, Distrito de Machanga, 6 September 1998.
Rafael, Amélia Chiriro. Machanga Sede, Distrito de Machanga, 8 September 1998.
Saveca, Jossias Mamba Mulhoi (Regulo de Hode). Hode, Distrito de Chibabava, 18 September 1998.
Simango, Filimon Dongonda, (Chefe de Dongonda). Dongonda, Distrito de Chibabava, 15 September 1998.
Simango, José Guacha. Machanga Sede, Distrito de Machanga, 7 September 1998.
Simango, José Paulo Maduca. Machanga Sede, Distrito de Machanga, 5 September 1998.
Simango, Martinho Manhacha Jackson. Machanga Sede, Distrito de Machanga, 5 September 1998.
Simango, Timóteo Mabessa. Machanga Sede, Distrito de Machanga, 4 September 1998.
Simango, Zacarias. Dongonda, Distrito de Chibabava, 15 September 1998.
Sitole, Ana Nyamunda, with Jorge Muchita Machava and Isaias Veremo Dhlakama. Chibabava Sede, Distrito de Chibabava, 14 September 1998.
Sitole, James. Moligue, Distrito de Chibabava, 17 September 1998.
Sitole, Marcos Siringuani. Buzi—Lado de Companhia do Buzi, Distrito de Buzi, 23 September 1998.
Tivane, Notissa with Dorica Pangananyi Moyani. Dongonda, Distrito de Chibabava, 15 September 1998.
Tuzino, Fernando Vitorino. Machanga Sede, Distrito de Machanga, 4 September 1998.
William, Mulenje Macama, Buzi Sede, Distrito de Buzi, 23 September 1998.

Inhambane Province, Mozambique

Group Interview with Germano Mauta Paulo Simango, António Mwando Chicunisse Simango e Cordeiro Miranda Mussequessa Simango, Mutinya, Distrito de Govuro, Provincia de Inhambane, 10 September 1998.
Rodrigues, João Bassopa. Mambone Sede, Distrito de Govuro, Provincia de Inhambane, 10 September 1998.

Eastern Zimbabwe

Chibuwe, Peter. Nyanyadzi, Hot Springs, Zimbabwe, 31 July 1999.
Dhlakama, Catherine. Chikore, Zimbabwe, 30 June 1999.
Dhlakama, Hlaibandhla. Mabhiza (Rimbi/Checheche), Zimbabwe, 11 July 1999.
Dhlakama, Mucherechete. Zamchiya, Zimbabwe, 13 July 1999.
Dhliwayo, Chendinofira. Mhakwe, Zimbabwe, 30 July 1999.
Dhliwayo, (Mbuya). Mhakwe, Zimbabwe, 30 July 1999.
Dhliwayo, Mwachitama. Rimbi, Zimbabwe, 11 July 1999.

Dhliwayo, Ndaiziyei. Jenya West, Chikore, Zimbabwe, 8 July 1999.
Dube, Daisy. Mundanda, Zimbabwe, 21 July 1999.
Dube, Maramwa. Checheche, Zimbabwe, 10 July 1999.
Dziwandi, Marien. Nyanyadzi, Hot Springs, Zimbabwe, 1 August 1999.
Gapara, Siyanzi Raphius, and Ellen Gapara. Chikore, Zimbabwe, 1 July 1999.
Gugu, Eva. Checheche, Zimbabwe, 10 July 1999.
Gumbo, Notase. Majehwe, Zimbabwe, 3 July 1999.
Hlabiso, (Sekuru). Matyukira, Vhimba, Zimbabwe, 25 July 1999.
Hlabiso, Sofi. Matyukira, Vhimba, Zimbabwe, 25 July 1999.
Jenya, Joyce. Rimbi, Zimbabwe, 11 July 1999.
Jenya, Meltah. At Chief Musikavanhu, Zimbabwe, 6 July 1999.
Khosa, Philemon. Pfidza Township, Chikore, Zimbabwe, 28 June 1999.
Kumbula, Losi. Garahwa (Checheche), Zimbabwe, 10 July 1999.
Kunjenjema, John. Chikore, Zimbabwe, 30 June 1999.
Mafuta, Mukanyi. Vhimba, Zimbabwe, 27 July 1999.
Mahaka, Chizii. Chinyaduma, Chirinda, Zimbabwe, 18 July 1999.
Makasha, Munyembezi. Chikware, Vhimba, Zimbabwe, 26 July 1999.
Makowe, Neli. Nyanyadzi, Hot Springs, Zimbabwe, 1 August 1999.
Makuyana, Jona Mwaoneni. Zamchiya, Zimbabwe, 14 July 1999.
Makuyana, Mwatanisa. Bangira, Chikore, Zimbabwe, 8 July 1999.
Mandivhana, Sarah. Vhimba, Zimbabwe, 27 July 1999.
Manyuni, Idah. Pfidza Township, Chikore, Zimbabwe, 28 June 1999.
Manzini, Nyadzani. Chikware, Vhimba, Zimbabwe, 26 July 1999.
Maorere, Chamusi. Chikware, Vhimba, Zimbabwe, 26 July 1999.
Maposa, Zisoyo. Jenya West, Chikore, Zimbabwe, 8 July 1999.
Marijeki, (Mbuya). Mhakwe, Zimbabwe, 30 July 1999.
Mashava, Luka and Eresi Mashava. Mhakwe, Zimbabwe, 30 July 1999.
Matyukira, Watch. Matyukira, Vhimba, Zimbabwe, 25 July 1999.
Mauwa, Chakai Oscar. Nyanyadzi, Hot Springs, Zimbabwe, 31 July 1999.
Mhlanga, Mubayi. Zamchiya, Zimbabwe, 13 July 1999.
Mhlanga, Munorwei Watch. Majehwe, Zimbabwe, 5 July 1999.
Mlambo, Albert. Gaza, Chipinge, Zimbabwe, 23 July 1999.
Mlambo, Esther. At Chief Musikavanhu, Zimbabwe, 6 July 1999.
Mlambo, Farisa. Chinaa, Zimbabwe, 1 July 1999.
Mlambo, Jackson. Garahwa (Checheche), Zimbabwe, 10 July 1999.
Mlambo, Mannered, and Dorothy Mlambo. Emerald, Zimbabwe, 20 July 1999.
Mlambo, Mary. Majehwe, Zimbabwe, 3 July 1999.
Mlambo, Moyasi. Emerald, Zimbabwe, 20 July 1999.
Mlambo, Mukapera. Chikore, Zimbabwe, 7 July 1999.
Mlambo, Nemasi. Majehwe, Zimbabwe, 5 July 1999.
Mlambo, Unganai. At Chief Musikavanhu, Zimbabwe, 6 July 1999.
Mlambo, Vanhuvaone. Tuzuka School At Chief Musikavanhu, Zimbabwe, 6 July 1999.
Mtetwa, Chinungu. Zamchiya, Zimbabwe, 13 July 1999.
Muganga, Mary. Chimanimani, Zimbabwe, 9 July 1999.
Muhlaba, Mwatama. Vhimba, Zimbabwe, 27 July 1999.
Muhlanga, Annah. Chinyaduma, Chirinda, Zimbabwe, 18 July 1999.
Muhlanga, Magoti Edward. Zamchiya, Zimbabwe, 14 July 1999.
Muhlanga, Marimanjira. Chirinda (at Chief Mapungwana), Zimbabwe, 17 July 1999.

Muhlanga, Muchemanenjira. Zamchiya, Zimbabwe, 14 July 1999.
Muhlanga, Mwaitireni. Mt. Selinda, Zimbabwe, 20 July 1999.
Muitire, Mwaoneni. Matyukira, Vhimba, Zimbabwe, 25 July 1999.
Mukokota, Phoebe. Chikore, Zimbabwe, 30 June 1999.
Mukombe, Siyani, and Rhodah Moyocha. Chinyaduma, Chirinda, Zimbabwe, 18 July 1999.
Mulambo, Ndapota. Rimbi, Zimbabwe, 11 July 1999.
Mundeta, Allen. Chikore, Zimbabwe, 29 June 1999.
Mundeta, Simon, and Mbuya Mundeta. Chikore, Zimbabwe, 28 June 1999.
Munedzi, Bertha. Mhakwe, Zimbabwe, 30 July 1999.
Munedzi, Ruben Gocha. Mhakwe, Zimbabwe, 30 July 1999.
Mureka, Ndodini. Vhimba, Zimbabwe, 27 July 1999.
Murombo, Fibiauwe. Chikware, Vhimba, Zimbabwe, 26 July 1999.
Mushoma, Riyarwi. Chinaa, Chikore, Zimbabwe, 1 July 1999.
Mutigwe, Celani, and Phillip Mutigwe. Chikore, Zimbabwe, 29 June 1999.
Mutisi, Mwatambudzeni. Chinyaduma, Chirinda, Zimbabwe, 20 July 1999.
Muyambo, Albert. Checheche, Zimbabwe, 10 July 1999.
Muzodini, (Mbuya). Matyukira, Vhimba, Zimbabwe, 25 July 1999.
Ndangana, Muhlanganiso. Bangira, Chikore, Zimbabwe, 8 July 1999.
Ngorima, Mwaamba. Chikware, Vhimba, Zimbabwe, 26 July 1999.
Ngwenduna, Hlanganipai. Matyukira, Vhimba, Zimbabwe, 25 July 1999.
Nkomo, Robert Open. Nyanyadzi, Hot Springs, Zimbabwe, 1 August 1999.
Nyananda, Mavisi. Nyanyadzi, Hot Springs, Zimbabwe, 1 August 1999.
Rwizi, Rushike. Rupise, Hot Springs, Zimbabwe, 31 July 1999.
Sibindi, Simon. Chimanimani, Zimbabwe, 29 July 1999.
Sigauke, Ndagumirwa. Zamchiya, Zimbabwe, 13 July 1999.
Simango, Amundidi. Shekwa, Zimbabwe, 2 July 1999.
Simango, Mateus. Zamchiya, Zimbabwe, 14 July 1999.
Simango, Nyamadzawo. Shekwa, Zimbabwe, 2 July 1999.
Sithole, Eva. Chinaa, Zimbabwe, 1 July 1999.
Sithole, Freddy. Chikore, Zimbabwe, 29 June 1999.
Sithole, Gilbert. Shekwa, Zimbabwe, 2 July 1999.
Sithole, Nyau. Shekwa, Zimbabwe, 2 July 1999.
Sithole, Sarai Nyabanga. Zamchiya, Zimbabwe, 13 July 1999.
Sithole, Sekai. Chikore, Zimbabwe, 29 June 1999.
Sithole, Taingwa Inox. Chikware, Vhimba, Zimbabwe, 26 July 1999.
Sithole, Wilson. Garahwa (Checheche), Zimbabwe, 10 July 1999.
Tarangwa, (Sekuru), and Muvhamba, (Sekuru). Pfidza Township, Chikore, Zimbabwe, 28 June 1999.
Woka, John, and Grace Chirawu. Chimanimani, Zimbabwe, 29 July 1999.
Zauta, Zuwarimwe (with Garikai Chaendepi and Mary Chaendepi). Chimanimani, Zimbabwe, 29 July 1999.
Ziomo, Machona. Chikware, Vhimba, Zimbabwe, 26 July 1999.

INDEX

Achebe, Chinua, 92
Acholi, 27
adornment: clothing, 19, 71–73;
  hairstyles, 23, 76–77, 80; houses,
  77–78, 79, 146n117; jewelry, 19, 23,
  70, 73–74, 80, 156n71; *nyora*
  (scarification), 23, 70, 71, 75, 76, 80,
  110, 156n71; *pika* (tattoos), 23, 70–71,
  75–76, 80, 110, 145n89, 145n90,
  156n71. *See also* beauty; cultural
  practices; material culture
Afrikaners, 26
ambira, 89, 152n102
American Board Mission, 118n35. *See
  also* missionaries
Angoche, 30
Anlo-Ewe (group), 28–29. *See also*
  Greene, Sandra
Appiah, Kwame Anthony, 3, 26, 92, 113
archaeological evidence, 5, 28, 36,
  37–38, 127n87
Atkinson, Ronald, 27

Bantu dialect. *See* Shona language
barbel, 70, 76, 142 *(Epigraph One)*
Barreto, Francisco, 32, 45, 71, 73,
  125n45
Barreto, Manuel, 32–33
Barth, Fredrik, 26, 54
Barwe state, 31, 32, 42, 46, 47, 74, 76
Bayão, Sisnando Dias, 51, 133n115
Bazaruto archipelago, 42
Beach, David, 56, 57, 119n39, 127n83,
  129n8, 153n13, 154n23
beauty, 23, 142n1; identity through,
  70–71, 80; *pika* and *nyora* as signs of,
  75–76; and Ndau men, 102
beer, 30; brewing as symbolic ritual, 23,
81, 90; ceremonial aspects of, 61, 66,
  82, 84, 85, 69; drinking to promote
  community, 78, 147n1
Beira, 116n10, 121n78, 124n38, 160n47
Biafran War, 92
Bilene, exodus to, 24, 61, 64, 95, 102,
  104–5, 107
birth rituals, 53, 62–63. *See also* cultural
  practices
body art. *See* adornment
Braudel, Fernand, 27
bridewealth, 53, 57, 58–59, 60–61, 62, 63,
  101, 136n45. *See also* cultural
  practices; marriage; women
British colonialism, 3, 34, 60, 78, 91. *See
  also* colonialism; independence
Brubaker, Rodgers, 2
Budya, 17, 50
Buhera, 50
bumphi totem, 57
burial rituals, 53, 63, 64–65, 69, 85, 86,
  104, 140n149
Buweni, 47
Buzi River, *4* (map), 4, 41, 47, 48, 51, 95,
  129n15
Bwanyi, 61, 72, 73, 143n24

capitão-mor, 47, 128n3
Castigo, Pedro, 20
Changamire, 11, 34, 45–46, 47, 49, 67,
  83. *See also* Rozvi
Changana. *See* Shangaan
chibitzi. See xibitzi
Chibuene, 50
Chibvumani ruins, 7, *8* (photo)
chidzviti, 102
chiefs, 7, 42, 52; and courts, 87–89;
  under Gaza Nguni, 98–99, 104; in

ROCHESTER STUDIES in
AFRICAN HISTORY and the DIASPORA

Toyin Falola, Senior Editor
The Frances Higginbotham Nalle Centennial Professor in History
University of Texas at Austin

In an examination of historical patterns over four centuries, Elizabeth MacGonagle reveals both continuities and changes in the crafting of identity in southeast Africa. This work challenges conventional approaches to the study of ethnicity and "tribalism" in Africa by showing that contemporary ethnicity is not merely a creation of the colonial and postcolonial eras, but has much deeper roots in the precolonial past. By focusing on collective historical experiences that affected ethnic identity before the influence of European colonialism, MacGonagle contends that the long history behind ethnicity reveals African agency as central to the formation of "tribalism."

With this first comprehensive history of the Ndau of eastern Zimbabwe and central Mozambique, MacGonagle moves beyond national borders to show how cultural identities are woven from historical memories that predate the arrival of missionaries and colonial officials on the African continent. Drawing on archival records and oral histories from throughout the Ndau region, her study analyzes the complex relationships between social identity and political power from 1500 to 1900.

Ndauness has been created and recreated within communities through marriages and social structures, cultural practices that mark the body, and rituals that help to sustain shared beliefs. A sense of being Ndau continues to exist into the present, despite different colonial histories, postcolonial trajectories, and official languages in Zimbabwe and Mozambique. MacGonagle's study of ethnic identities among the marginalized Ndau sheds light on the conflicts and divisions that haunt southeast Africa today. This compelling interpretation of the crafting of identity in one corner of Africa has relevance for readers interested in identity formation and ethnic conflict around the world.

Elizabeth MacGonagle is assistant professor of African History at the University of Kansas.